Achieving Effective Desegregation

Real Estate Research Corporation is a professional consulting organization that counsels decision-makers on social and economic trends, real estate investments, and related public and private policies. In public affairs counseling, RERC specializes in developing pragmatic recommendations that offer alternative methods of resolving complex social and organizational problems. RERC is headquartered in Chicago and has eleven regional offices across the country.

Lexington Books Politics of Education Series

Frederick M. Wirt, Editor

Michael W. Kirst, Ed., *State, School, and Politics: Research Directions*
Joel S. Berke and Michael W. Kirst, *Federal Aid to Education: Who Benefits? Who Governs?*

Achieving Effective Desegregation

Al Smith

Anthony Downs

M. Leanne Lachman

Real Estate Research Corporation

Lexington Books
D.C. Heath and Company
Lexington, Massachusetts
Toronto   London

The project presented herein was performed pursuant to a Contract from the U.S. Office of Education, Department of Health, Education and Welfare, for the Cabinet Committee on Education. However, the opinions expressed herein do not necessarily reflect the position or policy of the U.S. Office of Education or the Cabinet Committee on Education, and no official endorsement by the U.S. Office of Education or the Cabinet Committee on Education should be inferred.

Library of Congress Cataloging in Publication Data

Smith, Al, 1940–
  Achieving effective desegregation.

1. School integration– United States. I. Downs, Anthony, joint author.
II. Lachman, M. Leanne, joint author. III. Title.
LA210.S48   370.19'342   72-13496
ISBN 0-669-85464-6

Published simultaneously in Canada.

Printed in the United States of America.

International Standard Book Number: 0-669-85464-6

Library of Congress Catalog Card Number: 72-13496

Table of Contents

Foreword

For almost two decades education has been heavily involved in the difficult and emotionally charged process of eliminating racial segregation from the public schools. Although progress has been made, the task is still far from complete. Many of the difficult problems associated with achieving unitary school systems remain unsolved. Also, great frustration accompanies the growing realization that much that once appeared to be progress has disappeared into thin air as resegregation takes over. Little is gained if after all the turmoil we return to the point of beginning. In spite of the difficulties encountered, the national direction established in 1954 remains an unchanging challenge to teachers, administrators, and citizens generally. There is nothing to suggest, however, that the problems we face should not be approached with skill and understanding in order that the results will be lasting and positive rather than transitory and divisive. Certainly there is little doubt that desegregation and related educational and social issues will continue to demand and receive priority attention during the years immediately ahead.

The temptation is ever present to dwell upon the failure of past efforts. Instead it is now urgent that we direct our efforts toward the achievement of desegregation which is effective, lasting, and educationally meaningful.

This volume, *Achieving Effective Desegregation,* is most valuable because it proposes a positive educational approach. From this vantage point it is obvious that this is the only approach which will accomplish lasting results. The fact that desegregation is a continuing process rather than a one-time event is appropriately emphasized. The specific, detailed, and forward-looking suggestions will prove helpful to school systems throughout the nation—those presently involved and those yet to begin the desegregation process.

The authors of the report have surveyed the field and addressed practical, detailed suggestions to the various educational and community groups most directly involved in desegregation efforts. Recommended procedures take into account traditional educational processes which over the years have assured educational progress through community assistance and made permanent because of community approval. The same can be true of desegregation.

Throughout the report the point is repeatedly made that positive, dedicated leadership can mean the difference between success or failure of the desegregation process. This publication, *Achieving Effective Desegregation,* will prove to be a valuable tool in the hands of those who work to assure an unencumbered educational opportunity for all.

John W. Letson
Superintendent
Atlanta Public Schools

Achieving Effective Desegregation

1 The Basic Nature of Effective Desegregation

What is Effective Desegregation?

The Supreme Court has stated that, "The measure of any desegregation plan is its effectiveness."[1] Therefore, only *effective desegregation* can accomplish the purposes sought by the long series of federal court actions on the desegregation of schools.

In order to describe how to achieve effective desegregation, it is first necessary to define this concept clearly. However, this is not easy. As President Nixon has said, "Few public issues are so emotionally charged as that of school desegregation, few so wrapped in confusion and clouded with misunderstanding."[2] Yet the way effective desegregation is defined is critical. It will help determine how school authorities seek to achieve it, and how others measure their success.

Therefore, the definition used in this document has been very carefully developed from all the findings of this study, including an analysis of the relevant Supreme Court decisions and Acts of Congress. The result is a rather complex definition. Yet it is both precise and comprehensive:

> Effective desegregation is a process of educational change which eliminates any inequalities in the educational opportunities provided by the state in a public school system which are caused by race, color, or nationality. This process involves three separate elements, all of which are essential to its success. They are (1) meeting specific desegregation requirements established by the Supreme Court, (2) avoiding any undue disruptions in school and community life, and (3) achieving the positive goal of quality unified education for all students.

The remaining sections of this chapter explore exactly what this definition means.

Detailed Explanation of This Definition

The basic definition of effective desegregation can be more fully understood when examined in detail, as follows:

1

"Process of educational change." Effective desegregation is not a single event, or a one-time shift in school conditions. Rather, it is a whole series of activities, events, and changes occurring over a long period of time—at least several years. Eventually, this process will gradually merge into the general educational process.

In almost every school system, effective desegregation requires many fundamental changes in previous conditions. These changes involve not only school attendance patterns, but also the attitudes, beliefs and behavior patterns of both majority-group and minority-group students, teachers, administrators, and parents.

"Which eliminates any inequalities in . . . educational opportunities . . . caused by race, color or nationality." Up to now, the Supreme Court has not required public school authorities to eliminate inequalities in educational opportunities caused by factors other than race, color, or nationality, even if state action outside school systems contributed to those causes.[3]

"In the educational opportunities provided by the state." The Supreme Court has not stated that school systems must act to create equal educational results or even equal education—but equal educational opportunities. This is a highly ambiguous term. However, most experts believe it means *at least* equal resources devoted to education per pupil regardless of race. In our opinion, educational opportunities offered to different students are not equal insofar as state action is concerned unless the following three conditions are all met:

1. The quantity of publicly-supplied educational resources made available to each student is approximately the same.
2. The quality of those resources is approximately the same.
3. Those resources are adapted to the particular needs of each student to approximately the same degree.

Since students have very different needs, achieving equality of educational opportunities within a school district does not mean providing identical publicly supplied resources to every student. In fact, such uniformity would in most cases be a denial of equal educational opportunity. It would not result in equal adaptation of the resources concerned to the particular needs of the students.[4]

The requirement of equality applies only to educational opportunities provided by the state.[5] Most educational research indicates that the social situations of students are more important in determining their educational achievement than the schools they attend. However, the Supreme Court's rulings have definitely not required state action to offset inequalities of educational opportunity arising from such non-state-caused factors.

"In a public school system." All the Supreme Court's rulings concerning racial desegregation in elementary and secondary schools up to this time have applied to individual school districts only.[6] Thus, a public school system consists of all the schools and other facilities administered by a single public school district. Public authorities are obligated to eliminate inequalities in educational opportunities provided by the state caused by race, color or nationality in all the schools or other facilities within each district. But they are not obligated to eliminate such inequalities occurring among districts or in larger areas, such as an entire state.

Future Supreme Court decisions or legislative actions may change some of the meanings set forth above. However, these explanations represent what we believe is the clearest definition of effective desegregation possible at this time.

The Basic Purpose of Effective Desegregation

The basic purpose of school desegregation is to insure that every school provides "equal educational opportunities" to all who attend it.[7] President Nixon further explained this purpose in his statement of March 24, 1970:

> "As we strive to make our schools places of equal educational opportunity, we should keep our eye fixed on this goal: To achieve a set of conditions in which neither the laws nor the institutions supported by law any longer draw an invidious distinction based on race; and going one step further, we must seek to repair the human damage wrought by past segregation. We must give the minority child that equal place at the starting line that his parents were denied—and the pride, the dignity, the self-respect that are the birthright of a free American."[8]

Both scientific research and common sense prove that equality of opportunity in any area of life is not something which a person can create himself; it depends upon the attitudes and behavior which others adopt towards him. The "human damage wrought by past segregation" which President Nixon mentioned took place because one group of people treated another as though they were inferior. Psychological and educational research has proved that such treatment, repeated often enough by persons considered significant by those affected, tends to act as a self-fulfilling prophecy. It causes those treated as inferior to feel rejected and lose confidence in their own abilities. As a result, they fail to develop a strong motivation to perform well, or high expectations concerning what they can do. Thus, treating others—especially children—as though they were inferior often causes them to exhibit inferior performance.

This kind of experience has occurred time and again to members of America's minority groups. But they are not its only victims. Millions of disadvantaged American children of all ethnic backgrounds have suffered the adverse consequences of at least some open or unconscious rejection in public schools. This has occurred because most public schools are dominated by middle-class school boards and teachers. They often place disproportionate emphasis upon meeting the needs of the college-bound and the established residents of the community. Consequently, public schools have frequently failed to develop adequate curricula and educational methods designed to serve children of varied backgrounds and different aspirations. These children often have occupational goals, personal interests, and capabilities quite different from those of the college-bound middle-class child. In many instances, quite unconsciously, schools have "turned off" many of these children and caused them first to become disinterested, then to perform badly, and eventually to drop out.

In order to give all such "disadvantaged" children—not just minority-group children—what President Nixon called "that equal place at the starting line that his parents were denied," and to instill in each such child "the pride, the dignity, the self-respect that are the birthright of a free American," members of the dominant groups in public schools must treat both lower-income white children and minority-group children with respect and dignity, and with positive expectations about their abilities and worth. This will require certain changes in attitudes, behavior, and educational content closely related to those necessary for effective desegregation. Thus, many white Americans would benefit from the very same type of changes in public education—and in the behavior of the dominant groups in public schools—that are needed by minority groups.

Regarding such groups, desegregation of public schools cannot become truly effective unless there are significant changes in the present attitudes and behavior of many white students, teachers, and administrators toward minority-group students, teachers and administrators. Thus, effective desegregation is not just a matter of physical proximity among members of different groups in the same schools. It also requires that those schools create a positive atmosphere in which American children from all racial and ethnic groups, and all economic levels, can develop the basic attitudes of both self-confidence and mutual respect and understanding that are vital for the successful operation of our democratic society.

Therefore, efforts to achieve effective desegregation cannot be considered successful merely because children of both majority and minority groups are attending the same schools. As President Nixon put it, "From an educational standpoint, what matters most is not the integrated school but the integrated classroom."[9] Hence, if the federal government really wants to make desegregation effective, it must remain interested and informed about what happens in schools even after they have been physically desegregated. Certainly the federal government cannot and should not seek to control what happens in public schools across the nation. But neither should it consider the goal of equal educational opportunity as fully achieved once children from majority and minority groups are attending school together. Some specific recommendations about what kind of continuing interest it might exhibit are presented later in this book.

The degree to which desegregation in a particular school succeeds in meeting some of the other criteria of effectiveness—such as avoiding violence and any decline in academic performance—will also be greatly influenced by the nature of inter-group relations within that school. If minority-group children continue to be regarded as inferiors and rejected, however subtly, then trouble is very likely to occur. When it appears—in the form of protests or violence or declining academic achievement, many will blame desegregation itself. However, the first cause to look for is the way the minority group has been treated after physical desegregation took place. When both majority group and minority-group children share the same schools, it is no longer possible for the majority group to escape tasting the fruits of its own treatment of the minority group.

Specific Desegregation Requirements
Established by the Supreme Court

One of the three basic elements needed to make desegregation effective is meeting the specific desegregation requirements established by the Supreme Court. The Court itself has been reluctant to spell out any single operational definition of desegregation because of the tremendous variety of conditions in thousands of school districts. In fact, the Court has stated, "There is no universal answer to complex problems of desegregation; there is obviously no one plan that will do the job in every case."[10] Nevertheless, the Court's many rulings on this subject up to this time (July 1, 1971) have established a certain minimum set of conditions for desegregation. *All* of these conditions must be achieved in order to satisfy the Court that a previously established dual system no longer exists. In some cases, even attaining all these conditions may not satisfy the Court. Also, future Court decisions may add more conditions to the minimum requirements established so far, or alter those described below.

The following eight conditions (given short titles for convenient reference) constitute all the universally-required conditions we have been able to identify up to this time:

1. Unified Administration. Administration of the entire school system as a single, unified entity.[11]
2. Equal Facilities and Programs. No marked difference in the quality of facilities or the nature of the programs offered at schools primarily attended by members of different races.[12]
3. Equality and Racially-Balanced Faculties. No marked difference in the proportions of majority-group and minority-group faculty members in any schools in the system, or in the quality of faculty members assigned to schools primarily attended by members of different races.[13]

4. Non-Discriminatory Student Assignment. No assignment of pupils to or within schools by race, color, religion, or nationality.[14]
5. No Racially-Identifiable Schools. Absence of any clear identifiabilityof any particular schools as either "white" or "Negro" because of differences in the composition of their faculties, facilities, or programs.[15]
6. Minimum Racial Disproportionality of Students. Presence of only the minimum feasible number of schools in the system attended by members of only one race, or substantially disproportionate in their racial composition from the racial composition of the students in the system as a whole. "Minimum number" means the number which remains unavoidable even after employment of extensive bus transportation of students, school pairing, non-contiguous attendance zoning, and all other practical remedies. Such remedies should be used even if they are administratively awkward, inconvenient, and even bizarre, or impose burdens on some persons.[16]
7. Optional Majority Transfer. Provision for optional transfer of those in the majority racial group of a particular school to other schools where they will be in the minority, with free transportation for those exercising this option.[17]
8. Non-Discriminatory School Construction and Abandonment. No use of school construction and abandonment to perpetuate or re-establish the dual system.[18]

The Supreme Court has applied these eight conditions only to school systems where a racially segregated system was formerly established by law. The Court has said specifically that, "We do not reach in this case the question whether a showing that school segregation is a consequence of other types of state action, without any discriminatory action by the school authorities, is a constitutional violation requiring remedial action by a school desegregation decree."[19] Moreover, the Court has carefully qualified all of its statements to apply only to "state-imposed" segregation; that is *de jure* rather than *de facto* segregation.

Nevertheless, we believe it is reasonable to presume that any desegregation attempts, even entirely voluntary ones applied to *de facto* segregation, would have to conform at least roughly to the above eight conditions to be considered effective.

Avoiding Disruption of School and Community Life During Desegregation

The second basic element required for effective desegregation of public schools is carrying out the entire process in a manner that neither unduly disrupts or weakens the public school system, nor causes undue violence or hostility in the life of the local community. This element is essentially negative; that is, it consists of successfully avoiding certain undesirable outcomes. Nevertheless, it is just as essential in making desegregation effective as meeting the specific requirements established by the Supreme Court. If those requirements were met through actions which caused frequent local violence, intensive interracial hostility in the community, and a major withdrawal of both black and white students from the public schools, desegregation could certainly not be considered successful.

Achieving this basic element of effective desegregation requires attainment of the following five conditions (given short titles for convenient reference):

1. Non-Violence. The absence of any serious violence in the community or in the schools caused by desegregation. "Serious violence" is that which goes beyond the normal degree of personal physical contacts typical of adolescents, especially that which results in serious injury or death.
2. Non-Withdrawal. No marked immediate or long-run decline in the number of either white or Negro students attending the system after it desegregates as compared to beforehand.
3. Maintenance of Financial Support. No marked reduction in local public support for school-oriented bond issues or tax levies.
4. Maintenance of Academic Achievement   No significant decline in the academic achievement levels of either white or Negro students in the system after desegregation as compared to beforehand.
5. Non-Polarization of the Community. No significant or prolonged polarization of community sentiment concerning the public schools, or marked increase in interracial conflict or hostility within the local community, during or after initial desegreation as compared to beforehand.

These five conditions are all desired outcomes, rather than plans of action. The relationships between these outcomes and the actions necessary to achieve them are discussed in later sections of this handbook.

Achieving Quality Unified Education

The third basic element required for effective desegregation of public schools is the most important of all, because its achievement is the real purpose of desegregation. It is the provision of quality, unified education to all students in the public school system concerned. The Supreme Court indicated the significance of this element in *Brown v. Board of Education of Topeka* as follows:

"Today, education is perhaps the most important function of state and local governments. Compulsory school attendance laws and the great

expenditures for education both demonstrate our recognition of the importance of education to our democratic society. It is required in the
performance of our most basic public responsibilities, even service in the
armed forces. It is the very foundation of good citizenship. Today it is a
principal instrument in awakening the child to cultural values, in preparing
him for later professional training, and in helping him to adjust normally
to his environment. In these days, it is doubtful that any child may
reasonably be expected to succeed in life if he is denied the opportunity of
an education. Such an opportunity, where the state has undertaken to
provide it, is a right which must be made available to all on equal terms.[20]

Analysis of the many sources used in this study indicates that:

Quality unified education in desegregated schools must be based upon a
combination of three essential ingredients: (1) genuine unity of purpose,
efforts, and basic values within the system and within each school, regardless of race, color, or nationality; (2) positive appreciation of diversity
concerning the talents, capabilities, cultural values, and approaches of different individuals and groups, also regardless of race, color, or nationality;
and (3) constructive inter-group activities that generate mutual respect and
understanding among members of both majority and minority groups in
each school.

This combination forms the affirmative aspect of effectively desegregated
education, as contrasted with the essentially negative nature of the second
element described above. Without these positive ingredients, the educational
opportunities offered in desegregated schools to majority-group and minority-
group students cannot really be equal.

What do genuine unity and positive appreciation of diversity, and constructive inter-group activities really mean concerning desegregated education? Genuine unity means treatment of all students and teachers in each school as equally-
valued members of a single whole which derives its identity from all of them, and
serves the interests of all rather than just one segment. A simple example
illustrates this meaning. In many school systems, desegregation plans have called
for the closing of a formerly all-Negro school and the transfer of all its students
to a formerly all-white school, resulting in a combined school with about equal
numbers of Negro and white students. If the newly desegregated school retains
the same name, athletic team names, school colors, school songs, and student
government that it had when it was all-white, it thereby ignores those same
elements which the Negro students had in their former school. Then those operating this school have failed to achieve genuine unity. Instead they have based the
identity of the school as perceived by its students upon the interests of only part
of its members. On the other hand, school authorities could regard the newly-
desegregated school as something requiring a new identity. They could therefore

work with both white and Negro students to select a new school name, new athletic team names, new school colors and songs, and a new student government. Then they have achieved genuine unity, at least regarding these elements.

How such seemingly superficial aspects of education are treated in desegregated schools may seem to be trivial, but it is not. On the contrary, items like school colors and songs are preceived by nearly everyone as symbolic of the fundamental attitude of school authorities towards the formerly separated groups of students now attending the same school. Of course, genuine unity applies to more fundamental aspects of education too. For example, genuine unity cannot be achieved in a desegregated school if majority-group and minority-group students are taught in separate classrooms, or prevented from interacting in extracurricular activities (sometimes because these activities are cancelled).

In fact, achievement of genuine utity requires a strong positive effort by school administrators and teachers to overcome the psychological and other remnants of many decades of racial separation. For desegregation is indeed a fundamental change in the educational situation of any school system, especially one with relatively large numbers of minority-group children. The specific actions best suited to produce genuine unity are discussed later in this book.

A second critical ingredient in effectively dealing with the new situation caused by desegregation is positive appreciation of diversity. This means the clear and open recognition that many different talents, capabilities, occupational interests, cultural values, and personal approaches to life are desirable in a democratic society, and must therefore be valued and encouraged in the public school system.

American public education has traditionally emphasized a relatively homogeneous outlook in each school. One of its historic functions has been to impart a single relatively uniform "American" language and viewpoint to children coming from households with a tremendous diversity of incomes, cultural values, languages, and occupational interests. The need for "homogenizing" children from diverse backgrounds was especially strong in schools serving large cities after major waves of immigration from Europe. Later, this tendency towards a relatively homogeneous educational viewpoint in each school was encouraged for a directly opposite reason. It was the spatial separation of different groups into residential enclaves in which most families had about the same socio-economic status, incomes, and basic cultural outlooks, and often the same ethnic or nationality backgrounds. Wherever such relatively homogeneous enclaves are served by separate public school districts—as in many metropolitan-area suburbs—there has been a strong tendency to develop a relatively homogeneous educational viewpoint. Culturally, this tendency was accentuated wherever white and minority-group students were legally separated in different schools. The courses and textbooks in white school systems emphasized a strictly white dominated worldview.

However, several recent developments in American education have created a strong need to alter this traditional posture to more positive appreciation of diversity. Racial desegregation of schools is only one of these developments. Another is the need to impart higher status to occupations not requiring a college degree. We face potential future shortages in such occupations, and it is becoming clear that not all young people—not even all those from middle- and upper-income households—are well-suited for higher education as traditionally conceived in America. Still other developments encouraging greater diversity in public schools are:

> the proliferation of more varied life-styles among young people and in American society generally;
>
> greater legal recognition of individual rights among all groups (including students);
>
> the general desire among minority groups to strengthen their own identities by stressing their past cultural achievements.

All of these forces require shifting emphasis from various types of educational homogeneity to a greater positive appreciation of diversity. Specific forms of such appreciation could include broadening curricula by adding more vocational and business training, placing greater stress on the importance of personal respect in human interrelations, and providing more opportunities for young people to mix working with schooling.

Two other reasons for positive appreciation of diversity are more directly related to achieving effective desegregation. The first is the need to create a supportive educational environment for minority-group students so as to improve their academic performance. After surveying all available studies concerning the impact of desegregation upon academic performance, Nancy H. St. John concluded that:

> "The most plausible hypothesis is that the relation between integration and achievement is a conditional one: the academic performance of minority group children will be higher in integrated than in equivalent segregated schools, providing they are supported by staff and accepted by peers."[21]

Many experts have emphasized the importance of teacher expectations upon the academic performance of children.[22] The higher the performance the teacher expects and believes a child can attain, the better the child performs, on the average. This means it is vital that teachers exhibit an accepting and encouraging attitude towards all types of students from all types of backgrounds.

Positive appreciation of diversity is also essential in assisting minority-group members overcome the feelings of powerlessness and inferiority derived from their historically low-status position in America. This requires a clear recognition of minority-group cultural achievements, identity, and values by all important groups in the school system—including majority-group students, teachers, and administrators.

Some minority-group members believe that just appreciating diversity is not enough to insure equal educational opportunities for minority-group children. Rather, they feel the historic powerlessness of minority-group members over their own conditions of life can be meaningfully overcome only if they play a significant role in shaping educational policies and programs in public schools. Professor Edgar Epps expressed this view as follows:

> "Effective desegregation requires that minorities be assured an influential role in educational decision-making. This includes school personnel policies and practices, attendance policies and practices, pupil placement procedures, disciplinary policies and practices, curriculum, student elections and extracurricular activities, budgetary matters, and educational objectives."[23]

There are many different ways in which positive appreciation of diversity can be developed. Some of the specific techniques involved are discussed later in this book.

The third necessary ingredient of quality unified education consists of constructive inter-group activities. They are all forms of behavior in which members of both majority and minority groups participate together in an atmosphere that creates mutual respect and understanding among them. Such behavior can include normal classroom activities, sports, other extracurricular activities, assemblies, field trips, work experiences, special academic projects, and inter-group meetings or seminars. The most important will usually be classroom interaction throughout the day in classes containing members of both groups learning together. This means that deliberate separation of whites from minority-group members within a school in different classrooms, clearly different parts of the same classroom, or in different academic groups that are racially homogeneous, will prevent effective desegregation. Such separation blocks true equality of educational opportunities, and prevents the positive attitude and behavior changes which effective desegregation should generate.

However, in some situations, school districts meeting all the desegregation requirements set forth by the Supreme Court will still have some schools with entirely or almost entirely white or minority-group enrollments. This is most likely in districts with large majorities of minority-group students, as in some rural parts of the South, and in many big cities in both South and North. It will also be the prevailing condition in thousands of school districts across the nation where *de facto* segregation means there are very few minority-group students in the schools.

It will be impossible for the students in these one-group schools to experience constructive inter-group activities among themselves. To provide such experience, school authorities would have to arrange such activities with students from one or more other schools containing members of other ethnic groups. These activities could occur in any of the schools concerned, or outside those schools, as in museums or special interracial learning centers.

In theory, the basic attitude, behavior, and learning-condition changes required for effective desegregation could be created solely through such non-school-located relationships, if they occurred often enough. Therefore, effective desegregation would not absolutely require normal daily attendance of students from majority and minority groups at the same schools. This is relevant because such attendance sometimes requires very great physical dislocation and inconvenience for the students concerned. However, in practice, it is extremely difficult to change the attitudes and behavior patterns of members of both groups towards each other, and members of the minority group towards their own capabilities, without their daily presence in the same classrooms.

The inability to physically desegregate classrooms in all parts of the school districts mentioned above is often not the fault of school authorities. Rather it results from widespread racial and economic housing segregation typical of most large metropolitan areas. Trying to achieve effective desegregation of schools in many of these huge areas dominated by *de facto* segregation often brings school authorities to the limits of what schools alone can be expected to accomplish. As President Nixon stated, "Past policies have placed on the schools and the children too great a share of the burden of eliminating racial disparities throughout our society. A major part of this task falls to the schools. But they cannot do it all or even most of it by themselves. Other institutions can share the burden of breaking down racial barriers." Until some of those other institutions, such as those in housing and employment, cause major changes in the spatial distribution of whites and minority groups in large metropolitan areas, it is doubtful whether the schools alone can achieve effective desegregation throughout such areas. True, many school systems could do much more than they are now doing. But the ultimate challenge of achieving effective total desegregation is one that must be met through the combined actions of all parts of society—not just the public schools.

The Time Phases of Effective Desegregation

Because desegregation is a process rather than an isolated event, it occurs over time rather than in one instant or one month. Moreover, it involves fundamental changes in educational conditions and in personal attitudes and behavior patterns. So a great deal of time is required to make desegregation effective— probably several years at the very least.

Our analysis of desegregation efforts across the nation reveals that this timing dimension is widely misunderstood. Especially in areas desegregating under court orders, there is a strong tendency to focus attention upon a single event—opening day. Many school officials regard successful implementation of that event as the major action required for effective desegregation. Creating a harmonious opening day is indeed important, but it is only one step in desegregation. If school authorities then relax thier efforts, they are likely to be rudely reminded of the continuing nature of desegregation by later unpleasant developments. These could include student violence and dissension; protests by either white or minority-group parents or both; a sizable loss of either white or minority-group students from desegregated schools; or the decisive defeat of badly needed school bond issues.

To illustrate the importance of time in achieving effective desegregation, we have divided the process into three phases: planning, initial implementation, and positive development. These three phases overlap, but they are distinctive enough to serve as a useful guide.

The planning phase begins as soon as a school district has decided to desegregate, either voluntarily or under court order. It is most intensive between that moment and the day the schools first open on a desegregated basis. However, desegregation planning must continue—though less intensively—throughout the two later phases in order to make desegregation truly effective.

The initial implementation phase begins at the same moment as the planning phase, but becomes most intensive after the first plan has been formulated. Nevertheless, it is vital to start initial implementation efforts immediately after deciding to desegregate. In fact, participation in developing the plan should be the first stage of implementation. (Participation in the decision to desegregate could be an even earlier stage.) As will be shown later, the success of any desegregation plan is greatly enhanced if those most affected by it—especially both white and minority-group teachers, administrators, and students—actively participate in designing it. Initial implementation therefore begins very early. It continues well beyond opening day as the schools and the larger community become adjusted to the new situation. This phase encompasses most of the initial teacher training, community relations efforts, student orientation, administrative changes, curriculum changes, and other actions discussed in detail later in this book. This phase gradually transforms itself into the third phase described below.

The positive development phase should also begin as soon as it is decided to desegregate. Those planning and initially implementing desegregation must have a clear idea of what quality unified education is, and build it right into the entire desegregation process. Otherwise, they are not likely to produce it. As the schools and the community become adjusted to their new desegregation condition, focus on planning and initial implementation will fade out. Then the positive development of genuine unity and positive appreciation of diversity should become dominant. As this positive development proceeds, desegregation itself should merge with the general educational purposes of the school by influencing the ways in which those purposes are pursued.

These three phases have varying intensities. All three begin at the same moment, but have different life-cycles. The planning phase becomes most intensive immediately. It drops sharply in intensity after opening day, but remains in existence for a long time. The initial implementation phase becomes most intensive after the first plan is developed. It remains at high intensity until a few months after opening day, then gradually disappears. The positive development phase gradually builds to a dominant position shortly after opening day. It lasts for several years, eventually merging into the school's general educational development.

To make desegregation work, a school system must pursue all three of the basic elements of effective desegregation throughout each of these three time phases. In other words, its planning, initial implementation, and positive development efforts should all be aimed at *simultaneously* meeting the specific desegregation requirements established by the Supreme Court, avoiding undue disruption of school and community life, and achieving quality unified education for all students.

The Relationship Between Racial Desegregation and Economic and Social-Class Desegregation

The type of public school desegregation involved in all Supreme Court rulings to date is *not* aimed at counteracting prior segregation based upon economic or social-class status. A great deal of research has been done concerning the impact of both racial and social-class segregation and desegregation upon student performance on achievement tests. This research clearly indicates that the economic and social-class backgrounds of the students in each school are far more significant determinants of the impacts of either segregation or desegregation upon educational performance than their racial backgrounds. Specifically, minority-group students from relatively disadvantaged backgrounds show the greatest educational improvement when integrated in classrooms where students from middle-class and upper-class backgrounds form more than 50 percent of the total.[24] Conversely, as one study stated:

> "Classroom social class composition has a negative effect on the outcomes of instruction when the more advantaged student population constitutes less than a substantial majority."[25]

In commenting on the relative influence of racial and other factors, another researcher said that:

> "The research seems to show that . . . family background, social and economic status, and community characteristics appear to be by far the more important predictors of achievement in school."[26]

Therefore, he concluded that:

"School desegregation apparently would improve Negro students' academic performance only if it were combined with social class integration."[27]

These findings will be discussed in more detail in Chapter 2. However, they have several crucial implications concerning the basic nature of effective desegregation.

In many parts of the United States, the percentage of persons with relatively low economic and social-class status is much higher among minority-group members than among the white majority.[28] Therefore, racial desegregation in many public school districts results in the merger of two groups of students with quite different average economic and social-class status into the same schools. Certainly not all minority-group students are of relatively lower economic and social-class status. Nor are all white students of middle-class or higher status. In many rural Southern school districts, and some urban school districts, almost all students in *both* groups who would merge into desegregated schools are from low-income households. Nevertheless, on the average, there is a significant economic and social-class differential between these two groups of students.

Moreover, as noted earlier, most local school boards throughout the United States have predominantly middle-class members,[29] and many teaching staffs are largely middle-class. Many serious problems arising from desegregation result from attempts by these mainly middle-class institutions to educate children from relatively disadvantaged homes. Consequently, many of the educational methods likely to prove most relevant in achieving effective desegregation are those useful in teaching children from relatively disadvantaged backgrounds, regardless of race, color or nationality. Many educators believe that present methods of teaching relatively disadvantaged children are seriously deficient.[30] Nevertheless, they are the ones most relevant to many desegregation situations. True, some specifically race-related educational methods, courses, and teacher responses are extremely important for effective desegregation. But it is vital that those seeking to accomplish effective desegregation realize that many of the obstacles to doing so are based upon the economically-disadvantaged and socially lower-class backgrounds of many students from both majority and minority groups, rather than upon their racial characteristics.

One implication of these considerations has been almost totally ignored by the courts, and largely ignored by officials creating desegregation plans. To achieve maximum effectiveness in creating quality unified education, desegregation plans must take economic and social-class factors into account, as well as racial factors. This is vital because the economic and social-class composition of desegregated schools and classes will also certainly have a stronger influence upon the educational performances of their students than their racial composition.

Notes

1. *Davis v. Board of School Commissioners of Mobile County,* No. 436, Decided April 20, 1971, p. 4.

2. *Statement by the President on Elementary and Secondary School Desegregation* (The White House, March 24, 1970), p. 1. This is referred to hereafter as *President's Statement of March 24, 1970.*

3. This limitation on what the Supreme Court requires is explicitly stated in *Swann v. Charlotte-Mecklenburg Board of Education*, No. 281, Decided April 20, 1971, pp. 18–19. (This case is referred to hereafter as *Swann.)*

4. The Supreme Court has ruled that non-uniform treatment of students within a district based upon their race is unconstitutional, *unless* race is being taken into account to counteract past segregation. See *McDaniel v. Barresi*, No. 420, Decided April 20, 1971, pp. 2–3, and *Swann*, pp. 14, 23.

5. *Swann*, pp. 27–28.

6. Insofar as we could determine, the Supreme Court has not explicitly stated this condition. However, all of its actions so far have applied to districts, and each action applies to the entire district. See *Swann* and *Green v. County School Board of New Kent County*, 391 U.S. 430–439. (The latter is referred to hereafter as *Green.*)

7. *Brown v. Board of Education of Topeka*, 347 U.S. 483, pp. 493, 495. (This case is referred to hereafter as *Brown I.*)

8. *President's Statement of March 24, 1970*, p. 18.

9. *President's Message to the Congress Proposing Enactment of the Emergency School Aid Act of 1970*, May 21, 1970, p. 3.

10. *Green*, p. 439.

11. *Green*, p. 436.

12. *Swann*, p. 14

13. *Swann*, pp. 14–16.

14. Section 2000c of Title IV of the Civil Rights Act of 1964, 42 U.S.C., and *Brown I, passim.*

15. *Swann*, p. 14.

16. *Swann*, pp. 21–26.

17. *Swann*, p. 22.

18. *Swann*, p. 17.

19. *Swann*, pp. 18–19.

20. *Brown I*, p. 493.

21. Nancy H. St. John, "Desegregation and Minority-Group Performance," *Review of Educational Research*, Vol. 40, No. 1, p. 128.

22. For example, see Kenneth B. Clark, *Dark Ghetto* (New York: Harper Torchbooks, 1965), pp. 111–153.

23. Edgar G. Epps, "Notes on Desegregation," p. 7. This is an unpublished paper written especially for this study.

24. Robert P. O'Reilly, ed., *Racial and Social Class Isolation in the Schools* (New York: Praeger Publishers, 1970), p. 312.

25. *Ibid.*, p. 317.

26. David K. Cohen, "Defining Racial Equality in Education," *UCLA Law Review*, Vol. 16, No. 2 (February 1969), p. 258.

27. *Ibid.*, p. 268.

28. Numerous studies of this subject have been conducted during the past few years. For example, see "Poverty Increases by 1.2 Million in 1970," *Cur-*

rent Population Reports: Consumer Income, U.S. Bureau of the Census, Series P-60, No. 77, May 7, 1971, especially Table 5, p. 6.

29. Robert T. Stout, "The Processes of Desegregation," p. 5. This is an unpublished paper written especially for this study. Stout's source is George S. Counts, *The Social Composition of Boards of Education* (Chicago: University of Chicago Press, 1927). Although this is an old source, Stout says, "No subsequent study has demonstrated any basic change."

30. Edmund W. Gorden and Doxey A. Wilkerson, *Compensatory Education for the Disadvantaged* (New York: College Entrance Examination Board, 1966), pp. 156–182.

2

Principles of Achieving Effective Desegregation

This chapter and the others following it set forth a *prototype*—an idealized version—of the process of achieving effective desegregation in an individual school district. The "model" it contains has four basic parts:

1. A set of general principles about how to achieve effective desegregation (in this chapter).
2. A diagrammatic description of all the specific planning activities and tactics required to achieve effective desegregation, arrayed along a time line depicting the entire process (in Chapter 3).
3. A discussion of the desegregation planning process, keyed to the diagrammatic presentation mentioned above (also in Chapter 3).
4. A detailed discussion of the most effective tactics to use in achieving effective desegregation, divided into five categories: administrative measures, community relations activities, teacher training measures, student adjustment measures, and curriculum adaptation (in Chapter 4).

The principles, activities, and tactics included in this prototype, and the way they are laid out along the time line, represent conclusions derived from our extensive survey of existing knowledge about desegregation. True, no district ever behaved precisely in accordance with this idealized model, insofar as we know. Nevertheless, we have constructed this model because we believe that a prototype can provide the following benefits better than a purely narrative description of findings:

1. Useful guidance to officials designing new desegregation plans.
2. A "check-list" for officials reviewing desegregation plans already drawn up to determine how complete they are and whether the actions they include have been programmed in the most effective sequence.
3. A means of measuring and evaluating the progress of desegregation efforts in any district. This can be done by officials of that district and by "outside" observers, such as federal officials, local citizens, and state officials.

The Reliability of This Approach

Education and learning theory are marked by a great deal of uncertainty. There is considerable consensus about what the basic objectives of public-school

education are, but not about their relative importance. Moreover, much uncertainty exists concerning the causal relationships between particular educational methods (such as homogeneous grouping, or class-size variations) and
desired (or undesired) results related to the objectives of education. Therefore,
it would be wrong to claim that employment of the specific tactics described in
the prototype will always lead to effective desegregation, or any of its elements.
Undoubtedly, under some conditions, these tactics will not produce the desired
outcomes.

Nevertheless, our survey revealed that certain causal relationships relevant
to achieving effective desegregation have been reasonably well established by
experience in a variety of school districts. Many of these relationships are
essentially negative; they indicate that certain actions will surely impede effective desegregation. Moreover, all the positive relationships are highly conditional.
They describe actions that will contribute to effective desegregation but are not
strong enough to achieve it alone unless many other conditions are also met.
Inclusion of a specific tactic amounts to saying, "If a district does this, it increases the probability that effective desegregation will occur, and if it fails to do
this, it reduces the probability."

The specific causal relationships built into the prototype have not all been
empirically verified to the same extent. In some cases, carefully designed
empirical studies have confirmed a given relationship with high statistical
validity. Other relationships have been derived from very few field observations,
or from deductive reasoning employed by ourselves or authors writing in this
field. However, we have tried to exclude all specific principles and tactics which
are not strongly supported either by statistical evidence or by highly persuasive
field observations or deductions.

One question concerning this approach is sure to arise: how can a single
prototype for achieving effective desegregation possibly apply to all the immensely different school districts across the nation? The Supreme Court itself
has said "There is obviously no one plan that will do the job in every case."
Nevertheless, all desegregating schools are remarkably similar regarding those key
conditions most important in shaping the basic process required to achieve
effective desegregation. Clearly, they need many different physical desegregation
plans, as the Supreme Court observed. But concerning the desegregation process,
one set of basic principles is almost universally applicable. This is true because
nearly all school districts undergoing desegregation have two sets of common
traits: certain empirical conditions inherent in the way American public schools
are structured and operated, and certain relationships inherent in the process of
physically mixing white and minority-group students and staffs in formerly
segregated schools. The empirical conditions concerning schools include the way
they are administered, the presence of certain extracurricular activities, the
range of classroom sizes, their relationship to other elements of the community
and the educational backgrounds of teaching staffs. The relationships relevant

to interracial mixing include widely held attitudes in the white and black populations, the psychological dynamics of the interaction of formerly separated groups with varying mores and outlooks, the influence of nationwide race relations developments upon student perceptions, and some impacts of mixing students with very different social-class backgrounds (regardless of race) in the same classrooms.

The interactions of these two sets of nearly universal characteristics give rise to nearly universally applicable principles and tactics related to achieving effective desegregation. This does not mean the prototype set of tactics will perfectly fit every school district. But it does mean that each tactic is a response to forces or conditions likely to arise in every school undergoing desegregation.

Undoubtedly, detailed plans for desegregation in different districts will vary greatly. They involve such immensely differing traits as total population, racial composition, and geographic size and shape of the district. Hence the prototype does not attempt to provide specific contents for the plan elements dealing with these variables. True, in some cases, large differences in these variables may alter the fundamental factors on which the tactics in the prototype are based. Yet we believe such variations are surprisingly few. The prototype has much more universal applicability—as a guideline, not a rigid set of requirements—than at first seems plausible.

In hundreds of school districts—especially in the South—desegregation has already begun. It may even have been in progress for several years. Clearly, this prototype cannot be used for initial planning in these districts. Nevertheless, the prototype can still be used in such districts to determine whether all the key principles have been followed, and all the most important tactics have been performed in approximately the proper sequence. No matter how long a school district has been engaged in desegregation, the opening day of each school year represents an opportunity to introduce any major elements needed for effective desegregation that have been omitted from past efforts. In fact, changes and innovations can be made at many points during the school year. So valuable ideas can perhaps be gained from the prototype and applied "in midstream" even in districts which started desegregation long ago.

General Principles Concerning How to Achieve Effective Desegregation

Achieving effective desegregation requires a thorough understanding of certain general principles concerning (1) the nature of desegregation itself, (2) the attitudes toward it which public officials ought to adopt, and (3) those actions and relationships likely to make it work well. The most important such principles derived from this study are set forth briefly in the following paragraphs. It is vital that public officials responsible for carrying out desegregation study and absorb all of these principles. Our study proves that failure to follow them is almost certain to greatly reduce desegregation effectiveness.

The basic ideas in these principles could be organized in several ways. For the convenience of officials using them, we have employed an outline form combined with relatively brief explanations of each principle, and we have classified the principles into three categories. However, those using these principles should realize that many are applicable to more than one category.

Principles Concerning the General Nature
and Background of School Desegregation

1. Racial desegregation of public schools is a major social change in most communities, rather than a purely—or even primarily—educational development. For many people, school desegregation has profound social implications that outweigh its educational consequences. Desegregation is often seen by those opposing it and those favoring it as a symbol of greater racial equality between whites and minority groups. Many also view desegregation as a forerunner of other changes in minority-group status or in the nature of racial relations, rather than as a mainly educational development. This widespread perception of school desegregation as a broad social change means school officials engaged in desegregation must be far more concerned with relations between the schools and the rest of the community than is usually the case regarding shifts in educational policy.

2. Major changes in any long-established institution nearly always result from outside pressures rather than purely internal developments. This is certainly true of racial desegregation in public schools. It almost invariably begins with pressure applied on local school authorities by some other group, whether a civil rights organization or a federal court. Once desegregation has begun, it may develop its own internal dynamism moving it towards ultimate effectiveness. Nevertheless, it is likely that continued pressure of some kind from outside each school system will remain an important ingredient in moving that system towards truly effective desegregation even after the system's officials have assumed desegregation leadership. Top-level school officials should recognize and adapt to this relationship, rather than fight it. They can do so by establishing good communications with local civil rights advocates or other groups acting as outside change-agents (as well as with many other groups in the community). Such relations usually work better if the outside change-agents are locally based than if they are based elsewhere. Other parts of the community are more willing to recognize locally originated pressures as legitimate. In fact, the existence of strong locally based pressures for change can provide top-level school officials with useful leverage in accomplishing constructive improvements they want in spite of those who oppose any departures from the *status quo*.

3. Community conflict concerning the desirability of school desegregation is greatly reduced if desegregation is considered inevitable. This principle has two important corollaries:

   a. Strong statements by federal and state leaders—including state education officials—about the inevitability of school desegregation, and clear commitments by them to achieving it effectively, greatly reduce pressures on local school officials to delay or oppose desegregation. President Nixon has already made such statements about *de jure* desegregation. Also, the recent actions of the federal executive branch in pressing for strong desegregation plans have demonstrated a commitment to at least physical desegregation among schools. Moreover, governors of several Southern states have made strong statements about the necessity of desegregating schools rapidly, peacefully and effectively. This has unquestionably increased the chances of doing so within their states. Conversely, where top state officials oppose desegregation or remain silent about it, local opponents of desegregation are encouraged to increase their pressure upon local school officials to delay or hinder it.

   b. School boards and superintendents in *de jure* districts can reduce local controversy about desegregation by taking the position that it is inevitable and must be done, rather than by trying to gain local consensus about whether it is desirable. This approach is especially effective if the community is highly polarized on this subject. However, it is only applicable in districts where *de jure* segregation has existed in the past, since desegregation is not now legally required where segregation is *de facto* in nature. In *de jure* districts, the assumption of inevitability shifts public attention away from the highly controversial issue of whether or not desegregation should be done, to the much more technical issue of how to do it best. Most citizens are willing to leave resolution of that issue to professional educators.

4. Desegregating public schools is both so important and so complex that it requires thorough and very detailed advanced planning to accomplish it effectively. Therefore, as soon as the decision to desegregate has been made, school officials should quickly develop detailed plans for every part of the desegregation process—especially those parts that occur up to a few months after opening day. This is necessary to avoid unnecessary disruptions or conflicts that can arise simply through oversight of seemingly trivial items. In one district, failure to build a new trophy case for athletic awards previously won by black students caused a significant incident. To avoid missing such details, school authorities ought to create and use a "check-list" containing every action they believe is necessary. The prototype in this report provides an excellent basis for developing such a "check-list."

5. Desegregation often clearly reveals to the entire community for the first

time the inadequate total level of resources previously devoted to public education. In many districts, the school buildings, equipment, and even teacher skill-levels available to minority-group students in segregated schools have long been inferior in average quality to those used by whites. When desegregation occurs, these lower-quality facilities become mixed into the general educational system used by both whites and minority-group students. Hence many white students, parents, and educators become directly exposed for the first time to the inadequacies which the dual system has historically provided for minorities. In fact, they find themselves suffering from those inadequacies. This often generates strong pressures in white elements of the community for general improvements in school quality—especially in physical facilities. It may also lead to large-scale withdrawal of white students from the public school system. Consequently, desegregation may create strong pressures for federal assistance in funding general educational expenditures, as well as those specifically related to desegregation.

6. Many administrators and citizens think desegregation is largely completed if they get past the first opening day and the following few weeks successfully. In reality, it is a process requiring such major changes that it almost always takes years to carry out effectively. It is natural for school administrators in particular to concentrate their initial efforts on opening the newly desegregated schools without major incidents, and getting through the first few months successfully. Once this has been accomplished, many shift their attention to other concerns, believing desegregation is largely completed. Nothing could be further from the truth. Effective desegregation requires major changes in deep-seated attitudes and behavior patterns among students, teachers, and administrators of both majority and minority groups, and also among parents and community leaders, insofar as their relations to the schools are concerned. These changes never occur overnight, or even during the first year of school desegregation. Therefore, careful and thorough attention to desegregation-related planning and activities must continue long after the first year of desegregation if it is to be ultimately effective. In fact, such attention should become a permanent part of the general educational process.

Principles Concerning School-Community
Relations During Desegregation

1. The primary purpose of school-community relations programs connected with initial desegregation is to reduce the widespread uncertainty that naturally prevails throughout a community before any planned major social change. Members of each group in the community—including both white

and non-white students, parents, teachers and others—are unsure about what desegregation will really be like. They do not know precisely what behavior is expected of them, how they will be treated by school authorities and other participants, what behavior is expected of others, what particular class-room and other arrangements will exist, and what the ultimate consequences will be. Such uncertainty breeds both anxiety and mutually conflicting expectations about behavior; so it can lead to serious trouble. To alleviate this uncertainty, school authorities must take the initiative in establishing clear, explicit policies in writing, and making sure that all relevant persons both outside and within the school system are well informed about those policies before opening day. Such clarity and explicitness are not common in American public schools. In many districts, basic school objectives and many key policies are never written out or widely circulated. Some school officials believe that such vagueness gives them maximum flexibility in dealing with specific problems. However, this is a grave error in newly de-segregating districts because of the unusually great uncertainty and anxiety there. Clear and explicit policies given wide circulation are absolutely essential to achieving effective desegregation with minimum conflict and disruption.

The specific written statements which should be prepared in order to reduce uncertainty are discussed in detail in Chapter 4 under Administrative Measures. Many of these policies should not be formulated by the board and the superintendent alone. Rather, they should be worked out with the help of key teachers, staff members, students, parents, and others, as dis-cussed further below. But the essential responsibility for reducing un-certainty rests squarely on the board and the superintendent. The importance of reducing uncertainty both outside and within the school system cannot be overestimated. It is one of the most critical principles in achieving effective desegregation, especially during the first year.

2. School systems undergoing desegregation must greatly reduce the traditional isolation of the schools from the rest of the community prevalent in most areas. The broad non-educational implications of school desegregation focus community interest on the schools. But because schools are isolated from the community and have poor communications with it, confused expectations and beliefs arise about what is happening inside the schools. If the traditional isolation of the schools continues, these distorted beliefs and rumors will spread unchecked through the community. They can quickly create serious conflicts and disturbances. Reducing school isolation to prevent this outcome is especially important before and during the first year of desegregation. School authorities should communicate much more intensively than usual with others, both by telling them what the schools intend to do, and what desegregation will be like, and by listening to their reactions and suggestions.

Many other forces in society besides desegregation are also pressuring schools to reduce their general isolation. These forces include a desire for greater community control over schools in big cities, the charge that big-city school systems are unresponsive to the true needs of their students, the need for more efficient use of educational facilities now employed only part of each day and each year, and the need to more closely integrate school and work experiences.

3. How broadly school authorities should at first communicate with other local elements depends upon whether they are desegregating voluntarily or involuntarily, and how polarized community opinions are on this issue. Specifically:

    a. Where desegregation is purely voluntary, widespread contacts between school authorities and many other community elements are essential right from the start of the issue-resolution period. Voluntary school desegregation will work only if the community arrives at a fairly strong consensus supporting it. That requires a long participatory "dialogue" involving all relevant community groups.

    b. Where desegregation has been ordered by a court, and intense feelings about it strongly divide the community, school authorities should probably communicate at first mainly with small groups of key leaders. They might include the newspaper publisher, the mayor, major businessmen, key civil rights leaders, and other "influentials" who will not immediately denounce the school authorities for proposing desegregation. The purpose of this limited approach is to win the support of these leaders without providing an open forum for emotional attacks on desegregation that would heighten community tensions. However, a greater degree of participation in desegregation planning is necessary within the school system itself, as described below. Experience shows that thus "playing it close to the vest" until just before opening day has often minimized disruptive controversy and emotional debate until desegregation has become an accomplished fact—when they become pointless. However, this strategy requires switching to an intensive communications effort throughout the community right after opening day to reduce whatever uncertainty still remains because of initially restricted communications.

    c. Where desegregation has been ordered by a court but community feelings against it are not strong, school authorities should carry out a much broader initial communications process about it than the one just described. However, they do not need to engage in the intensive, community wide "dialogue" required for voluntary desegregation. Because of the court order, they can take the position that desegregation is inevitable, rather than trying to create a voluntary consensus supporting it. Undoubtedly, other specific community characteristics will also influence the style of communications most appropriate in any given district.

4. The single most important factor influencing the quality of desegregation achieved in any district is the nature of the leadership provided by the local school board and superintendent. If they take the initiative in developing their own desegregation plans right after the decision to desegregate has been made, and continue to exercise strong positive leadership far beyond opening day, then chances of achieving effective desegregation—or at least peaceful physical desegregation among schools—are excellent. But if they vacillate, or leave the development of desegregation plans to outsiders, or fail to exert strong leadership after a plan has been formulated, the probabilities of frequent disruption and ineffective desegregation are greatly increased. In almost every American school district, the vast majority of citizens are accustomed to leaving governance of the schools to the local board of education and school superintendent. Therefore, when a court orders the district to desegregate, if either the board or the superintendent or both quickly seize the initiative by creating and promoting an effective plan, they are likely to be supported by most local citizens. This is especially probable if desegregation seems inevitable. But if the board and superintendent refuse to take the initiative after a court order has been issued, their inaction creates a vacuum concerning what the schools should do. Local citizens and outsiders with strong opinions for and against desegregation quickly try to fill that vacuum. But they have no power to make binding decisions about how the schools should behave. Therefore, what results is not a resolution of the issue, but a heightening of tensions, conflict, and uncertainties. This creates a climate in which violence, school disruptions, and intense racial hostilities both within and outside the schools are all too likely. Moreover, that climate will never shift to one favoring effective desegregation until the board or superintendent gets solidly behind some desegregation plan and exercises strong and unwavering leadership to implement it.

Experience shows that plans drafted by "outsiders" are rarely as effective or as strongly supported as those drafted by local school authorities themselves. Thus, the effective support and strong positive leadership of the local board and/or the superintendent are the *sine qua non* of effective desegregation, not only during the planning period, but also during initial implementation and positive development. The faster local school authorities take positive action after the decision to desegregate has been made, and the more unwavering their support for accomplishing desegregation effectively, the less the chances that anti-desegregation forces within the community will succeed in rallying enough support to create significant disruptions. Once the school board itself realizes that desegregation must eventually be carried out, it should resist any temptation to avoid the "political heat"

of actively supporting desegregation. The longer it vacillates, the greater
the difficulties that the school system will face in ultimately achieving
effective desegregation. This conclusion has been repeatedly validated by
experience in many parts of the country.

5. Desegregating an entire school system simultaneously appears to be more
effective than desegregating it a little bit at a time. Some school systems
have desegregated gradually—often starting with the two highest grades one
year, doing two more the next year, etc. This approach has been widely
employed in rural areas, and often works reasonably well. But it also post-
pones the necessity of everyone in the community facing up to desegregation and learning to accept it as the "natural" condition. Moreover, when
some parts of a school system are desegregated and others are not, it is
very difficult to obtain compliance with a single set of rules concerning
interracial relations, student behavior, extracurricular activities, and student
government. The prolonging of segregated classes in some parts of the
system also allows those opposed to desegregation to cling emotionally to
the past. And the retention of segregation in some classes, plus evident
reluctance at ending it, perpetuates the feeling among minority-group students that they are considered inferior by those responsible for educating
them. All of these conditions constitute serious barriers to *effective* desegregation. In contrast, simultaneously desegregating the entire system removes these
barriers immediately. At first, it may seem a more traumatic experience. But
afterwards *everyone* can concentrate on adjusting to school desegregation,
rather than some doing so while others are still in segregated classes.

6. Before and into the first year of desegregation, school authorities should
consider establishing proper community relations as their top priority job,
and creating the proper climate within the schools themselves as of second
priority—though still vital. As time passes and the community accepts
desegregated schools as "natural," school authorities should make establishing the proper climate for effective desegregation within the schools their
most important task. A suggested time-sequence for shifting the priorities of
various desegregation activities is presented on an accompanying page. This
chart was taken from a paper by Dr. Elias Blake, Jr., but it conforms to
other findings we have surveyed. Initially, obtaining community acceptance
of desegregation has top priority so an overall climate can be established
within which schools can function without undue disruptions or tensions.
Formulating effective school policies is a vital part of creating that climate,
as explained above. It is also critical for creating the proper atmosphere
within the schools themselves. Staff interpersonal relations also have
relatively high priority early in the process, since the attitudes and example
exhibited by teachers and staff vitally affect student perceptions about how
much equality of opportunity really exists within the school. Eventually

student interpersonal relations assume top priority, because affecting them is the ultimate purpose of effective desegregation.

7. Although school authorities should use both formal and informal methods of communicating with the general community, major emphasis should be placed upon creating an effective network of informal channels. Formal channels include TV and newspaper announcements; large public meetings; written notices sent out to parents or the community; and published official documents. Informal channels include small meetings in the homes of parents; visits by teachers, school workers, and administrators to homes and club meetings; personal counselling with parents and students; informal picnics or box-lunch dinners for groups of parents; and telephone "rumor centers" manned by volunteers for answering individual questions. The more parents and community leaders are made part of such informal channels, the greater will be the ability of school officials to tell the community what they are planning and doing and to learn what its members want or are concerned about. These networks should be set up in the pre-opening-day period. They can then be used to inform people about what desegregation will be like and what behavior is expected of all concerned, and to answer their questions about it.

   Active participation by the superintendent and all principals in such informal communications is vital to their success. If most people are aware of such participation, and feel they could easily see these key officials if they wanted to, they will feel greatly reassured even when they have no specific problems.

8. School officials should establish close working relationships with other public officials whose efforts are important to achieving effective desegregation—especially the police and social welfare agencies. As soon as the school board even starts considering desegregation, initial conversations with law enforcement officials should be held to obtain firm support for whatever course the board adopts. Once the decision to desegregate has been made, but before it is announced, a joint policy statement on law enforcement in and around the schools should be worked out with local law enforcement officials. This should be announced almost at the same time as the decision to desegregate. Specific procedures should be planned for the most likely types of incidents in or near the school requiring police action and constant communication maintained on an informal basis even when nothing untoward is happening. Similarly, school officials should establish close relationships with social welfare workers providing services to students' families, and with health care workers operating clinics or other facilities used by those families. Greater knowledge of the backgrounds and needs of students will enable school officials to better understand them and provide them with more appropriate educational support.

Principles Concerning the Achievement of
Effective Desegregation Within the Schools

1. Racial desegregation is such a significant change in many formerly segregated
   schools that they should be regarded as truly new schools. This is particularly important where desegregation has resulted in many minority-group
   children attending formerly all-white schools, or many white children
   attending formerly all-black schools—but it is basically applicable to almost
   every desegregated school. The school buildings may be the same as before,
   and the classroom formats and subjects may remain unchanged. But many
   crucial aspects of desegregated schools are so new and different that the
   basic quality of life and education in them is changed. These new aspects
   include the new status of legal equality for minority-group children, the
   new racial composition of the student body, and the new racial composition
   of the teaching and administrative staffs. Moreover, many students in any
   desegregated school have departed from their former school, to which they
   had built up some loyalty, and are "strangers" in a completely different
   school. They have no loyalty to this different school's name, record, athletic
   teams, or traditions. If the school retains these elements just the same as
   before, then those who were there formerly are familiar with it, but the
   newcomers feel like aliens. To create genuine unity in a desegregated school
   with a sizable fraction of both whites and minority-group students, it is
   almost necessary to give that school a new name, new colors, and new team
   names so that both groups will be on the same footing in regard to the
   school's identity. Then both groups can begin establishing loyalty to the
   same entity, and it will impart equal status to each of them. If possible,
   student leaders of both groups should be consulted in creating this new
   identity—which may be formed from an amalgam of the colors and symbols
   of the schools both groups formerly attended. If a new identity of this
   type is imparted to the school, this will dramatize the importance of desegregation to students, staff, parents and the entire community.
2. Desegregation creates a greater need than ever in schools to emphasize
   certain non-academically oriented functions of education for children. These
   include the building of confident self-images and feelings of self-respect,
   the development of respect and consideration for others regardless of
   their race, social status or academic skills, the ability to live and work in
   harmony with others who are "different" from oneself, and the development of familiarity with and skills in democratic decision-making. These important purposes have often been unduly subordinated to imparting
   academic skills and preparing a selected group of students for entry into
   college. However, there are three reasons why such non-academically
   oriented purposes need to be emphasized in a desegregated school. First,
   many white and minority-group students in this school have suddenly

*Priorities for Key Problem Areas in Desegregation
at Different Times in the Desegregation Process*

Time Period	Priority Ranking of Problem Areas
From Initial Desegregation Decision to About Half-Way Through the First Desegregated School Year	1. Community Relations 2. School Policies 3. Staff Interpersonal Relations 4. Student Interpersonal Relations
From About Half-Way Through the First Desegregated School Year Well Into the Second Year	1. School Policies 2. Staff Interpersonal Relations 3. Student Interpersonal Relations 4. Learning Programs 5. Community Relations
From Well Into the Second Year of Desegregated Schools Onward	1. Student Interpersonal Relations 2. Staff Interpersonal Relations 3. Learning Programs 4. Community Relations 5. School Policies

Source: Dr. Elias Blake, Jr., "A Re-Definition of Education Problems Occasioned by Desegregation and Title IV of the Civil Rights Act of 1964," Written for the National Conference on Equal Educational Opportunity in America's Cities, Washington, D.C., November 1967.

Note: The time periods shown above have been altered from those given in the original paper so as to conform to the time-line in our analysis.

transferred from some other school that they had traditionally attended, so they naturally feel somewhat uprooted and anxious. Second, the new situation of attending school with members of another race traditionally separated from one's own has a natural tendency to raise anxiety among all students. Third, many white and minority-group students come from disadvantaged backgrounds that have not prepared them well for coping with a curriculum heavily oriented towards college preparation.

As a result, if desegregated schools do not concentrate very intensely upon performing the non-academically oriented functions described above during at least the first year or so of desegregation, they will create attitudes and behavior patterns in many students that will discourage good academic performance in the long run. As emphasized repeatedly in this study, students who feel inferior, who are humiliated or rejected by their classmates, who never experience any academic successes in school because the course

content and method of decision-making are unfamiliar to them are not
motivated to do their best in terms of academic achievement. Furthermore,
they may build up resentments and frustrations, or simply lower their own
efforts in ways that reduce the ability of their fellow students to attain
their maximum potential academic achievement too. Thus, it is doubly in
the interest of those who want *all* students to do their best in terms of
academic achievement to have the schools place heavy emphasis upon key
non-academically oriented functions in the early parts of the desegregation
process. This certainly does not mean that the schools should neglect the
teaching of traditional academic subjects. In fact, improvements in academic
achievement are an important incentive for desegregation, especially among
minority-group students and parents. It does mean that they should put that
purpose in better balance with the others set forth above than is traditionally
the case. Transmitting to white and minority-group parents the importance to
all their children of this emphasis will require a very well-thought-out community relations program.

   This principle has many key implications for all aspects of school structure
and activities, as set forth in Chapter 4. One point worth mentioning here is
the importance of providing easy access for all children to extracurricular
activities. Many students who are not academically inclined can do very well
in sports, dancing, drama, and other non-academic activities that can impart
feelings of self-confidence and participation they do not find in their classroom experiences. Yet the very students who most need these activities are
often excluded from them because they feel inferior, are rejected by their
classmates, lack money, or are shy about joining something new. School
officials should arrange extracurricular activities so that participation by
all students is convenient. Furthermore, officials should take positive steps
to encourage such participation, such as insuring bi-racial sponsors of clubs,
etc. Above all, officials should not cancel activities as part of the process of
school desegregation or as a concession to the fears of white parents—
thereby depriving students who need non-academic means of gaining dis-
tinction from enjoying opportunities they formerly experienced in segregated schools.

3. Desegregation reinforces a need for greater diversity of curriculum content
   and value acceptance in American public schools that has already been
   generated by other cultural and social forces unrelated to race (as noted in
   Chapter 1). Specifically, desegregation often tends to bring together in one
   school system enough white and minority-group children not likely to
   attend college so that they form a relatively larger proportion of total enrollment than before. Moreover, desegregation increases the diversity of
   viewpoints, social backgrounds, and cultural experiences represented among
   the children in a single school. Therefore, desegrated schools typically
   need greater curriculum diversity in terms of both course content (such as

the addition of vocational subjects) and educational methods (such as more emphasis upon group-oriented activities). In many school systems, the consolidation of formerly separated schools creates a larger average school size than before. This larger-scale school is organizationally capable of supporting greater diversity. Thus, desegregation generates both a need for greater diversity in the schools, and the means of meeting that need.

4. Effective desegregation cannot be achieved unless the school administration itself creates a powerful example by providing equal opportunities for all its staff members, regardless of race, color or nationality. Studies of the methods of desegregation considered most effective by many school administrators and education experts indicate that direct personal contacts among members of different racial groups are the single, most powerful means of improving race relations. In contrast, appeals to general principles of human equality are ineffective. In short, actions speak louder than words. This principle has the following corollaries:

   a. Effective desegregation within the schools is seriously undermined if a school district discharges a disproportionate number of minority-group teachers and staff members as part of the desegregation process. The replacement of Negro principals, coaches and teachers by whites who are no better qualified (if as well qualified) is a striking message to the student body and the entire community that top-level school officials consider minority-group members inferior to whites, regardless of what they say about racial equality. When desegregation of schools begins this way, it is difficult to establish a climate of true equality of opportunity credible to the minority community.

   b. Similarly, school administrations must assign staff positions of importance to both white and minority-group members and have teachers from both groups teaching students from both groups, if they want to establish an example of equal opportunity for their students. Always having black staff members act as "assistants to" and never as superiors to whites, or never having black teachers in mainly white classrooms, tends to undermine achievement of real equality of opportunity.

   c. Where teaching and administrative staffs have much lower proportions of minority-group members than the student enrollment in a district, it may be desirable to deliberately recruit a disproportionate number of new minority-group staff members in order to raise their representation on the staff closer to that of the student body. It is especially important to have a significant number of minority-group men on the staff to provide models for minority-group boys.

5. Within the school system, encouraging the active participation of students, teachers, other staff members, and parents in both the preparation and implementation of specific desegregation plans is the most effective way to improve the quality of those plans and their acceptance by the people

they affect. In almost all human activities, those who are responsible
for accomplishing any task will do so much more enthusiastically if they
have helped design the task than if they are simply handed orders and told
to execute them. Because of the complexity of desegregation planning,
and the need to avoid generating excessive controversy in the initial
planning process, such participation should often be restricted at first to a
few key leaders from each group. However, if those leaders are well chosen,
their participation in designing the plan will greatly enhance its legitimacy
in the eyes of everyone else. Moreover, their suggestions will usually increase the plan's sensitivity to the interests of all the groups concerned. It
is particularly important to obtain active participation of minority-group
students, teachers, and parents in the planning process. Their participation is both a vital symbol of their newly equal status in the school system,
and an effective means of insuring that minority-group desires, fears, and
interests are given adequate weight in the formulation of the plan itself.

The use of participatory planning within the school system will represent a
major change in established behavior for many highly centralized school
districts. However, employment of relatively secretive, highly centralized
planning concerning desegregation cannot work in the long run. Desegregation requires major changes in the attitudes and behavior of all staff members and many students if it is to be effective. The probability of such
changes is nearly zero if they are simply ordered from above. True, requirements for rapid development of the initial desegregation plan, plus a
need to concentrate administrative efforts on community relations before
opening day, may make it difficult to establish participatory planning at
first. Until such planning becomes an integral part of the desegregation
process, however, that process is not likely to become effective.

6. The development and promulgation of clear and explicit rules concerning
student and teacher behavior in all facets of school life—especially classroom
discipline—should be completed as soon as possible in order to reduce
uncertainties within the school system. Copies of such rules should preferably be passed out to all students on opening day, and certainly not more
than ten days later. Students experiencing desegregation for the first time
are especially uncertain and confused about what behavior is expected
of them, and what they can expect from members of groups with whom
they have never before attended school. Therefore, it is of critical importance to set forth—*in writing*—simple and impartial rules applicable to most
situations likely to arise in normal classroom and extracurricular activities.
Moreover, strong efforts should be made to insure that all students and
parents read and understand such rules so that no incidents occur out of
ignorance. This stress on clear and explicit behavioral rules may also
represent a departure from established practices in the school system. It
may even seem to be unnecessary or demeaning to the students. This is

especially likely if many come from permissive, upper middle-class homes and have caused few behavioral problems in the past. Nevertheless, the mixture of such students in classes with others from entirely different home backgrounds—often much more authoritarian in character—creates a new situation. That situation is fraught with possibilities of conflicts arising simply out of mutually inconsistent behavioral expectations, rather than ill will. The only way to create consistent behavioral expectations among students from such different backgrounds suddenly thrown together in a novel situation is to provide them all with explicit rules they can fully understand.

7. Student disciplinary problems and practices are a major cause of both uncertainty and feelings of ill will in desegregated schools for white and minority-group students and parents alike. In addition to clear and explicit rules concerning disciplinary matters, school officials must provide: strict impartiality of treatment regardless of race (though taking into account other individual traits), swift disciplinary action, and constant accessibility of top-level officials (especially principals) to students, teachers, and parents for both disciplinary action and airing of grievances. It is particularly important that any incidents that reputedly involve unfair treatment because of race or color be quickly investigated and followed up with either corrections of distorted views or remedial actions, as appropriate. Such vigilance is necessary to prevent rumors of race-related conflict or prejudicial treatment from spreading through the community, and to establish a reputation for firm fairness among all groups. Furthermore, teachers who are not skilled at handling severe disciplinary problems should be able to receive *immediate* assistance from higher-level staff personnel specializing in such problems.

8. Desegregation creates a need for most school principals to shift the nature of their roles somewhat by spending more time in direct contact with students, teachers, and parents and less on administrative matters. School boards and superintendents should be aware of this need and support proper responses to it. In desegregated schools, many teachers of both races are reluctant to discipline students of the other race because they do not know what disciplinary behavior those students expect, and they fear being considered discriminatory. Hence, they either fail to exercise proper discipline in such instances, or turn them over to the principal. This means that the principal must make himself immediately accessible to *all* his teachers *all* the time so he can handle such cases with dispatch. Moreover, he must be equally accessible to students of both races who believe they are being treated unfairly by teachers or other students. Such "instant accessibility" is crucial to both these situations because a key characteristic of all effective justice—whether punitive or remedial—is close proximity in time to the alleged offense. For the same reason, the principal must also be

easily accessible to parents who come to the school because they believe
their children are not being treated fairly. This triple need for accessibility
takes up more of the principal's time and makes it more difficult for him to
schedule periods of sustained and uninterrupted activity on administrative
matters.

Desegregation increases uncertainty and confusion among teachers as they
face new problems with their students and need advice and guidance about
how to carry out curriculum and organizational changes in their approach
to teaching. Moreover, the newly desegregated faculty needs leadership
to insure that proper interracial attitudes and behavior patterns are established. For these reasons, the principal in a desegregated school must spend
more time than formerly working closely with his teachers, and acting as
their professional educational leader, rather than just as an administrator.

Specific techniques that the board and superintendent can use to support
the principal's shift in roles are set forth in Chapter 4.

9. Although officials in desegregated districts should make every effort to
avoid potentially inflammatory incidents in or around the schools, they
should also be well prepared in advance to cope with such incidents if they
happen—for, sooner or later, they usually do. In terms of avoiding undue
disruption, all the principles set forth in this chapter can be considered
means of *preventative planning.* But our analysis of desegregation experience
throughout the nation indicates that, even in districts that have exercised
great care in planning, there is likely to be some kind of "incident" within
the first three months that is interpreted by the community at large—often
wrongly—as a "racial" incident caused by desegregation. Among the incidents
that have aroused intense community feelings are the following: a protest
demonstration by black students angry because their athletic trophies were
not displayed in the desegregated school, a fight between a group of white and
black adolescent boys, a fight between larger groups of black and white high
school students at a football game, the slapping of a white woman teacher by a
black girl in class, the expulsion from school of black students but failure to
punish white students when both engaged in a fight at the school, the
arrest and jailing of a black girl for swearing at her teacher, black students
extorting small sums of money from younger white children outside the
school, and black girls acting aggressively in gym class by pushing white
girls. Some of these incidents resulted from truly reprehensible racial discrimination. But most were simply typical actions of normal children of
various ages, formerly found in segregated schools among members of the
same racial group. However, in a community with a long tradition of racial
separation, and some citizens who intensively oppose desegregation, it is
easy for such typical behavior to be interpreted as a dire result of "mixing
the races" in school. Rumors fly, and much of the good will and acceptance

carefully built up over months of work by school officials is jeopardized in a few hours.

That is when a thorough program of community relations can pay big dividends. First, if law enforcement action is necessary, the local authorities should be called upon to act immediately—but in a racially impartial way, as previously agreed upon in discussions with school officials. Second, the local media can present the facts in a calm manner, rather than as "scare" headlines. Third, school officials can use their previously established informal communications networks—including a "rumor center"—to "get the word out" to both whites and blacks about what *really* happened, and how its causes were in fact related to racial tension—if they were. Fourth, school officials can meet directly with any aggrieved parties and with anyone who feels his or her children are "threatened" by remaining in a school where "such things happen." If school officials have prepared all their supporters in the community for rapid action in the event that such an incident occurs, they can effectively counteract it and dampen untrue rumors very rapidly—before they have damaged the acceptance of desegregation already built up throughout the community.

Typically, when incidents happen, the first one usually occurs either on opening day or about eight to ten weeks later. By then, white and minority-group students have become familiar enough with each other to abandon some of their initial caution and mutual avoidance. No matter how thorough a district's preventative planning against incidents has been, it is certainly prudent for its officials also to develop an incident-response plan that can be put into immediate effect—just in case.

10. All the desegregation-related policies and activities in schools described above should become permanent parts of the educational process. In order to promote effective desegregation, they must be built into the normal, day-to-day life of the school and remain integral parts of that life into the indefinite future. They cannot be viewed as one-time-only expedients adopted just to promote harmony during the first year of desegregation, and then forgotten or even gradually de-emphasized, if the schools concerned are to achieve effective desegregation. This conclusion applies to such things as emphasis upon curriculum diversity; meaningful participation in the planning of school policies and programs by students, teachers, and parents; non-discriminatory policies regarding the hiring, retention, and promotion of teachers, administrators, and support staff members; use of clearly written rules and policies; and greater emphasis by principals upon their roles as student and teacher counsellors. By encouraging widespread adoption of these policies and activities, desegregation cannot only become effective in itself, but also can contribute to the general improvement of American public education.

Conclusion

In most desegregating districts, the decision to desegregate was forced upon the community by federal court order, against the desires of the dominant elite and much of the population. It is easy—perhaps natural—for the attitudes of school officials and many citizens towards desegregation to be heavily influenced by this coercive origin. Yet the Supreme Court's consistent rulings on this subject surely indicate that once a district has been ordered to desegregate, the process becomes inevitable in that district—in some form or other.

If school officials and the local citizenry want to gain the greatest possible benefit from their school system, they will seek to make that form *effective* desegregation. The basic perspective most likely to enable any district to achieve effective desegregation is viewing the entire desegregation process as a positive opportunity to improve the quality of education offered in the local schools, not only for minority-group children, but for everyone. If the principles described in this chapter are followed, a significant improvement in educational quality should accompany desegregation. In contrast, if district officials take a basically negative viewpoint towards desegregation, its occurrence may not help the quality of their schools. The more negative their perspective, the less likely they are to gain any benefits from desegregation. The more positive their perspective, the larger their likely benefits will be.

In the remaining chapters the authors set forth a prototype planning process, and specific desegregation tactics, that will enable school officials approaching desegregation with a positive perspective to achieve it effectively.

3

Planning and Timing Effective Desegregation

This chapter describes the way all the basic steps in the process of achieving effective desegregation should ideally occur over time, with special emphasis on desegregation planning. It is built around a time-line chart on which all these steps have been laid out in chronological order, with the key relationships among them clearly indicated. School officials and others can use this chart to plan achieving effective desegregation and to evaluate desegregation planning and progress for any given district.

These two functions are possible because the chart presents a prototype, or idealized version, of how the desegregation process ought to occur if it is to be effective. The chart, and the remainder of this chapter, are thus parts of the prototype desegregation process described at the beginning of Chapter 2. For reasons discussed there, this chart can be directly applied to almost any school district in the United States engaged in desegregation, regardless of its particular characteristics (such as size, shape, school enrollment, percentage of minority-group students, etc.). Similarly, the desegregation planning process described in this chapter is also applicable to almost any district. Certainly, officials of a particular district can vary specific elements in the entire process in order to meet local circumstances. However, we believe that any really large deviation from the process as described in this chapter is likely to reduce the effectiveness of the desegregation ultimately achieved in the district, or increase the time it takes to achieve truly effective desegregation, or both.

The first major section in this chapter presents a detailed discussion of the basic characteristics of effective desegregation planning. This discussion sets forth many of the key ideas about such planning derived from the knowledge surveyed in this study. It is followed by the time-line chart and a discussion of the specific components of that chart. A certain amount of repetition of contents is found in these two discussions, and both of them also significantly overlap the various parts of Chapter 4. However, such repetition is unavoidable.

The Basic Characteristics of Effective Desegregation Planning

Effective desegregation planning has thirteen basic characteristics, which are depicted in a chart on an accompanying page. These characteristics are discussed in detail in the following sections, which contain most of the substantive anal-

Effective Desegregation Planning Is:

1. An on-going process
2. Based on strong, positive administrative leadership
3. Rooted in explicit, written school board policies
4. Comprehensive but not complete
5. Moderately long-range
6. Evolutionary
7. Flexible
8. Based upon factual research
9. Action-oriented
10. Participatory
11. Evaluation-oriented
12. Realistic
13. Understandable

ysis about effective desegregation planning in this chapter. More detailed information about the timing and contents of specific steps in the desegregation planning process follow the chart.

Why Effective Desegregation Planning Is a Process

As explained in Chapter 1, effective desegregation is a process of educational change. Effective desegregation planning is determining what actions are necessary to bring about that educational change in a given district. But the process of achieving effective desegregation takes a long time—usually several years. Moreover, the first part of that process—the time between the decision to desegregate and opening day—is an extremely busy period for school officials. It would be unrealistic to believe that they can sit down right after the decision to desegregate and prepare a complete, detailed, and comprehensive plan covering all the years of action necessary for effective desegregation. No one has the foresight required to draw up such a plan without greatly revising it later. And school officials in particular—though they must do some important planning immediately—are too harassed during this period to prepare a complete and final plan that would extend over three or more years. Therefore, effective desegregation planning is itself a process that occurs over time. The desegregation plan should not be static and rigid, but dynamic and flexible. It is not a single document prepared once-and-for-all but a series of documents, each of which builds upon but alters those that preceded it. It is vital for all school officials to understand the dynamic nature of effective desegregation planning. Only if such planning is viewed as a changing process can it be carried out successfully.

Why Effective Desegregation Planning Must Be
Based upon Strong, Positive Administrative
Leadership

As every administrator knows, drawing up a plan and putting it into effect are two different things—often worlds apart. It is especially hard to carry out a plan involving a major social change in a community where there is strong opposition to that change. Therefore, unless any desegregation plan is forcefully followed up with strong, positive administrative leadership, it will not be translated into reality.

For some parts of a desegregation plan, it may seem obvious to the entire community that there is little chance that they will not become reality. This seems true, for example, of plans concerning the assignment of students to specific schools, and bus transportation for students. Moreover, these elements of desegregation plans are likely to be covered by a court order when a district is under such an order. Nevertheless, experience in several districts proves that many white parents have simply refused to send their children to the schools they were assigned to by the desegregation plan. Instead, they send their children to some other school through various subterfuges. Unless school officials keep alert to the possibility of such evasion, and move quickly to stop it, the effectiveness of the entire desegregation plan could be seriously undermined.

Many other far less visible parts of a desegregation plan will require even more vigorous administrative leadership to become reality. For example, simply stating in a plan that the curriculum will be changed, and that teachers will adopt a new approach towards discipline, will not alter the life-long habits and practices of experienced teachers, both white and black, whose behavior is not consistent with the plan. Unless all the elements in the plan are strongly supported and followed up by school administrators who want them to occur, the plan will remain nothing but paper. That is why strong, positive administrative leadership is the single most important ingredient in achieving effective desegregation, as noted in Chapter 2. The need for such leadership in gaining acceptance of desegregation within the entire community is thoroughly discussed elsewhere in this handbook, especially in Chapters 2 and 4.

Why Effective Desegregation Planning Is
Rooted in Explicit, Written School Board
Policies

The ultimate legal and administrative authority for all action taken within a school system lies in the policies governing that system set forth in writing by the school board. In many districts, the number of explicit, written policies adopted by the board, and the degree of detail they cover, are sparse indeed. The board may believe that using only very broad general policy statements, loaded with ambiguity, allows it to retain maximum flexibility in making actual decisions. Or it may not believe that detailed policies need be established by the board—that they should be the prerogative of the superintendent. Or the board may simply have never gotten around to considering what its policies really are concerning a great many aspects of education or school activities.

However, effective desegregation requires a complete re-examination of all the activities carried out within the school system to be sure they: a) are free from any negative constraints that inhibit attainment of equal educational opportunities, and b) are designed to make the maximum possible positive contribution to that attainment. Since all activities within the school system are legally based upon the school board's policies, the most important ultimate determinant of whether those activities will conform to the two conditions just mentioned is the nature of those board policies. That is why continuing the practice of not writing down the policies that govern many key school activities will actually inhibit effective desegregation. Many school activities or arrangements carried over from practices in segregated schools inhibit effective desegregation. Yet if no explicit policies come out from the board repudiating such activities, or requiring a new approach to them, the old and destructive habits may persist for years. Therefore, it is critically important for the school boards of desegregating schools to: a) draw up a complete list of all the policies they ought to have; b) carefully examine the written policies they do have and adjust them to achieve the two purposes related to desegregation described above; c) create new policies in writing to fill any gaps indicated by comparing what exists with the idealized list, insuring that these new policies also serve the same two desegregation-related purposes; and d) forcefully announce the entire resulting set of new and revised policies to the community, the school staff, and the students, insuring that each group receives and understands those policy statements relevant to its interests.

This formal creation and statement of school board policies in writing establishes the underlying foundation that all desegregation planning must have in order to be carried out effectively. It needs this foundation because:

1. Such policies provide the legally-binding basis supporting all desegregation plans.
2. Written policies provide clear guidance to planners concerning what objectives they ought to seek, and what constraints exist shaping the ways they may seek those objectives.
3. When planners can clearly support their plans by citing written board policies that back up those plans, this gives much greater psychological force to plan implementation efforts. It "legitimizes" the plans and provides stronger motives for everyone in the school system to carry out those plans.

4. Such policies provide a means for settling some disputes that may arise over implementation of resulting plans.

Why Effective Desegregation Planning Is Comprehensive But Not Complete

To be truly effective, desegregation must affect nearly all parts of the activities that occur in a school, and influence many of the ways those activities are structured. Thus, the specific elements that must be included in any effective desegregation planning are comprehensive in nature. They include the following:

Administrative policies and procedures.
Student location and school assignment.
Teaching personnel—composition and training.
Administrative personnel—composition and training.
Curriculum.
Student activities (including extracurricular activities).
Physical facilities.
Community relations.
Relations with other government agencies (especially law enforcement and welfare agencies).
Student transportation.
Evaluation methodology.
Student guidance program.

Specific plans concerning the best ways to modify existing or past behavior so as to achieve effective desegregation should be drawn up for each of the above elements or they should at least be included in overall planning. Planning only the physical desegregation of schools cannot accomplish effective desegregation. A plan for physical desegregation alone would cover student school assignment and student transportation, and perhaps some community relations planning. The Supreme Court also requires that desegregation plans include teacher and administrative staff desegregation. Just incorporating these five elements into a desegregation plan cannot possibly produce effective desegregation. All twelve of the above elements are essential to its achievement. That is why effective desegretation planning must be comprehensive. However, desegregation plans need not always discuss every aspect of each element—only those specific aspects relevant to desegregation. True, desegregation may drastically alter almost every aspect of some elements. This is likely to be true of student transportation, for example. But other elements—such as the use of physical facilities—may be only slightly affected. That is why effective desegregation is comprehensive but not complete. The precise degree of completeness relevant to each element will vary greatly from one district to another.

Why Effective Desegregation Planning Is Moderately Long-Range

Effective desegregation takes years to achieve—probably at least five years in most districts. Therefore, initially planning its achievement requires looking quite far ahead. On the other hand, experience proves that detailed plans made by school officials and teachers for periods much more than a year ahead are difficult to carry out without substantial revision. Therefore, avoiding such revisions requires a relatively short-range plan.

Making desegregation planning moderately long-range by using a three-year planning horizon represents a reasonable compromise between the two objectives discussed above. This means a district should prepare plans that cover desegregation-related school activities for the three school years following the initial decision to desegregate. A three-year horizon is far enough ahead to allow for rational and efficient planning of certain activities that need continuity over a long time. An example is an in-depth in-service education program for teachers covering aspects of education relevant to desegregation. On the other hand, a three-year horizon is not too far away to make normal human foresight useless as a guide to the future. This recommendation that a three-year planning horizon be used in desegregation planning is *not* based upon any particular experience in desegregating districts. Most of them used shorter horizons, although several districts surveyed have continued in-service training for periods up to five and six years. Thus, the length of the training period in this study has been established as a reasonable period in which the typical school district could achieve effective desegregation.

Why Effective Desegregation Planning Is Evolutionary

Effective desegregation planning is evolutionary because of the practical impossibility of putting together a fully-comprehensive, three-year plan right at the start of the entire desegregation process, and because of the need for continual modification of whatever plan is created at the outset. The period between the initial decision to desegregate and the first opening day is usually that of the greatest emotional, political and personal stress in the community—as upon school officials—especially in districts under court orders. It would not

Specific Stages in the Evolution of Effective
Desegregation Planning

1. FIRST-YEAR PLAN
   a. Initial Plan
   b. First-Year Teaching Plan
   c. First-Year Student Activities Plan
2. Interim, Ad Hoc Planning—First Round
3. COMPREHENSIVE PLAN
   a. First-Round Evaluation
   b. Federal Funding Applications
   c. Final Comprehensive Plan
4. Second-Year Plan
5. Interim, Ad Hoc Planning—Second Round
6. Third-Year Plan
7. Interim, Ad Hoc Planning—Third Round
8. Transformation into General Educational Planning

OR

Continuation of Some Form of Explicit Desegregation Planning

be realistic to expect school administrators to develop a full-blown plan covering all twelve elements during this initial period.

Instead, school officials should develop a desegregation plan that evolves through several stages as shown in the chart at the top of this page. Two of these stages—the First-Year Plan and the Comprehensive Plan—have been underlined because they are the two really major planning efforts required for effective desegregation. The other six stages are important, but require far less effort than these two—and are mainly derived from them.

These stages can be described in more detail as follows:

1. First-Year Desegregation Plan
   The First-Year Plan consists of three parts, drawn up separately by three different groups. The Initial Plan is prepared under the direct supervision of the district school administration, perhaps using outside consultants for technical assistance. It is drawn up first. The First-Year Teaching Plan should be prepared by a joint bi-racial committee of school administrators and teachers. It can be started after the Initial Plan has been started, but both must be finished in time to be put into operation before opening day of the first year of desegregation. The third part is the First-Year Student Activities Plan, which can be started at the same time as the First-Year Teaching Plan. This student-oriented plan should be drawn up by a joint bi-racial committee of school administrators and students. It also must be completed before opening day.

Further details about these three parts are set forth below.

a. Initial Desegregation Plan
    Work on this plan should be started immediately after the official
    decision to desegregate the district. The plan must be completed in time
    to put its main components into effect before opening day, as noted
    above. In some districts, this means the Initial Plan must be prepared
    rapidly on a "crash" basis. In other districts, much more time is
    available. However, at a minimum, this Initial Plan must cover the
    elements shown below, which are discussed in more detail in various
    parts of Chapter 4:

    Many administrative policies and procedures.
    Student location and school assignment.
    Desegregation of teaching personnel, and assignment of teachers to
        specific schools and positions.
    Desegregation of administrative and other non-teaching personnel, and
        assignment of them to specific schools and positions.
    Whatever adjustments in physical facilities are required for initial school
        operation.
    Extensive community relations.
    Cooperation with local law-enforcement agencies.
    Complete student transportation plan.

    All of the above elements—plus others covered by the other two parts
    of the First-Year Plan—are necessary in order to prepare for opening day,
    open the school successfully, and move effectively through about the
    first eight to ten weeks of school without substantially revising the
    original plans. If time permits, other elements might also be added.

    This handbook contains detailed discussions of most of the above
    elements that must be included in the Initial Plan, except for the
    physical-planning aspects of assigning and transporting students to
    specific schools. Chapter 4 does not contain any discussion of the
    relative merits and disadvantages of such techniques as school pairing,
    central schools, consolidation, and use of geographic attendance
    zones. These subjects and the technical skills to prepare such plans are
    highly developed and accessible through Title IV-sponsored consulting.
    The subjects themselves have already been discussed in great detail in
    several publications easily available to local school officials; so it would
    be pointless to reproduce them here. The most significant of these
    publications are:

Office of Education, *Planning Educational Change,* Volume I, *Technical*

Aspects of School Desegregation (OE-38014), Washington, D.C., (U.S. Government Printing Office Catalog Number FS 5.238:38014); price - 45 cents. This booklet has very detailed instructions about how to create plans for student assignment, with illustrations of various alternative arrangements. It is an excellent practical guide.

U.S. Commission on Civil Rights, *Racial Isolation in the Public Schools,* Volume I (Washington, D.C., 1967), pages 140 to 183. (Available from the U.S. Government Printing Office for $1.25 per copy in paper cover.) This chapter of a larger report contains a more theoretical discussion of various approaches to assigning students to specific schools in desegregation, including some illustrations. It is less oriented towards detailed practical instructions concerning how to go about such planning.

The Initial Plan must be drawn up so quickly, and is so technical in nature, that it is almost impossible to have broad participation of non-administrators in its preparation. However, after it is prepared but before it is published, it should be reviewed by the two committees that prepare the First-Year Teaching and First-Year Student Activities Plans. This review is mainly to inform these representatives concerning the nature of the Initial Plan, rather than to obtain suggestions for revision. However, any really outstanding suggestions they make should certainly be used.

b. First-Year Teaching Plan
    This part of the First-Year Plan should cover the following elements:

    In-service teacher training, with special focus on training to be conducted before opening day. This should include some human relations seminars, courses, or other instruction.
    Curriculum modifications, including changes in what is taught, how the teaching is structured, and what educational methods are used.

    These elements should be developed by a joint committee of selected school administrators (probably principals) and teachers. The plans they originate should be subject to final review and approval by school administrators.

c. First-Year Student Activities Plan
    This part of the First-Year Plan should cover the single element of desegregating student activities. It should include deciding upon possible creation of a new identity for the school through designation of new school colors, songs, athletic team names, and school names. A joint and bi-racial committee of principals and students (and perhaps some teachers) should consider these matters, developing means of insuring bi-racial participation in all student activities. Concerning a possible

new school identity, the committee can either recommend an immediate set of resolutions to the school administration (which should have final approval), or recommend that several alternative resolutions be put to a vote of the students after the school opens. (The latter device has *not* been tried anywhere, insofar as we could determine.)

All three parts of the First-Year Plan should be developed with a one-year time horizon, rather than a three-year horizon. This will allow desegregation planners to concentrate their energies upon properly handling those components of the plan necessary to successfully navigate the first year, without having to worry about longer-range considerations. Moreover, when a district is first engaging in desegregation, it usually does not yet have sufficient experience to know what ought to be done past the first year.

2. Interim, Ad Hoc Desegregation Planning—First Round
    The next evolutionary stage in desegregation planning consists of making small, incremental additions to, or revisions in, the First-Year Plan before the Comprehensive Plan has been completed. The latter is described below. However, before it can be completed, there will undoubtedly be occasions when modifications in, or extensions of, the First-Year Plan will become necessary. For example, further planning for desegregating student activities will be required as more such activities approach on the school calendar. All such *ad hoc* changes constitute alterations in what the First-Year Plan called for. However, experience shows beyond question that needs for such changes will arise constantly. It is far better to meet those needs with a series of interim changes in the plan, and the practices based upon it, than to stick to the original plan rigidly at the expense of closer adaptation to these emerging needs.

3. Comprehensive Desegregation Plan
    The third evolutionary stage in the desegregation planning process is development of the Comprehensive Desegregation Plan for the district concerned. This is the long-range plan that should encompass all twelve elements of the desegregation process as described earlier in this chapter, and plan them over a three-year time period (that is, until the end of the third year of desegregation). As indicated on the time-chart set forth later in this chapter, work on the Comprehensive Desegregation Plan should commence sometime before the middle of the first school year, say about the beginning of December. Preparing this plan will probably require several months. It may not be completely finished until sometime during the summer between the first and second years of desegregation, although it might be finished in the late spring of the first year.

This plan should include all those elements that may have been omitted from the First-Year Plan. If the First-Year Plan contained only the components described earlier, then the following additional components will be incorporated in the Comprehensive Plan:

Some administrative policies and procedures not revised earlier in the year.
Major realignment of the curriculum, concerning both its structure and its contents.
Major adjustments of, or additions to, physical facilities.
Intensive teacher in-service education regarding most of the aspects of education affected by desegregation.
Consideration of program evaluation methods.
Development of a guidance program for students.

During the process of preparing the Comprehensive Plan, several other activities closely related to this plan will take place, as shown on the time-chart. These activities can be viewed as sub-stages in the evolution of desegregation planning within the district. They include the following:

a. First-Round Evaluation
    As discussed later in this chapter, a series of tests concerning a number of the dimensions of effective desegregation should be given to district students in the spring of each year after the schools have been desegregated. If similar tests had been given when the schools were segregated, this would allow comparisons of achievement performance and attitudes so as to determine some of the impacts of desegregation. If similar tests had not been given in the past, then this first round of testing would establish a statistical base for comparisons with tests administered in succeeding years. Some of the results of this first round of evaluation may serve as useful inputs to the Comprehensive Plan by providing insights concerning what activities it ought to contain or what goals it should emphasize.

b. Federal Funding Applications
    In the spring of the first year of desegregation, school officials will probably want to prepare funding applications for various federal educational aids to be used during the following school year. Some of the required information can be taken from that gathered for the Comprehensive Plan. Conversely, the Comprehensive Plan may include activities to be financed with federal funds stemming from these applications.

c. Final Version of Comprehensive Plan
    This is the final product of the planning process just described. Since

the first year of desegregation is over or almost over by the time this
final version is completed, it focuses upon the second and third
years, along the lines discussed above.

Since no school district that we surveyed had actually developed a Comprehensive Plan of the type described above, the need for such a plan may
seem questionable. Why go to all the work of carrying out another and even
more extensive planning process, when just a few additions to, and modifications of, the First-Year Plan would be more in keeping with the actual
experience of desegregating school districts? The Comprehensive Plan has
been built into this evolutionary planning process because it meets several
key needs that cannot be adequately met by the First-Year Plan alone.
Specifically, these needs are:

*The need to develop plans for long-range components of effective desegre-
gation*, such as teacher training programs with an integrated curriculum
scheduled over two to three years. The First-Year Plan has a one-year time
horizon, and administrators are usually too busy when drawing it up to
develop reliable three-year plans.

*The need to evaluate the experiences gained during the first year of deseg-
regation, and to incorporate the results into plans for future years.* This
may call for extensive changes in certain ideas or procedures that appeared
desirable when the First-Year Plan was drawn up, but have proven unwork-
able or inefficient. It may also require the addition of many new elements
which were not thought of when the First-Year Plan was designed, but
which experience has shown to be vital.

*The need for a more thorough and reflective consideration of desegregation
than may have been possible under the sometimes hectic conditions before
opening day.* In many districts, the original planning is done under great
pressures of time and community conflict. Plans that are to influence the
school's behavior for years to come should be created when more thorough
and less harried consideration is possible.

The need for broader participation in the desegregation planning process.
The pressure of time described above often compels district officials to
minimize the number of people who participate in developing the First-Year
Plan—especially the Initial Plan. Moreover, school officials may deliberately
restrict such participation to reduce potential community conflict before
opening day if the community is highly polarized concerning desegregation.
But after the community has lived with desegregated schools for six months
or more, chances of creating intensive conflict by encouraging broad
participation in the planning process are greatly reduced. Hence, for both
timing and political reasons, participation in desegregation planning can be
much broader when preparing a Comprehensive Plan than when preparing

the First-Year Plan. The advantages of broader participation are discussed later in this chapter.

The need for greater continuity from one year to the next. Whereas the First-Year Plan focuses solely on one year, the Comprehensive Plan looks on the entire three-year period—including the year almost over when this plan is drawn up. This allows the planners concerned to develop programs with much greater continuity over time than a one-year planning horizon permits.

In order to meet all of these needs satisfactorily, any school district must go through an extensive plan-revision process around the end of the first year. The approach embodied in this chapter simply expands that revision process somewhat to produce a more comprehensive—and hence more effective— result than would emerge from merely revising the First-Year Plan.

4. Second-Year Desegregation Plan
   During the summer between the first and second years of desegregation, or perhaps in the spring of the first year, a specific plan for the second year should be prepared. This constitutes the fourth stage in the evolution process. Like the First-Year Plan, the Second-Year Plan should have a one-year time horizon. However, it will differ from the First-Year Plan in the following respects:
   a. The Second-Year Plan should be fully comprehensive; that is, it should include all twelve elements described earlier in this section, and cover all aspects of each relevant to desegregation. Hence, it will not be a "minimal contents" plan like the First-Year Plan.
   b. The Second-Year Plan will essentially be derived from part of the Comprehensive Plan, which covers the remainder of the period, from opening day of the first year to the end of the third year of desegregation. The Second-Year Plan will be prepared right after a draft of the Comprehensive Plan has been completed. So it may not be necessary to prepare much of a separate plan for the second year. Of course, this was not possible when the First-Year Plan was formulated.
   c. The Second-Year Plan will probably not contain as intense a focus of activities and concern upon the first few weeks after opening day as the First-Year Plan.

5. Interim, Ad Hoc Desegregation Planning—Second Round
   This fifth stage consists of occasional modifications in, and additions to, the Second-Year Plan to meet changing circumstances during the second year of desegregation.

6. Third-Year Desegregation Plan
   During the summer between the second and third years of desegregation, or

in the spring of the second year, the Third-Year Plan should be derived
from the Comprehensive Plan. The Third-Year Plan is very much like the
Second-Year Plan. It has a one-year time horizon, covers all twelve elements,
and can be derived for the most part from the Comprehensive Plan. How-
ever, the Third-Year Plan will be formulated over one year after the
Comprehensive Plan was originally drawn up. Therefore, preparing the
Third-Year Plan is likely to take more time and effort than preparing the
Second-Year Plan.

7. Interim, Ad Hoc Desegregation Planning—Third Round
    This is the seventh and final stage in the desegregation planning process—
    unless the district decides to continue preparing explicit desegregation plans.
    This stage is analogous to the second and fifth stages described above.

8. Transformation of Desegregation Planning into General Educational Planning
    After the third year of desegregation, school districts can either a) con-
    tinue with a series of further desegregation plans, b) transform them into
    general education plans, or c) cease performing such planning altogether.
    Which course to take depends in part upon how effective desegregation has
    been during the first three years. This in turn can be measured by the annual
    evaluation described earlier. If the district decides to continue explicit
    desegregation planning, it may choose to prepare another three-year
    Comprehensive Plan. Or it may decide to revise the Comprehensive Plan
    each year, maintaining a running three-year horizon, and develop its annual
    plan directly from the revised Comprehensive Plan.

Why Effective Desegregation Planning
Is Flexible

The reasons why effective desegregation planning must be flexible have been
stated in the preceding discussion.

Why Effective Desegregation Planning Is
Based Upon Factual Research

Desegregation planning involves many highly technical considerations. It
also deals with complex relationships among both tangible persons and things—
like children, buses, and school buildings—and highly intangible things—like
academic achievement, human relations, and self-images. Moreover, the decisions
made in desegregation directly affect the lives of hundreds or perhaps thousands
of people in each district; so these decisions should certainly not be approached

casually. Both these factors emphasize the need to base effective desegregation planning upon careful, thorough, and accurate factual research.

Every desegregation plan should be built upon a solid base of factual data concerning such variables as the following:

1. The number, age, location, racial character, and socio-economic status of the children in the district. None of the many school district desegregation plans we examined took account of the socio-economic status of the children concerned, even though there is overwhelming evidence that this variable has a critical impact upon the quality of education in any given school. Therefore, school officials drawing up desegregation plans, or reviewing plans drawn up for them by consultants, should definitely examine the socio-economic status or social class mixture of students in each school proposed by any plan under consideration, as well as the racial mixture in that school.

2. The number, size, location, physical capacity, facilities, and condition of all the school buildings and other facilities in the district.

3. The number, experience, racial character, skill-levels, past assignments, and general capabilities of the teachers and administrative staff members in the district, and of other non-teaching, non-administrative personnel.

4. Results of past achievement tests and other tests concerning the non-achievement ingredients of effective desegregation for all the students in the district, as related to key student characteristics, such as race, socio-economic status, school socio-economic status, school racial mixture, etc.

5. The number, condition, and capacity of the transportation vehicles available in the district.

6. The nature and extent of use of specific curriculum materials and teaching methods in various schools and classes within the district.

7. Drop-out and retention rates in all the schools in the district, analyzed in relationship to other key relevant variables set forth above.

8. The nature, quantity, and condition of special educational facilities and materials available in each school (such as movie projectors, tape recorders, and library materials) as related to the racial and other characteristics of that school.

9. Any available measures of public opinion concerning the quality of education now being received by the children attending various schools in the district, or other relevant aspects of the local schools.

10. Recent trends concerning the most important of the above variables.

Procurement of all the above information should provide a reasonably sound basis for making most of the planning decisions required for effective desegregation planning.

Because certain technical skills are required to obtain and analyze all the above data rapidly, and to formulate alternative possible plans from those data, it may be desirable for the district to retain the services of one or more desegregation consultants during preparation of the First-Year Plan and the Comprehensive Plan. Most Southern states have University Desegregation Centers that offer such services, or can direct local district officials to those who do. A listing of the regional Title IV offices that handle referrals to University Desegregation Centers is included in Chapter 4.

Why Effective Desegregation Is Action-Oriented

All too often, planning results in the production of attractive documents, or lengthy statements and reports, which are promptly filed and forgotten. Yet the real purpose of planning is to influence actual behavior and events. Some types of desegregation planning are clearly not likely to go unused. They concern activities that are highly visible and must be performed every day—such as the student bussing program set forth in the transportation plan. But other types of planning—such as that which seeks to encourage more minority-group participation in extracurricular activities—do not have any such built-in implementation. Only systematic and persistent follow-up efforts will make these plans work.

Therefore, a key part of every plan should be a section on how the planned activities will be implemented. This should indicate:

Who is responsible for implementation.
What they are supposed to do.
When and where they should do it.
How their activities will be financed.
What reports they are to make concerning their actions (if any reports are required).
Who is responsible for supervising or evaluating the results.

When these ingredients of implementation are clearly set forth, definite accountability for results is established. Then administrative officials know who is responsible for success or failure. This acts as an added incentive for achievement of the desired results in most cases.

Why Effective Desegregation Planning Is Participatory

As indicated earlier, many parts of the effective desegregation planning process involve significant contributions from people other than school administrators themselves. True, the latter should have final responsibility for whatever plans are adopted. But teachers play a key role in formulating the First-Year Teaching Plan and the Comprehensive Plan; students play a similar role in formulating the First-Year Student Activities Plan and the Comprehensive Plan; community residents help work out certain portions of the Initial Plan concerning community relations; and officials of other agencies also help formulate parts of the Initial Plan. In all these instances, the participation of non-school officials in desegregation planning is likely to make its results more effective because:

People who must help carry out a plan are more willing to do so when they have had a part in creating it. They identify with its objectives far more than if they are just handed a ready-made plan and asked to carry it out.

Participation in planning is an excellent means of communicating the nature of the problems involved, and helping people become better informed about them. This is especially important concerning desegregation, since it helps reduce uncertainty about what is likely to happen in desegregated schools.

When school administrators ask people to participate in desegregation planning, and make use of the ideas they contribute, those people become convinced that they and their views are valued by the administrators. This makes them far more likely to support or even advocate to others the plans so developed, and the school system in general.

The quality of the plans developed through such participation is likely to be much greater than if cooperation did not occur. Non-administrative participants often have far more accurate knowledge than school administrators concerning the needs, beliefs, and behavior patterns of key actors in the community. For example, students can often tell much better than school administrators how other students will react to a certain action.

Participation often increases the "legitimacy" of the plans it generates in the eyes of others who did not participate themselves. They know that people like themselves—or representatives of their interests or points of view—were involved. Therefore, they believe the resulting plans are more likely to take account of their needs than if no such participation had occurred.

All of these functions of participation in planning are especially crucial to achieving effective desegregation, which has as one of its key ingredients a positive, cooperative attitude towards the schools and what happens inside them among all parents, students, teachers, and administrators. People are far more likely to exhibit a cooperative attitude if they, or others like them, have participated in planning desegregation in some way than if the plans they must live with are arbitrarily imposed upon them without prior consultation. Thus, the crucial role of attitudes in achieving effective desegregation requires that planning for it be as participatory as possible.

Why Effective Desegregation Planning Is
Evaluation-Oriented

It is impossible to determine whether the desegregation process in a given school district is working effectively unless specific and systematic efforts are made to evaluate its progress objectively. Whereas physical desegregation is relatively easy to observe and measure, effective desegregation requires many non-physical ingredients that cannot be observed directly, and are extremely difficult to measure indirectly. These ingredients include:

The strength of self-images among both white and minority-group students, especially those who are disadvantaged.

The nature of interracial attitudes in the school.

The success of the school in teaching children to participate in democratic decision-making processes effectively.

The degree of genuine unity achieved in the school.

The degree of respect for diversity generated by the school among its students.

The academic achievement of its students.

Only the last of these ingredients can be measured objectively and quantitatively with much accuracy. Even so, the causal factors related to it are open to widely varying interpretations.

Nevertheless, any school seeking to achieve truly effective desegregation must institute systematic means of evaluating its progress concerning all of the above variables as best it can. It should perhaps add others to the list of those requiring periodic measurement, or at least estimation. The most intangible are the factors required to reach the goal, the more necessary it is to try measuring them objectively and systematically—because the less helpful casual observations become. Therefore, the prototype desegregation process as illustrated on the time-chart in this chapter contains an annual evaluation of student performance and student condition regarding all the variables listed above. This annual evaluation becomes part of desegregation planning when its results influence plans for future activities. Such "feedback" should occur each year after the test results are available.

In performing such evaluation, it is critically important to include a broad spectrum of variables in the measurement process, and not to rely almost entirely on data concerning academic achievement, simply because they are the most readily obtainable. Academic achievement is a very important non-physical ingredient in effective desegregation, but it is by no means the only important one. Measures of the others should be developed by using a variety of techniques, perhaps including opinion surveys. It is especially important to educate the general community concerning the broad spectrum of variables that must be measured for an accurate evaluation of progress towards effective desegregation. Otherwise, the community may erroneously judge that progress solely in terms of the impact of desegregation upon academic achievement.

An additional component in the evaluation program concerns two activity items: the actual frequency with which individual teaching techniques were used during the year, and the actual degree of student participation in all extra-curricular activities. Information about these two types of activity should be gathered as part of the annual evaluation process, though not necessarily at the same moment as the academic and non-academic testing described above. Perhaps it would be more appropriate to gather these data at the end of each school year. The number of times that individual teaching techniques were used will indicate the degree to which teachers are actually implementing plan recommendations. This tabulation will also provide a data base for evaluating judgments about the effectiveness of techniques. For example, teachers may say that intensive tutoring in reading has not had a positive effect on student skills. Yet the fre-quency data may show that such tutoring has only been used for two short intervals during the year. Then administrators might decide to test this technique further before abandoning it. Tabulation of student participation in extra-curricular activities will show the extent of minority-group participation in clubs, sports, musical events and student government. This is a significant measure of the achievement of effective desegregation in a school.

All tests and tabulations in the evaluation program should be analyzed in terms of minority and majority groups. In school districts now, achievement tests are not usually identified and separately tabulated by race and ethnic group, so there is no way of readily determining whether or not differences exist between racial groups within a district. A knowledge of variations in achievement levels between white and minority-group students in the same grade in a district is essential if corrective programs are to be introduced. Similar knowledge is equally vital in evaluating the non-academic measures described above.

Why Effective Desegregation Planning Is Realistic

Realistic planning does not formulate goals that cannot possibly be reached within the time-frame of the plan. School officials who develop realistic plans thereby reduce the risk of generating expectations in the minds of local citizens that cannot be met in practice. Experience indicates that many parents have unrealistic expectations concerning the effects of desegregation. Some black parents have unrealistically high expectations about how much better-educated their children will be than they were in segregated schools. Some white parents have unrealistically low expectations concerning the effects of minority-group children on the quality of education their children will receive. Realistic officials must cope with both of these erroneous impressions by stating the facts clearly and calmly, and by maintaining open communications with all parents.

Realism also implies willingness to reveal certain facts to the public—such as student achievement scores, school crime and delinquency rates, and other sensitive variables. These should not be hidden or avoided, but published in a straightforward, factual manner without undue fanfare. The way they are handled by the press will be greatly influenced by the school's media policy, as discussed in Chapter 4.

Why Effective Desegregation Planning Is Understandable

No matter how sophisticated the techniques of analysis used in desegregation planning, it will not be effective unless its results are stated in terms easily understandable to those who are affected by the plans created. Therefore, all desegregation plans should be written in relatively simple language, and the use of jargon or highly technical wording should be avoided.

Elements of Desegregation Prototype Chart

The following prototype chart sets forth the step-by-step process for achieving effective desegregation within an individual school district. It is difficult in narrative form to fully convey the planning-and-action process required to carry out school desegregation. However, a network diagram is easy to follow and easy to use as a guide both for district planning and for evaluation of progress.

The diagram presents a complex process as a series of specific related activities. This method of presentation helps local school officials answer the questions, "Where do we start?" and "What do we do next?" Each activity logically follows from one or more that came before and, in turn, advances the process to the next specific activity.

The time schedule shown along the bottom of the chart for the first school year is designed to assist local administrators in scheduling their planning for future action. In a process as lengthy and as involved as achieving effective desegregation, it is quite common for people to become too deeply absorbed in one aspect while neglecting another. The network diagram should help local administrators avoid this by indicating when activities should begin so as to assure a proper progression through the whole sequence. There is a considerable amount of leeway in the timing of many activities. However, the diagram sets certain limitations because some activities must be completed before others can begin.

It should be emphasized that this prototype chart represents only one possible way in which the various steps in the planning-and-action process can be laid out in relation to each other. There are many variations of this layout and among these relationships. In fact, the diagram will often have to be modified somewhat to fit particular characteristics of specific districts. Nevertheless, the basic sequence of major steps in the planning-and-action process illustrated on the chart should occur in most districts that are purposefully working toward effective desegregation. A chart could also be prepared at a much greater level of detail—and individual districts may wish to do this—but the prototype included here covers what the authors believe to be the critical steps.

Timing On The Prototype Chart

The time sequence shown on the prototype chart covers only two of the four broad time periods that we have identified as stages in the desegregation process. The four phases of desegregation in most districts are as follows:

1. Issue Resolution Period—From the time the issue is first raised locally (e.g., a court case is filed or a strong public statement is made by a powerful local action group) until the decision is made by the school board to desegregate.
2. Pre-Opening Period—From the time of the desegregation decision until the first opening day of desegregated schools. This period is detailed on the chart.
3. Post-Opening Period—This is generally the first year of operations of the desegregated schools. The sequence of events for this time period is also shown on the chart. The most critical time in the first year of operations is the post-opening day period of about eight weeks when students and faculty members are settling into their new routines and the unusual is gradually becoming the usual.
4. Revision Period—After the first year of desegregation, there is generally a need for operational revisions in curriculum, teacher training, student grouping, administrative policies, and community relations. It is at this time that the Comprehensive Plan can best be formulated. This plan should be scheduled for revision as unanticipated events occur and as the attitudes and achievements of students and teachers are periodically evaluated. The revision period extends until effective desegregation has been achieved in the school district, covering the Second-Year and Third-Year Plans described earlier. To show this time period (which may take from three to ten years) on the chart would simply have involved repetition of most of the events of the first year, but with less emphasis on adapting to the new. We do suggest in the text, however, some of the specifically different actions that should be taken in the second year and afterwards.

As mentioned earlier, a month-by-month sequence of events is shown on the chart for the first year of school desegregation. This timing is by no means absolute. For example, the evaluation program could certainly be undertaken in February instead of late March if that were more convenient within the framework of the local academic program. The prototype is designed as a general guide for sequencing events, not an inflexible blueprint. We believe that the timing is realistic in terms of both capability of accomplishment and the relationship of different types of activities to one another.

Symbols On The Prototype Chart

The prototype diagram uses symbols to express causal and priority relationships in a pictorial manner. These symbols are straightforward and easy to understand. The key to the symbols on the chart can be explained as follows:

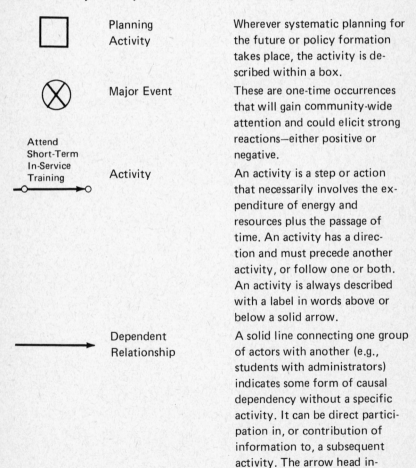

	Planning Activity	Wherever systematic planning for the future or policy formation takes place, the activity is described within a box.
	Major Event	These are one-time occurrences that will gain community-wide attention and could elicit strong reactions—either positive or negative.
Attend Short-Term In-Service Training	Activity	An activity is a step or action that necessarily involves the expenditure of energy and resources plus the passage of time. An activity has a direction and must precede another activity, or follow one or both. An activity is always described with a label in words above or below a solid arrow.
	Dependent Relationship	A solid line connecting one group of actors with another (e.g., students with administrators) indicates some form of causal dependency without a specific activity. It can be direct participation in, or contribution of information to, a subsequent activity. The arrow head in-

dicates the direction of dependency. No labels are placed on these lines.

_____ Continued   A dotted line indicates continued
            Normal Activity   existence and normal behavior
                               of the parties involved (e.g.,
                               faculty or community) but no
                               special action related to desegregation taking place.

All of the events and activities on the chart are numbered. There is no significance to the numbering sequence, though the order is from left to right. The numbers merely serve as identification for reference in the narrative portions of the chapter.

The events and activities on the prototype chart fall into five general categories:

1. Policy formation.
2. Development of plans.
3. Major events.
4. Independent activities.
5. Preliminary activities (those carried out in preparation for something in one of the four categories above).

The paragraphs below that describe the contents of the chart deal with these categories in turn, except for preliminary activities, which are discussed with the items they precede.

Policy Formation

Board Policy Statement

The first step in the actual process of desegregating a school district (after the decision to do so has been made by the board), is formation of a broad policy statement by the board. This statement firmly and positively declares that the district's schools and their staffs will be desegregated as completely as possible, starting on the opening day of the next school year.

In some communities, boards have divided this statement into two parts: a first statement announcing that the board is considering this issue, and a later statement declaring its decision.

In any event, it is crucial that this statement receive wide circulation throughout the community and full coverage in the press. A detailed discussion

of the nature of this statement is presented in Chapter 4 in the section on
Administrative Measures. Another discussion of how to publicize the statement
is presented in Chapter 4 in the section on Community Relations.

In addition, the board should formulate more explicit statements on
specific issues. Generally, the firmer the board is on more issues, the more ready
the community will be to accept desegregation as inevitable. Among the subjects
that should be covered in an initial policy statement by the school board are:

a. Employment, placement and tenure of teachers.
b. Filling of vacant teaching positions.
c. Assignment of teachers and principals to desegregated schools.
d. Bussing to achieve desegregation.
e. Transfer of students over attendance zone boundaries.
f. Distribution of different races in school organizations.
g. Distribution of teachers, by race, in district schools.

Often it will not be possible to issue policy statements on all of the above
subjects before the Initial Plan is prepared. If that is the case, then omitted
policies should be formulated and issued publicly as soon as possible after
planning has been undertaken.

In addition to verifying the certainty of school desegregation to the community, firm policy statements by the school board provide the superintendent
and his administrative assistants with strong support that will enhance their
positions as leaders in the desegregation process.

Each of the major plans prepared for the school district—the Initial Plan,
the First-Year Teaching Plan, the First-Year Student Activities Plan, and, later,
the Comprehensive Plan—will require policy decisions for implementation. At
each of these points, policy statements should be issued in an unequivocal
manner, preferably by the school board but at least by the superintendent.
Administrators may find it prudent to consult with selected groups of teachers,
principals, students, and community leaders prior to finalizing policies. However,
a fine line of authority exists at this point, because it is very important that
the superintendent assume a lead position.

Student and Staff Regulations

The second major policy formulation needed in the pre-opening period
consists of two sets of regulations: one for students, and one for employees—both
professional and support staff. These regulations should be available in writing
for distribution at student meetings and teacher in-service training sessions held
prior to opening day. A check list of the types of policy statements that should
be made is included in Chapter 4, but the level of detail necessary should be
mentioned here.

Teachers' regulations should cover such subjects as sick leave, discipline, and specific duties such as monitoring play yards, sponsoring student clubs, attending in-service training sessions, etc. (Teacher handbooks traditionally cover these points, but all regulations should be reviewed in light of desegregation.) Student regulations should be explicit on causes for suspension or expulsion, behavior at extracurricular functions, care of textbooks, etc. Regulations should also be issued to bus drivers, cafeteria workers, secretaries and custodians so that they can fulfill their roles in a constructive manner.

It was recommended by the Division of Equal Educational Opportunities of the Office of Education in a desegregation plan for Mobile County, Alabama, that, "Through personal observations, students see that nonprofessional service positions in their schools are not for members of one race and that harmonious working relationships can exist between members of both races."

The student and employee policies and regulations established in Step 12 on the chart would be re-evaluated annually, as indicated by Step 35 toward the right-hand side of the chart.

Development of Plans

The evolutionary desegregation planning process was described, along with the key plans needed in a district, in an earlier section of this chapter. In Chapter 4, specific details are provided on particular approaches that should be considered in planning for administrators, teachers, students, curriculum needs and community relations. Because those subjects are covered elsewhere, the emphasis here will only be on the timing of the interactions among various groups in the schools and the community related to this planning process.

First-Year Plan

Since the Initial Plan is frequently developed under conditions of stress, it must be prepared rapidly and with as little controversy as possible. Consequently, it is often best for a school district to place heavy reliance upon outside consultants in preparation of this document. As shown in the section of the prototype chart left of that reproduced below, participation in planning by a bi-racial committee from the community is optional. The determination of whether or not to involve such a committee would depend upon the degree of polarization in the district and the time available.

Our prototype shows the establishment of student and faculty advisory committees while the Initial Plan is being developed, but use of those groups only to review the Initial Plan to be familiar with it before it is announced publicly. This approach could certainly be varied to allow for more meaningful participation by these groups in preparing the Initial Plan. But there is often a

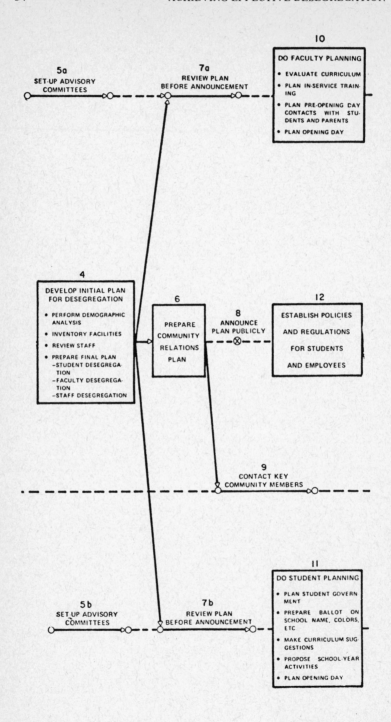

gain in support if a firm statement comes directly from the board, as long as it is immediately shared with those who will be most directly involved. The lack of prior consultation with faculty members and students in the development of the Initial Plan is balanced in the prototype by their participation in detailed planning of two other types immediately after the Initial Plan is announced (see Steps 10 and 11). The principals and teachers would assume responsibility for preparing the original draft of the First-Year Teaching Plan. They would evaluate and revise the curriculum, plan pre-opening day in-service training sessions, plan some of the opening day procedures, and plan for as much contact among teachers, students, and parents as could be arranged prior to the opening of school. (In all but the smallest districts, it is very likely that such contacts cannot be scheduled with most students. Then specialized contacts can be made instead—with key athletes by coaches, with music students by music teachers, and with community youth organizations by sponsoring teachers.)

Student advisory committees can be used for drafting a recommended First-Year Student Activities Plan (school administrators retain final approval rights over both this plan and that drawn up by the faculty). Prior to opening day, this student-principal committee could propose plans for student government organization, extracurricular activities, and opening day events. In addition, students could be encouraged to make curriculum suggestions and thereby participate to some degree in faculty planning. It might also be desirable for student committess to prepare a ballot on a new school name, colors, etc. so that voting could take place shortly after school opened. (We did not discover any precedent for this suggestion, but a voting plan like this would encourage democratic participation and make students a part of the planning for their new school situation.)

Another integral element in overall pre-opening day planning is developing the community relations part of the Initial Plan. As detailed a program as possible should be prepared for establishing communications among school personnel, parents and other community members. Possible elements of community relations plans are presented in Chapter 4. Our research indicates that favorable press coverage of desegregation is critical to the establishment of a constructive attitude on the part of community members prior to opening day. School officials should work closely with the media throughout this period. They should also work with key community leaders who could be instrumental in achieving simultaneous desegregation of local service organizations—groups like the YMCA, and public parks and recreation facilities. Again, various techniques that can be incorporated in community relations planning are presented in Chapter 4.

Comprehensive Plan

Long-range planning for achievement of effective desegregation within a school district should begin early in the first year of operations but after the

eight-week post-opening day period. In our prototype, we have scheduled planning committee formation to begin about November 1. We believe this is
realistic, but there will certainly be variation among school districts. The planning
committee should be bi-racial and composed of both administrators and faculty
members. Participation by a bi-racial community committee may or may not be
encouraged, depending upon the level of cooperation already established in the
district.

Formulation of the Comprehensive Desegregation Plan should begin about
mid-year. Development of a complete plan will usually take several months of
discussion and revision. On the chart, eight months elapse from the inception of
planning to completion of the final product in the summer between the first
and second years of desegregation. Applications for federal and state funding
would probably have to be prepared before the plan is finalized; so a draft
version of this plan should be prepared before the end of the first school year.
The focus in that draft should be upon the plan for the second year. It should
also be ready for announcement to students and faculty before they disperse for
the summer. This would allow time for the same sort of faculty and student
planning before the second-year opening day that was performed prior to the
first opening day, though perhaps with less psychological pressure. The focus
would be somewhat different the second time around, as shown in Steps 28
and 29. The faculty, for example, would recommend more extensive revisions in
curriculum, procedures and materials for the second year, after evaluating
student needs revealed during the first year of classes. Students should also be
asked to contribute suggestions for curriculum changes, particularly with
respect to course offerings.

Evaluation Program

A key input in preparing the Second-Year Plan and the Comprehensive Plan
will be the results of the evaluation program conducted in the spring of the
school year. If feasible, attitudinal evaluation could be performed twice a year—
in the fall as well as in the spring. As discussed earlier in this chapter, the evaluation program will be integral to all school district planning after the first year.
Revisions will be made in planning of curriculum, administrative policies and
teacher in-service training as the needs of students and faculty are determined. By
testing achievement and attitudes, and comparing results from year to year, both
deficiencies and progress can be detected. Corrective action can then be introduced, and other programs can be phased out if the need for them no longer
exists. Further details of such evaluation were presented earlier in this chapter.

The evaluation program should be conducted annually, even after effective
desegregation is achieved. Monitoring of student achievement, student and
faculty attitudes, and other key indicators improves general educational planning,
not just planning for desegregation.

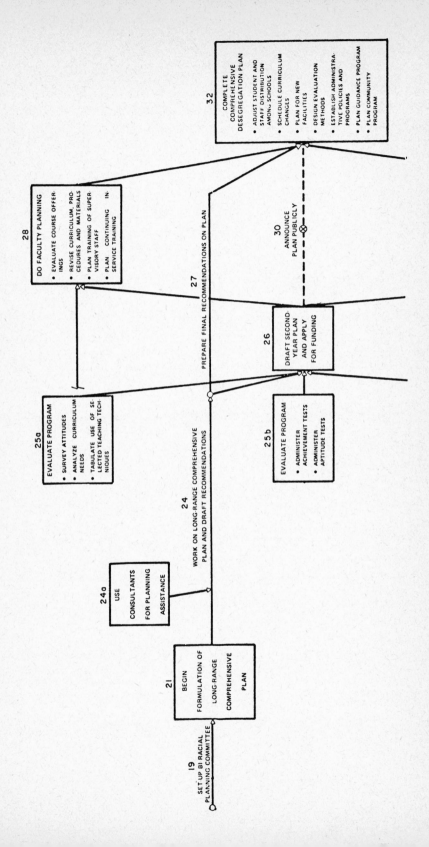

19 SET-UP BI-RACIAL PLANNING COMMITTEE

21 BEGIN FORMULATION OF LONG-RANGE COMPREHENSIVE PLAN

24a USE CONSULTANTS FOR PLANNING ASSISTANCE

24 WORK ON LONG-RANGE COMPREHENSIVE PLAN AND DRAFT RECOMMENDATIONS

25a EVALUATE PROGRAM
- SURVEY ATTITUDES
- ANALYZE CURRICULUM NEEDS
- TABULATE USE OF SELECTED TEACHING TECHNIQUES

25b EVALUATE PROGRAM
- ADMINISTER ACHIEVEMENT TESTS
- ADMINISTER APTITUDE TESTS

26 DRAFT SECOND-YEAR PLAN AND APPLY FOR FUNDING

27 PREPARE FINAL RECOMMENDATIONS ON PLAN

28 DO FACULTY PLANNING
- EVALUATE COURSE OFFERINGS
- REVISE CURRICULUM, PROCEDURES AND MATERIALS
- PLAN TRAINING OF SUPERVISORY STAFF
- PLAN CONTINUING IN-SERVICE TRAINING

30 ANNOUNCE PLAN PUBLICLY

32 COMPLETE COMPREHENSIVE DESEGREGATION PLAN
- ADJUST STUDENT AND STAFF DISTRIBUTION AMONG SCHOOLS
- SCHEDULE CURRICULUM CHANGES
- PLAN FOR NEW FACILITIES
- DESIGN EVALUATION METHODS
- ESTABLISH ADMINISTRATIVE POLICIES AND PROGRAMS
- PLAN GUIDANCE PROGRAM
- PLAN COMMUNITY PROGRAM

Major Events

The prototype chart shows several major events that will occur in the district before and during the first year of desegregation. These single occurrences will have communitywide impacts; therefore, they are points at which school administrators can solidify support for effective desegregation. We have included only four major annual events on the chart, the small number being an indication of the significance of these activities. All these events require a great deal of planning and preparation, as discussed below.

Announcement of Initial Plan

The first major event on the chart is the public announcement of the Initial Plan, shown as Step 8 on the prototype. This announcement should be made either by the head of the school board or by the superintendent of the district. In either case, description of the plan should be prefaced by reaffirmation of the board's firm policy statement regarding implementation of desegregation in the district. This will establish the tone of inevitability that must be conveyed in the presentation of the Initial Plan.

Prior to the public announcement of the Initial Plan, student and faculty committees should have been given opportunities to review the contents. It is important that the administration have knowledgeable supporters among students and faculty who can answer the immediate questions of their colleagues. Community support is also critical. As indicated in Step 9, influential members of the local community should be contacted just before public announcement of the plan. It is likely that some community leaders will have been consulted earlier. District administrators should be sure of the support of as many public officials, religious leaders, civic spokesmen, businessmen, newspaper editors, and broadcasters as possible. Informational packets should be prepared for distribution immediately before, or at the time of, public announcement of the Initial Plan.

Preparation of the Superintendent's Speech

The second major event is the preparation of the speech that the superintendent of schools will deliver on opening day. Like the Initial Plan announcement, the superintendent's speech can be extremely influential in establishing the attitude of the entire community toward school desegregation. If the superintendent's tone is firm and positive, community residents are less likely to attempt any strong objections to desegregation than if the superintendent says nothing at all about it or delivers a weak and conditional speech.

Although the speech will be delivered on opening day, it should be prepared in advance so that copies can be distributed to principals of local schools and to the press. The principals' opening day speeches and directions should be tailored after those of the superintendent so that a consistent message is conveyed to the community.

Opening Day

The most important single event in the process of desegregating a school district is the first opening day. This event must be planned with extreme care. In fact, as mentioned earlier, planning for opening day by administrators, faculty and students should begin immediately after the Initial Plan is announced. Parent-teacher organizations can be influential in the smooth handling of many opening day procedures if bi-racial groups of parents are assembled to greet parents accompanying students on the first day of school.

Opening day activities in the schools should be well organized and uncomplicated. If registration did not take place in a prior week, the registration process on opening day should be streamlined, and sufficient guidance should be provided to avoid confusion. The school transportation program should be well organized, with bus drivers fully instructed on procedures and courtesy towards all students, so that there is as much air of routine as possible. The principals should lead the student assemblies and explain all of the established rules of behavior in class, on the school grounds, and in extracurricular activities. Homeroom and classroom teachers should be made responsible for clearly explaining class procedures so that students are fully informed, but not confused, about the operation of the desegregated school. Policies and procedures should be clarified and reiterated throughout the early weeks of the school year.

Before opening day, close liaison should be established with local law enforcement officials so that there will be a swift, impartial, and effective response by them to any disorderly conduct associated with the beginning of desegregation. The likelihood of serious or violent opposition, or of initially peaceful demonstrations that might cause incidents, will vary greatly from district to district. If there are significant indications that some violence or demonstrations may occur, then school officials should work out a detailed contingency plan in advance with law enforcement officials. It is probably best for police or other such officials to be visible in areas where possible trouble is suspected, but not initially massed there in conspicuous force. However, the exact strategies to be used should be developed jointly by school administrators and the highest-level law enforcement officials. Clear communications channels should be kept open between them at all times during opening day and for the first few days thereafter.

The procedures described above (except perhaps those concerning law enforcement) should be followed on every subsequent opening day. There will always be new students and new procedures to be introduced. A standardized schedule simplifies administration of opening day events and also gives students a sense of security—starting school is always the same.

Districtwide Open House

The fourth major event shown on the prototype chart is a districtwide open house that would be scheduled about 10 weeks after opening day. The field surveys conducted for this handbook did not provide any examples of such an event; so it should be regarded as a desirable suggestion rather than a proven tactic. However, many desegregated schools maintain an open door policy for parent visitations throughout the school year. Also, most school districts do hold an open house for parents, usually in the spring.

A districtwide open house scheduled early in the school year would provide students and faculty members with a short-term goal that would necessitate cooperation and planning among all members of the school district. This type of activity would strengthen student identity with the newly desegregated schools, and would encourage teachers to devise means of including and representing students not of their own race. The open house would serve to reassure parents of both races that their students were receiving the same personal attention and treatment as in their prior schools. It could feature a central activity followed by refreshments and visits between parents and teachers, or it could be limited to parent-teacher visits. A central activity could be a group sporting event or a musical revue or skit with clear bi-racial participation throughout. The emphasis should be strictly on group presentations without star performers so there would be no allegation that one race was favored over the other.

To some extent, the desirability of a districtwide open house at this point in the year depends upon the intensity of feelings about desegregation that prevail in the community. It would certainly be unwise to hold an event shortly after opening day that might precipitate some type of incident in a highly-polarized community. However, if the community has accepted desegregation with relatively low-intensity opposition, then such a cooperative, bi-racial event could perform an important function both inside and outside the schools in the district. If successful, it could become an annual event.

Independent Activities

The prototype chart includes a number of independent activities carried out by one or another of the major groups in a school district. These activities range in duration from one or two days (e.g., attendance at orientation meetings) to the entire school year (e.g., recruitment of participants in student inter-group activities). Many of these activities are on-going and can be interrupted by major events or other more intense activities. Consequently, the timing of independent activities shown on the chart is by no means fixed. In some cases it is intended as an indication of the long-term duration of the activity or its general relationship to the scheduling of more discrete events.

In-Service Teacher Training—One important group of independent activities consists of the faculty in-service training sessions indicated in the following three steps from the chart. Steps 13, 22 and 33 represent differing intensities of the same type of event. In-service teacher training is discussed in detail in Chapter 4, but a summary of the purposes of the various sessions cited on the chart is appropriate here.

The short-term in-service training provided immediately before opening day would serve mainly to acquaint teachers of both races with one another and to explain to faculty members the most obvious problems they will be likely to encounter. Attempts would be made to reduce existing unfamiliarities with colleagues and students of other races, and to increase personal sensitivity to one's own unconscious prejudices. Emphasis would be placed upon the positive role that teachers can play in achieving effective desegregation.

Throughout the first school year, weekly in-service training sessions would be held for faculty members (Step 22). The format of these sessions would vary considerably, depending upon the current problems facing the teachers concerned. Sessions could be structured and focused upon selected published articles on teaching techniques in newly-desegregated classrooms. Or informal discussions could be held so that teachers could exchange instructive anecdotes. Or outside experts could be invited to speak on bi-racial relations. These are merely examples; the range of possibilities is limited only by the needs and ingenuity of the individual faculty.

In-service training sessions are consistently cited as essential ingredients in the process of achieving effective desegregation. Hence, it is important that a regular schedule be established for these sessions during the school year. Attendance should be mandatory. In the second year of desegregation, the in-service training sessions could perhaps be reduced to a bi-monthly schedule. It is even possible that a monthly schedule would be adequate by the third year. However, it is unlikely that less frequent meetings would prove sufficient until the district had been desegregated for a number of years.

As many teachers as possible should be encouraged to attend summer institutes held at neighboring universities or within the district itself (Step 33). These institutes are more intensive than those held in the schools and offer more specialized direction in specific subjects, and varying levels of instruction for different grades. By the second summer, the school district should encourage selected teachers and principals to take graduate-level university courses in specific teaching techniques, guidance counselling, etc., so that they can assume supervisory roles within their schools. Funds should be made available to assist with at least some of the expenses incurred by these professional staff members.

Student Meetings—Special efforts should be made to encourage student participation in the desegregation process. Aside from the student planning already discussed, orientation meetings can be held right before the school year begins. These meetings may be as short as the half day needed for registration. Or they can extend for a week and include planned recreational activities and informal encounter sessions with teachers. As mentioned earlier, pre-opening day orientation meetings also provide administrators with an opportunity to inform students of the policies and regulations that have been established for attendance, behavior and grade-level promotion.

Student involvement in inter-group activities is reflected in Steps 23 and 34 on the prototype chart. The recruitment of students of *all* ethnic groups for special-interest clubs, athletic teams, musical organizations, school publications and student government is an on-going process that should be emphasized throughout every school year. It is likely that administrators would devote more attention to the way in which some of the recruitment is handled in the first year than in later years when precedents have been set. Initially, special decisions should be made about the choice of cheerleaders and homecoming queens, for example.

The summer bi-racial program indicated by Step 34 is actually an optional activity. If the local park district or community organizations have extensive bi-racial programs, the school district would not have to become involved. Recreational activities can be introduced in summer academic programs, though, if few structured events of this type are available in the community.

Districtwide Communications—The three items on the chart labeled "communicate intensively" cover the critical eight-week period right after opening day. What happens in this span of time usually has a great impact upon the tenor of the rest of the year. So every effort must be made to assure that counter-productive behavior is kept to a minimum, and that students are engaged in constructive activities. Experience has shown that a key element in successful desegregation is reduction of uncertainty among teachers, students, parents, and other residents. Much uncertainty is based on simple lack of knowledge or understanding; so every effort must be made to encourage communications on all levels.

A vital pre-requisite for understanding among persons throughout the school district is open communication by administrators. Plans and regulations must be made public. Meetings and forums should be scheduled to explain the actions being taken and to answer questions raised by parents, teachers and students. Some districts have successfully introduced "rumor centers" to attempt to reduce exaggeration about actual or reported incidents. Newspapers can also be influential in reducing uncertainty and fear within the community.

Principals and administrators should be highly "visible" and readily available to answer questions and to reassure their staffs and their students throughout the early desegregation period (and after). Efforts should be made to keep students actively involved in projects, but routine should not be disrupted. The goal, after all, is to make the unusual seem usual.

Continuation of the Desegregation Process in Subsequent Years

The chart depicting the prototype desegregation process presented in this chapter covers only the time period from initial desegregation policy-formation by the school board to the opening day of the second year of desegregated schools. Yet the process of achieving effective desegregation takes years to complete. The second year of this process, and all those that follow it, have been omitted from the chart to simplify it graphically, and because charts of subsequent years would look very much like the one shown. Some differences would surely emerge. For one thing, as noted earlier, the intensive concentration of activity before opening day of the first year would probably not be repeated in subsequent years. Once the community has lived through a whole school year of desegregation, it is unlikely that it will be anywhere near as interested in opening day as it was when it had no such experience. Moreover, the Second-Year Plan will have been largely developed during the first year. So there will be no need for another document to be announced right before opening day, analogous to the Initial Plan. Thus, the general level of intensity of all functions specifically connected with desegregation will decline sharply in the second year as compared to the first, and may continue to decline in later years.

On the other hand, the influence of desegregation upon the general educational procedures used throughout the school system should increase sharply during the second year, and perhaps gradually in subsequent years. Everyone in the school system should learn during the first year of desegregation just what elements of his or her behavior, both personal and professional, are really inconsistent with harmonious, positive relations among all racial and social groups. In the second year, teachers, students, and administrators will have an opportunity to put these lessons from the first year into practice to a greater degree. Gradually, as everyone's experience with other groups grows, most relationships should improve, and all behavior within the schools should become more consistent with truly equal educational opportunities.

4

Techniques for Achieving Effective Desegregation

This chapter presents a detailed description of those specific techniques that our study revealed to be most useful for individual school districts trying to achieve effective desegregation. It also briefly describes the main problems and policies to which these techniques are related, and explains the relationships involved. Finally, it presents specific examples of many individual techniques (though by no means all of them) as actually used by individual school districts covered by the field investigations or literature surveyed by this study.

The chapter is divided into six major sections. This first section describes what is in the remaining five, how those contents were selected, and how they are organized. Each of the other five sections contains all of the problems, policies, and techniques relevant to one key aspect of desegregation. These five sections, plus their code abbreviations, are as follows:

Administrative Measures (ADM)
Teaching Techniques and Training (TEA)
Community Relations (COM)
Student Adaptation (STU)
Curriculum Adaptation (CUR)

Sources Of The Information In This Chapter

The basic sources of information used in preparing this chapter can be described as follows:

Survey of the Literature on Desegregation

We compiled and analyzed about 1,100 articles, unpublished dissertations, essays, pamphlets, journals, and government publications concerning racial desegregation of public schools, educating disadvantaged children, school administration, teacher training, classroom teaching practices, and related general education topics. Although we began searching the literature only for items directly related to school desegregation, it soon became apparent that achieving effective desegregation really involved specific ways of carrying out general educational techniques, rather than performing activities mainly related to race relations. Therefore, it was impossible to draw any clear line between literature on achieving effective desegregation and literature on general educational methods. We have had to use rather arbitrary judgment, plus the limitations on the resources available for document acquisition, to determine just how far to go in acquiring literature in the area of general education.

Rather than present a complete bibliography of all the items acquired in this study, we have set forth selected lists of those items most relevant to each major section of Chapter 4, and most likely to be useful to school officials. These limited bibliographies appear at the end of each of the five last sections.

Field Surveys in Ten School Districts

We conducted in-depth field surveys of ten school districts that had experienced school desegregation. These districts were selected because each had reputedly developed some unusual or highly effective technique for achieving desegregation, or had done especially well at desegregating overall. In each district, interviews were conducted with an average of twelve key school officials, teachers, students, and other local residents about a variety of facets of the district's desegregation experience. In these field surveys, we also procured a number of documents and examples that are used in various parts of Chapter 4.

The specific school districts visited were located in the following areas:

Chapel Hill, North Carolina
Clarke County, Georgia
Cleveland, Ohio
Colorado Springs, Colorado
Gainesville, Florida
Muskogee, Oklahoma
New Albany, Mississippi
Portland, Oregon
Providence, Rhode Island
Sacramento, California

Expert Essays

We commissioned brief papers of various aspects of desegregation experience by four well-established academic authorities in this area, two white and two black. The ideas and data set forth in these papers were used as inputs into our final analysis. The papers and their authors were as follows:

Mark Chesler, "Desegregation and Integration Within the School."
Edgar G. Epps, "Notes on Desegregation."

Robert T. Stout, "The Processes of Desegregation."
Daniel C. Thompson, "The Role of Leadership in School Desegregation."

Government Documents

We obtained all available information and statistical data on desegregation from the Office for Civil Rights of the Department of Health, Education, and Welfare, the Office of Education, the Department of Justice, and other government agencies. Visits were also paid to several University Desegregation Centers established under Title IV of the Civil Rights Act of 1964, and as much information and data as possible were obtained from them.

Expert Interviews

In the course of this study, a number of persons who have specialized expertise concerning one or more facets of school desegregation were interviewed in person or by telephone. Their ideas and the experiences they described have formed an important input for this study. We also submitted the first draft of the report to 35 experts for review and comment.

Special Consultants

At key stages in the process of preparing this handbook, especially during the research-design and draft-review stages, we obtained detailed advice and suggestions from two special consultants to this study, whose ideas and counsel have been extremely valuable. They are Professor David K. Cohen of Harvard University, and Professor John McKnight of Northwestern University.

Method Of Selecting the Specific Problems, Policies, and Techniques Included In This Chapter

As noted above, there is no simple and clear-cut way to differentiate techniques for achieving effective desegregation from those for achieving effective educational results generally. It is true that many of the administrative and community relations actions required for effective desegregation need not be carried out in the normal course of school affairs where desegregation is not an issue. But some of the actions most critical to achieving effective desegregation—such as the way teachers handle student discipline problems—are simply particular ways of carrying out general educational practices. Yet hundreds, perhaps thousands, of general educational techniques are employed daily by school teachers, principals, and other school officials across the nation. These techniques differ tremendously in level of detail. Furthermore, each technique may affect one or dozens of the many variables related to education, and its effects upon any one variable may vary enormously, depending upon other factors besides the technique itself.

In order to arrive at an organizational scheme for this portion of our analysis, we carried out the following steps:

1. Definition of what "effective" really means in relation to desegregation, as a basis for determining which techniques have been most "effective".
2. Examination of the dynamics of the desegregation process as revealed by experience.
3. Identification of those factors in the desegregation process considered to be the most critical in determining its success by past analysts and by participants in actual desegregation efforts.
4. Determination of what specific problems occurring in the course of desegregation seemed most important to those responsible for accomplishing, initiating, or analyzing it.
5. Identification of all the specific policies and techniques used in the process of desegregation that seemed to produce desirable results, and collection of as much data about them as feasible.
6. Examination of educational and other theory and research for indications of the specific policies and techniques most likely to work effectively in coping with the problems identified in Step 4 above.
7. Comparison of these theoretically-desirable policies and techniques for achieving effective desegregation with those actually used in desegregation, as determined in Step 2 above.
8. Determination of the combination of actually-tried and theoretically-desirable policies and techniques that seemed likely to provide the most effective means of solving the main problems associated with desegregation, as identified in Step 4 above. These are the policies and techniques included in this chapter.

This methodology was complicated by the fact that truly effective desegregation has probably not been achieved by any of the school districts we visited or read about. Moreover, existing data are inadequate to determine where else effective desegregation may have been achieved. Therefore, all of our analysis of how to achieve effective desegregation necessarily contains a large theoretical component that cannot be empirically verified. We are essentially trying to describe how to do something no one has ever done—or at least we could not identify where it had been done. This meant it was impossible to confine our suggestions about what techniques to use only to those that had been empirically verified by success. Instead, in order to give officials practically applicable advice, we had to include many techniques that might work, based upon our judgmental analysis of related experience and relevant theory.

A second complication is the high degree of uncertainty in educational theory and research. Educational experts warned us that it was impossible to say with much confidence that employment of any given technique would consistently produce any particular desired result. Too many other variables could negate the effects of that technique.

In light of the above considerations, we had to employ a methodology that relied significantly upon subjective judgments and analytic skill, rather than solely upon scientifically-validated conclusions. Initially, it was proposed that every technique included be fully documented with the specific sources from which data about its nature and effectiveness had been derived. However, that is not possible when the techniques have been selected through the methodology described above. Nevertheless, we have documented many techniques with specific examples, and others with footnotes to sources in the literature.

For the above reasons, the catalog of desegregation techniques in this chapter cannot be considered comprehensive and complete. However, some parts are more complete than others. We believe the sections on Administrative Measures and Community Relations contain thorough descriptions of the policies and techniques required for maximum contribution to effective desegregation in these specialized areas. However, the sections on Teaching Techniques and Training, Student Adaptation, and Curriculum Adaptation must be considered representative and illustrative rather than all-inclusive. These are the specialized areas in which techniques for effective desegregation are most closely intertwined with general educational techniques. There are hundreds or even thousands of the latter. Moreover, most can be broken down into finer and finer parts by changing the level of detail concerned. Hence, we certainly cannot guarantee that the catalog in this chapter contains all or even most of the techniques that might somehow be relevant to desegregation. However, we believe it does contain those which are most significant to achieving desegregation effectively.

How This Chapter Is Organized

The way each of the five remaining sections in this chapter is organized is illustrated by the outline shown on an accompanying page. Each section begins with a three-part general introduction. The first paragraphs present a short idealized statement of the roles that each of the categories (such as the curriculum) is supposed to perform in the public schools. These statements have been derived from general educational theory and are not specific to desegregation. The second part of the introduction briefly identifies particular problems regarding those roles that have been caused or aggravated by desegregation of schools. The last part of the introduction lists the main objectives that school policy ought to pursue in order to solve or reduce those desegregation related problems.

After the introduction, each section contains a series of major subject headings. Every heading is organized around one particular desegregation related problem within the general category concerned. The problem is stated, and then a series of proposed school policies are described that are responsive to the problem. Each such policy is set forth as a normative statement: "Someone should carry out this type of action." That summary sentence is followed by a brief general discussion of the policy, and then by a series of specific educational or other techniques that can be used to carry out the policy. Most of the techniques are named and briefly described. In many instances, an example of the technique is presented on one or more separate accompanying pages, which are set apart from the main text.

The accompanying outline can be used as a key to the code system for locating particular policies and techniques in this catalog. In each major section, every specific problem used for grouping policies and techniques is designated by a capital letter. As on the outline, the first problem in a section is designated A, the second B, etc. Under each problem, the specific policies are numbered in order (1, 2, 3, etc.). Every major section also has a code designation consisting of the abbreviation set forth above; thus, the code for the section on Curriculum Adaptation is CUR. Therefore, the third policy under the second problem in that section can be coded as CUR-B-3. Similarly, the fourth policy under the third problem concerning Administrative Measures would be coded ADM-C-4, etc. Specific techniques are not assigned separate code designations because this would result in coding too complicated for easy practical use, and because many techniques appear in more than one part of this catalog. Instead, the techniques are designated by the policy (or policies) under which they are grouped (e.g., CUR-B-3).

This coding system is designed to enable the reader to find specific policies or techniques quickly and conveniently, in spite of the length and complexity of Chapter 4. To make this possible, we have listed all the problems and all the techniques in two separate indexes, designating each problem and technique by code (or codes) where it is located. These indexes appear right after the introduction. The problem index is organized consecutively following the contents of the five sections. The technique index is organized alphabetically by the subject and/or name of the technique. Thus, to discover where the technique of team teaching is discussed, a reader should look up that term in the alphabetical technique index. Policies are not indexed because they are not stated in easily titled form.

Outline Organization of Sections in Chapter 4
One of Five Categories of Techniques

I. Introduction

    Idealized Statement of the Roles or Functions This Category is Supposed to Perform

    Basic Problems Concerning That Performance Caused or Aggravated by Desegregation

    Basic Objectives That Schools Should Pursue to Solve or Reduce Those Problems

II. Specific Problems, Policies, and Techniques

    A.   PROBLEM: Brief statement of first particular problem

          POLICY :   Normative statement of first policy responsive to
          (A-1)   the problem

        Brief discussion of policy

        Suggested techniques for carrying out policy

        1. First technique, with brief discussion of its nature, advantages and limitations

        2. Second technique and discussion

        POLICY :   Normative statement of second policy responsive to
        (A-2)   the problem

           SAME FORMAT AS UNDER POLICY (A-1)

    B.   PROBLEM: Brief statement of second particular problem

          POLICY.   Normative statement of first policy responsive to the
          (B–1)   problem

           SAME FORMAT AS UNDER PROBLEM A
                        ETC.

How To Survey The Contents Of This Chapter Rapidly

There is a relatively simple way to become acquainted with what is in this chapter without reading all of it. In each section, first read the general introductory statement, which is not over three pages long. Then skim through the remainder of that section, reading in full only the *PROBLEM* paragraphs. Under each *PROBLEM* paragraph, glance at the specific policies and techniques to get an idea of what they are like. Then go on to the next major section and repeat this process. In this manner, a reader can quickly discover how the entire chapter is organized and what its main points are.

Index of Problems in Chapter 4

Administrative Measures

	Code	Page
Improving Representation in the Decision-Making Process	ADM-A	91
Promoting "Inevitability" and Community Understanding	ADM-B	94
Overcoming Technical Deficiencies in Desegregation Planning	ADM-C	99
Reducing Uncertainty Within School Staffs	ADM-D	101
Revision of the Principal's Role	ADM-E	106

Teaching Techniques and Training

Improving Teacher Sensitivity to Diversity	TEA-A	117
Using New Classroom Management Techniques	TEA-B	124
Using New Curriculum Materials and Instructional Techniques	TEA-C	137
Improving Teacher Performance with New Supervisory Arrangements	TEA-D	149

Community Relations

Reducing Community Uncertainty About Desegregation Issues	COM-A	163
Implementation of a Positive Communications Program	COM-B	169
Gaining Community Participation in School Desegregation	COM-C	180
Obtaining Cooperation of Other Public Agencies	COM-D	186

Student Adaptation

Forming Democratic School Structures and Policies	STU-A	194
Teaching Skills and Knowledge Required for Good Citizenship	STU-B	196
Practice of Democracy in All Phases of School Life	STU-C	196
Improvement of Self-Images, Achievement and Interaction Through Student Activities	STU-D	199
Using Curriculum to Improve Behavior, Adjustment and Achievement	STU-E	210
Using Guidance Services to Improve Behavior, Adjustment and Achievement	STU-F	211
Maintaining Discipline in the Desegregated School	STU-G	214

Curriculum Adaptation

Index of Techniques in Chapter 4

Short Title Techniques

**Administrative Measures to Achieve
Effective Desegregation**

*School Organization And Problems
In Desegregation*

School organization is an administrative expression of community policies and educational theory. In order to prepare students for participation in community life, the structure and organization of the school system should represent a consistent expression of community and educational views on social organization, grouping of individuals, objectives of the learning process, and content of instruction.

The corporate form of school organization has been almost universally adopted throughout the United States. This type of organization provides for community representation on a school board responsible for policy planning and for a central administration to coordinate the decisions of school faculty and employees. Unlike most corporate organizations, the school system provides for a high degree of automony in decision-making at lower levels of the organization. The purpose of this decentralized structure is:

To allow adaptation of the instructional program to individual school-community needs.

To maintain authority and responsibility for adaptation of the content, method and organization of the instructional program as close as possible to the individual pupil.

To provide for immediate action on problems arising in the classroom.

To allow teachers and principals to enjoy a high level of professional autonomy.

To make the instructional process consultative in nature.

Basic Problems Caused Or Aggravaged By School Desegregation

1. School board policy decisions are intended to be comprehensive statements that meet the needs of all students in the school system. In many areas, however, the school board's composition is dominated by persons who represent only a small segment of community opinion. Often their policy decisions reflect their own views or are influenced by the views of persons who they feel represent leadership in the community.

2. School desegregation is not purely, or even primarily, an educational process, but a process of social change. In most communities, it demonstrates the narrow base upon which educational decisions have been made. In others, it threatens to disrupt the entire educational process when the school

board is unable to maintain its authority. Thus the process tends to cause school officials to narrow their objectives in an effort to control decisions—and maintain order in the school system.

3. In many communities, school desegregation can only be accomplished by creating "new schools". Such changes require the school board to draw upon leaders from all walks of community life and expend significant financial resources in order to restore public confidence in the school system. To accomplish this, it is often necessary for community leaders and school officials to make difficult adjustments in the community's established patterns of "doing business".

4. In most communities, desegregation poses a threat to the internal organization of the school. It creates pressures toward greater centralization of decision-making in the board and superintendent. Often this process alienates members of the faculty and staff who are uncertain of their positions in the transition. This problem is intensified among principals who ordinarily are involved in administrative decisions.

5. The process of school desegregation creates pressure toward diversification within the decentralized school structure. Most often this pressure results because of the desire of teachers to improve instructional techniques and develop stronger peer relations with minority-group staff members. This process may result in teachers taking mild advocacy positions and/or in divisions among the staff if principals do not assume rules as strong—but democratic—leaders in bringing about unity within their schools.

Basic Objectives In Desegregation To Remedy These Problems

1. School officials should take initiative in developing consensus among a broad cross section of community leaders prior to involving or informing the public of the district's intention to desegregate. This action should be taken as a means of maintaining the authority of the school board.

2. The school board should attempt to plan comprehensively for desegregation. This process should involve a wide range of community leaders as well as outside consultants.

3. An attempt should be made at the earliest date to enlist the loyalty of key staff members, particularly principals. Efforts should be made both publicly and privately to assure the community that all professional staff will be retained upon desegregation.

4. Plans should be made to reorganize the administrative duties of the principal to reflect increased faculty needs, including leadership, training and reinforcement. In some cases, the school board should consider hiring additional staff to relieve the principal of tasks in guidance, discipline and administration.

Specific Problems, Policies and Techniques

A. Improving Representation in the Decision-Making Process

PROBLEM: The usual school decision-making process is dominated by a
board/superintendent coalition, with decisions being made in
relative isolation from the people for whom policies are decided.
Because they represent the majority whites in most communities,
the board and superintendent often have no clear idea of what
the needs and wants of non-white, non-middle-class citizens may
be, or how to find out.

Regardless of whether a group of people achieves school board status
through election or appointment, membership in the school's decision-making
body is based, according to Robert T. Stout, on:

"... who you are rather than on what you are, not unlike membership in a
family-owned corporation. That is, 'being of the right sort' seems a better
predictor of membership than the ability to command a set of skills which
have relevance for the work of policy-making."[1]

The result has historically almost always been white and solidly middle-
class boards. Moreover, the superintendent chosen by the board to administer
their policies is usually selected because he is similar to them in background and
outlook.

The board/superintendent arrangement has worked fairly well, in that the
board, as a lay group, knows "what people want" and the superintendent, as a
professional, knows "how to do it". But desegregation, recognizing minorities as
distinct groups apart from "the people" represented by the board, presents a
new problem. The needs of minority groups must be determined and fulfilled.

POLICY.   Access of minority groups to the decision-making process should
  (A-1)   be improved.

If desegregation planning is to result in effective desegregation, access to, and
representation in, the decision-making process by a traditionally "voiceless"
group should be heightened. The fact that minorities are usually most affected
by desegregation makes improved access and influence even more imperative.

Increased representation in the planning process should take place within
the community through such means as formation of citizens adivsory committees
and appointment of minority members to the school board, and within the
schools by top-to-bottom staff desegregation.

Suggested Techniques

1.   Citizens Advisory Committee
A citizens advisory committee is a group set up for the express purpose of

advising and assisting the school board in planning for desegregation. To meet the dual objectives of reducing board isolation and improving minority-group influence, the committee should be bi-racial and as representative as possible of the community's social, political and economic composition. This type of committee should be involved in planning for all aspects of desegregation, not just the community relations aspect.

Impetus for the formation of a citizens advisory group should come preferably from within school administration—either from the board or from the superintendent. This provides the community with a positive indication that the decision-makers realize that knowledge of public opinions and preferences is important and necessary to policy deliberations. Active and effective citizens advisory committees have been set up through citizen efforts alone, but this has usually happened in districts where the board has displayed lack of interest in doing anything beyond making a decision to desegregate.[2] In most cases, if an advisory committee is to function properly, it needs the respect and confidence of administrators. The administration must feel that the committee is sincerely interested in the schools rather than in taking over school administrative or legislative authority.[3]

The "representative" bi-racial citizens advisory committee works well in a community where:

The schools are racially imbalanced rather than actually segregated.

Minorities are accorded equal treatment in hiring practices for school professionals.

There are minority professionals in the process of rising through school administrative ranks, or already present in the top echelons.

Racial mixing is usual in non-school facilities.

In communities where the above combination of factors is not present, or where the minority population is particularly small, the citizens advisory committee wil need to be more representative of minorities, to the point where they can in fact influence policy decisions. Edgar G. Epps suggests that guarantee of an effect on the outcomes of decisions "might require implementation of a 'security council' type of arrangement giving the minority a veto in sensitive areas involving personnel, discipline, pupil assignment, the inclusion of ethnic materials in the classroom, the determination of which schools to keep open or to close, and the location of new school facilities."[4]

If the community is small and the school board and/or the superintendent have been in office for a number of years, the selection of possible candidates for appointment to the committee should not be difficult. However, emphasis should be placed on making the committee representative. A black physician in a town where blacks usually fill low-status jobs is not representative, though the temptation to appoint him would be great because, from the standpoint of the board, he would be closer to being just like them. If racial isolation in a town, even a very small town, is so great that the administration truly cannot identify the minority leadership, minority clergymen or members of the school staff should be consulted.

If the district is large, the school board should direct the superintendent to conduct the research necessary to develop an accurate picture of all its components. He should submit a tentative list of community representatives for an advisory committee along with a brief explanation of why each person is being nominated.

In both large and small districts, it is recommended that an administrative employee serve as secretary to the advisory committee, since most of the members will not be able to devote the necessary time for the routine clerical and communications work.[5]

The operation of bi-racial citizens advisory committees, and the variety of activities that can be, and have been, undertaken by such committees are discussed in detail in the section of this chapter titled "Community Relations To Achieve Effective Desegregation".

2.   Complete Faculty Desegregation

Many suggestions for change and innovation within a district are generated by school staff, and then conveyed to the superintendent through his administrative staff. Unless the faculty is desegregated, from top to bottom, minority influence in this sphere of decision-making will not be possible.

The school board is responsible for accomplishing faculty desegregation at the same time as student desegregation.[6] The initial policy statement on desegregation made by the board (see discussion in Section B below) should include a statement of resolution to this effect.

If the minority staff is so small that many schools in the system with minority enrollments do not have minority staff members, even after faculty desegregation, the school board should consider adoption of a hiring policy giving preference to minority applicants. This policy would remain in effect until the proportion of minority staff members in the system approximated the proportion of minority students. Sacramento City Unified School District has adopted a policy like this with regard to both black and Chicano staff members, and there is evidence that Sacramento is not unique.[7] If a district decides that such a policy is desirable, it should include recruitment for principals and other administrative-level persons as well as teachers.

3.   Appointment of Minority-Group Board Members

If school board membership in a community is appointive, the appointing official or body should be encouraged by the district administration to begin appointing minority members if there are none on the board or if the present minority proportion of members is below that in the community's population. The superintendent can initiate the process by suggesting several names of minority citizens known to be interested in the schools and known to have influence in the minority community.

According to Robert T. Stout, many communities with elected boards have

unwritten agreements that a member whose term is about to expire will resign
and the "right" person will be appointed to fill out his term. The new appointee
is subsequently elected.[8] In a community where this process is standard, introduction of a minority member should be suggested by the superintendent as
soon as a seat is vacated.

POLICY .   A bi-racial student advisory committee should be created to advise
  (A-2)   on sensitive student-related aspects of planning for desegregation.

Students as a group, and minority students in particular, have generally had
decisions on in-school matters made for and about them, but not with them.
Therefore students are also a traditionally "voiceless" group about whose needs
and wants the board has had little information. Since students will ultimately
have to make desegregation work, their opinions should be sought in planning
for desegregation in a district. A discussion of the creation and possible activities
of student advisory committees is found in the section of this chapter on
Student Adaptation.

B. Promoting "Inevitability" and
Community Understanding

PROBLEM: School boards often do not announce that desegregation is being
                considered; and if a positive decision is reached to desegregate,
                actual plans are not made public. Boards tend to fear controversy
                and attempt to reduce it by limiting communication with the
                community.

Desegregation attracts community-wide interest, even among citizens who
normally do not become involved in what is happening in the schools. School
boards realize that they will be in the midst of any controversy that develops,
and they understandably fear polarization of their communities.

Acting with what Robert Stout terms "a concern for maintaining peace,"
many boards have conducted unpublicized deliberations on whether to desegregate. After deciding to do so, they have issued vague, general statements of
policy—or no statements at all. If the board has realized that, in order to
introduce the idea of "inevitability," a definite policy statement is necessary
(or a resolution of intent to comply in the case of a court order), and controversy
has ensued, the first reaction has often been postponement of one or more
steps in the plan as a pacification effort.

The idea behind these actions is, of course, to wait until the "right time".
However, given the intense interest of both proponents and opponents of
desegregation in seeing decisions made in their favor, that time will probably
never come.[9]

POLICY .   The school board should issue clear and unequivocal statements
  (B-1)   regarding policy deliberations and decisions.

Suggested Techniques

1.   Announcement of Policy Consideration
When a school board that is not under court order begins deliberations on desegregation, the public should be apprised of that fact through a published announcement stating that desegregation is being considered and explaining why. If the district is under court order to desegregate, a statement of "policy consideration" is not necessary and may actually be undesirable because it may give the community the false impression that the subject is still open to discussion.

In Sacramento, California, the school board announced that it was discussing desegregation and then appointed a citizens advisory committee to provide the "why". The committee was asked to identify barriers to equal educational opportunity and to define *de facto* segregation in Sacramento. Their findings were submitted and considered before a final decision was made to desegregate. The public was aware that research was underway and was consequently psychologically prepared for the results of the study.

2.   Announcement of Policy Decision
In any district, when desegregation becomes official board policy, a clear and detailed policy statement should be issued. Because of the inherent potential for conflict, school boards have sometimes viewed the announcement of the decision to desegregate as a greater problem than arriving at the actual consensus. Consequently, boards have buried the decision in the minutes of a meeting or issued vague, lengthy statements on "democracy" and "equality" without ever mentioning the words "desegregation" or "Negro".[10]

The key point for school boards to remember is that it is the fact of desegregation—not the policy statement—that causes potential for conflict. Available literature indicates that a definitive and public policy statement does not produce conflict, but in fact forestalls it by stressing the idea of inevitability. In contrast, failure to explicitly outline the board's decision keeps both proponents and opponents of desegregation agitating for a policy favorable to their respective positions. Complete information should therefore be published on the changes to be made, and a community relations program should be initiated to promote acceptance of desegregation.

The statement of policy on desegregation issued by the Pittsburgh School Board in 1965 is reproduced on a following page. It serves as a good example of firmness and clarity. The Montgomery County, Maryland Board of Education supplemented its statement with an indication of the extent of desegregation. The following principle was included: "The integration of Board of Education employees shall be accomplished at the same time as the integration of pupils."[11]

Many different policy statements must be prepared by the school board to cover all exigencies of desegregation. A sample checklist of policies is presented on a following page. As many as possible of the decisions needed to arrive at these policy statements should be made early in the desegregation process.

3.   Announcement of Timetable for Desegregation
The school board should adopt and announce a firm, unalterable timetable for desegregation. No activity, or threatened activity, happening in the community should be allowed to cause postponement of all or any part of the plan for desegregation once the date(s) for implementation has been announced.

Based on experiences with other communities, desegregation consultants can advise the board on the probability of disruption in the district and the form it might take. Among other things, the consultants will likely advise the board to prepare for potential disorder by:

Setting up a well-publicized rumor center staffed with bi-racial citizens who have been provided with correct and complete information on desegregation plans.

Reaching agreement with local law enforcement agencies on intervention tactics in case disruption should develop.

Details on establishing a rumor center and arriving at law enforcement policy are presented in the section of this chapter titled "Community Relations to Achieve Effective Desegregation".

POLICY.   School boards should take the initiative in establishing lines of
(B-2)   communication with the community.
A discussion of the methods that a school board can use to initiate community interest and participation in effective school desegregation is found in the section on Community Relations.

POLICY.   The interest of the local media in school desegregation must be
(B-3)   recognized and dealt with.
Desegregation, as a departure from the usual, is of particular interest to local reporters. Unless the district is in a large metropolitan area where only school news of an explosive nature is likely to be covered in detail, desegregation is usually viewed as not only interesting but worthy of prominent placement in the news.

Suggested Techniques

1.   Rapport with the Press
If the superintendent, or his public relations officer, has reached accommodation with the media, they welcome his suggestions for interesting feature stories and he benefits by their willingness to help him shape public opinion. If a racial incident, or one having possible racial overtones, should occur within

Example of School Board Policy
Statement on Desegregation

This report is addressed to all the people of Pittsburgh. It seeks to declare the position of the Board of Education on the subject of racial equality in the schools. It is a statement, as starkly honest as we can make it, of the progress so far and of the large unfulfilled hopes that we in the Board of Public Education have for Negro boys and girls in the Pittsburgh Public Schools. It is a statement of the frustrations and contradictions confronting the Board on this immensely difficult subject. The report is intended neither to pacify Negro citizens, nor to console or reassure white citizens . . .

We will disappoint the civil rights advocates who look for sudden integration but who give little help in concrete counsel toward solutions. We will startle the white citizens who seek to live in white isolation. We will disturb those, both Negro and white, who think that the social revolution of 1965 will pass over soon and that we will return to the old ways. We will not return to the old ways, and your Board of Education is determined that every possible resource of the schools shall be invested in the education of every Negro child for his ultimate, genuine integration by his own choice and by his own worth. We and our faculty declare ourselves in this report prepared to take every reasonable and rational means at our disposal to achieve this goal.

We believe that a lifetime of work remains to be done.

Source: Robert L. Crain, *The Politics of School Desegregation* (Chicago: Aldine Publishing Company, 1968), p. 98.

the schools, the superintendent is obliged to give the media the truth about the matter. He can also take this opportunity, though, to tell how the administration is coping with the incident.[12]

2. News Emphasis

Pre-desegregation reporting should be "tone" reporting, aimed at producing a positive atmosphere for opening day. For example:

The appointment of a citizens advisory committee is a factual story. However, with the inclusion of biographical details on the membership, it becomes a human interest story and introduces the idea of bi-racial cooperation.

The establishment of a rumor center also makes good copy. Staff members at the center can be interviewed concerning some of the calls they receive and how the calls are answered.

The superintendent or board chairman can be interviewed following announcement of a major policy decision for a description of the history behind the decision.

*Example of Types of Policy Statements Required
in Achieving Effective Desegregation*

Policy on Desegregation
1. Statement of decision to desegregate (if voluntary) or resolution of intent to comply (if involuntary).
2. Statement of the date on which the policy will be implemented, and the schools that will be included.
3. Statement that desegregation of faculty and nonprofessional staff members will occur simultaneously with student desegregation.
4. Statement of the method of transportation that will be used to achieve desegregation.

Faculty Policies
5. Statement (or statements) that professional staff will be hired, promoted, paid, demoted and dismissed without regard to race, color or national origin.

Policies and Regulations on the Conduct of Faculty and Staff
6. Statement to faculty and staff regarding their responsibility for making desegregation work.
7. Evaluation of faculty policy handbook for possible revision of policies regarding:
    Discipline and control of behavior.
    Referrals for guidance and other matters.
    Promotion of students.
    Appearance of classrooms.
    Plans and records.
    Evaluation of teachers.
    Responsibilities and duties of staff outside the classroom, such as monitoring and PTA attendance.

Educational Policies
8. Adoption of an in-service training program for teachers to meet personal and professional adjustment needs.
9. Evaluation of the existing curriculum for meeting the needs of the desegregated schools.
10. Statement on differential expenditures for the disadvantaged; i.e., equal educational opportunity is not identical educational opportunity.
11. Statement of policy on ability grouping.

Policies on Specifically Student Matters
12. Statement that all students will be integrated into the regular school program and encouraged to participate in all activities of the school.
13. Adoption and issuance of "Student Code," for distribution to students and parents.

14. Statement of transfer policy; i.e., students who make up a majority in one school will be permitted to transfer to a school in which they are a minority, but not if by so doing, they change their racial group from a minority to a majority in that school.

15. Consideration of the necessity for changing the name and other "traditions" (colors, mascot, songs) of a school or schools to reflect a changed identity.

16. Statement on the elimination of a dual bus system.

Source: Field Surveys by Real Estate Research Corporation, 1971.

The inaugural speeches of Governors Holton of Virginia and Carter of Georgia offered opportunities for positive reporting. They affirmed their support for desegregation as a matter of obedience to the law and support for democracy. Governor Holton followed up his speech by enrolling his children in the predominantly black Richmond schools, where his teenage daughter was subsequently elected cheerleader of her high school.

Opening day reporting should be factual reporting. Unless one of the schools is sponsoring a particularly unusual assembly, such as the dedication of a high school with a new "identity" or installing bi-racial student body presidents, the superintendent should encourage coverage of the day as a factual event.

Post-opening day reporting should emphasize the positive inter-racial contacts that are taking place daily. Aside from the usual reporting on athletic and beauty contests, the media can find a number of human interest stories in personal responses to desegregation.

The section of this chapter on Community Relations contains further discussion of school-media cooperation in working toward effective desegregation.

POLICY. (B-4)   The school board should communicate with opponents of desegregation.

A discussion of how school administrators can identify opponents of desegregation and establish channels of communication to them appears in the Community Relations section.

C. Overcoming Technical Deficiencies in Planning for Desegregation

PROBLEM: When viewed as a process rather than just accomplishing a satisfactory opening day, desegregation requires detailed short- and long-range planning. It must be based on a knowledge of the schools and the community far beyond simple computation of the numbers of black, white and brown students in the district. Even drawing up a plan for the physical rearrangement of students requires information on such tangibles as organization and finance of the school system, and on such intangibles as social class composition and attitudes of the community.[13] Many school boards do not realize the intricacy and complexity of desegregation and so do not prepare adequately.

If the board is using a citizens advisory committee to assist with planning, that group will need to have detailed information on the community, plus knowledge of what actions have and have not worked in other areas with a similar set of conditions.

The development of an effective desegregation plan also demands that:

An instructional program be established that will meet the needs of all students.

Teachers and other staff members be given in-service and/or sensitivity training.

Effective counselling and answering services be set up to respond to staff and community members' questions about the policies of the district.[14]

Not only must all of these factors be investigated, but they must be incorporated as integral parts of an overall plan. This poses a formidable task for a school board that has limited access to persons with technical skills to act as advisors. Unless the superintendent, who traditionally is vested with the responsibility for advising the board on technical matters, has been through desegregation before, it is improbable that all necessary steps will be covered. (See Chapter 3 for a discussion of the desegregation planning process.)

POLICY.   The school board should acquire the skills and knowledge of
 (C-1)   professional consultants in planning for desegregation.

Desegregation consultants are trained and experienced professionals who, upon request, provide assistance in dealing with problems related to school desegregation. Title IV of the Civil Rights Act of 1964 set up three different methods of providing consultative help to school systems and personnel:

Section 403 gives grants for technical assistance rendered by units in State Education Agencies, by school desegregation consulting centers in universities, and by field and headquarters staff of the Division of Equal Educational Opportunity of the Office of Education.

Section 404 provides for grants and contracts with colleges and universities for short-term or regular session institutes to train school personnel to deal effectively with school desegregation problems.

Section 405 gives grants to school boards for the purpose of in-service training or for hiring advisory specialists.

One college or university in each of the Southern states and in New Mexico has a desegregation consulting center. Numerous others have desegregation institutes set up for the express purpose of training school personnel to cope with desegregation. Locations of the consulting centers and institutes can be obtained by contacting a regional office of the Division of Equal Education Opportunity. These offices are listed on a following page.

Districts desegregating under court order are likely to have different consultative needs than districts desegregating on a voluntary basis. Professional help can be obtained by a district for any or all of the steps involved in effective desegregation.

POLICY.   Consultants should be used with, not instead of, citizen advisory
(C-2)   groups in planning for desegregation.

Consultants have the technical and professional expertise to plan for desegregation. Citizen groups know what the community wants and needs in a desegregation plan. The best long-range plan for effective desegregation will come through close cooperation between the lay and professional advisors.

D. Reducing Uncertainty Within School Staffs

PROBLEM: Desegregation is a unique educational change that requires
            administrative recognition of staff uncertainty and other personal
            and professional transition problems.

No other educational change enacted by school boards has required that the staff change their personal values, along with their methods of instruction, and that school personnel accept and enforce social as well as educational change. In most school districts, there will not have been a previous educational change that generated as much unsureness over whether the administration actually wanted the change accomplished, and over job security following the change. Because of the insecurity that desegregation causes, principals must be directed to pay attention to the personal attitudes of their teachers and the relationships among teachers resulting from those attitudes.

POLICY.   The superintendent should recognize the new personal and
(D-1)   professional needs of his staff arising from desegregation.

New personal needs of staff members arise because of general unfamiliarity in dealing with members of a different race or ethnic group and uncertainty about how to handle inter-racial contacts once they occur on a daily basis. New professional needs of staff members are generated by a number of factors, such as:

The larger number of students performing below the class norm. Some of them are actually below average, but most of them are not. The teacher must be able to tell the difference.

The lack of interest among students as dull work designed for younger students is given to slower older students.

The need to give personal attention to students with learning problems.

List of Title IV Regional Offices

Region III

Senior Program Officer
U.S. Office of Education
Div. of Equal Educational
   Opportunities
220 - 7th Street, N.E.
Charlottesville, VA 22901
(covers Delaware, District of
Columbia, Maryland, Virginia,
Pennsylvania, West Virginia)

Region IV

Senior Program Officer
U.S. Office of Education
Div. of Equal Educational
   Opportunities
Peachtree - 7th Building
Room 404
50 - 7th Street, N.E.
Atlanta, GA 30323
(covers Alabama, Florida,
Georgia, Kentucky, North
Carolina, South Carolina,
Mississippi, Tennessee)

Region V

Senior Program Officer
U.S. Office of Education
Div. of Equal Educational
   Opportunities
433 West Van Buren Street
Chicago, IL 60607
(covers Illinois, Indiana, Ohio,
Minnesota, Michigan, Wisconsin)

Region VII

Senior Program Officer
U.S. Office of Education
Div. of Equal Educational
   Opportunities
1114 Commerce Street
Dallas, TX 75202
(covers Arkansas, Louisiana,
New Mexico, Oklahoma, Texas)

Region IX

Senior Program Officer
U.S. Office of Education
Div. of Equal Educational
   Opportunities
760 Market Street
San Francisco, CA 94102
(covers Alaska, Arizona, California,
Hawaii, Nevada, Oregon, Wash.)

Northern & Western Branch

Chief, Northern & Western Branch
U.S. Office of Education
Div. of Equal Educational
   Opportunities
400 Maryland Avenue, S.W.
Washington, DC 20202
(covers Colorado, Connecticut,
Idaho, Iowa, Kansas, Maine,
Massachusetts, Missouri, Montana,
Nebraska, New Hampshire, New
Jersey, New York, N. Dakota,
Rhode Island, S. Dakota, Utah,
Vermont, Wyoming)

The sterility of traditional textbooks for non-middle-class, non-white students, and the inappropriateness of those books as examples for positive peer group relations.

The superintendent is responsible for noticing and responding to the new problems and needs of the staff. A desegregation consultant (such as discussed above) will be able to point out the probability of these staff problems and discuss their solution as part of the long-range desegregation plan. The superintendent cannot, however, expect that a consultant will solve the problems simply by being present. The purpose of a consultant is to teach teachers and principals ways of solving their own problems.[15] To meet the personal needs of staff members, a consultant will probably recommend the institution of some type of pre-desegregation sensitivity training. It is the superintendent's responsibility to recognize that several weeks of sensitizing may not be enough to overcome lifelong attitudes. Therefore, he may recommend longer in-service programs. A detailed review of in-service training programs appears in the section of this chapter titled "Teaching Techniques and Training to Achieve Effective Desegregation". The superintendent should also be cognizant of the possible need for extra staff—curriculum specialists, guidance counsellors, teaching aides, etc. If such personnel are required, it is up to the superintendent to make the appropriate recommendations to the school board.

POLICY. The school board should adopt an equal opportunity employment
(D-2)   policy that will be strictly enforced.

An equal opportunity employment policy states that an employee or an applicant for employment with the school system will not be discriminated against on the basis of race, color or national origin. The fate of black educators in Southern school districts following desegregation provides a vivid illustration of why such a policy may be needed.[16]

The superintendent should recommend to the board that an equal opportunity employment policy be incorporated in the district's policy handbook. Under Federal law (Title VI of the Civil Rights Act of 1964), discriminatory treatment in the desegregation of faculties is illegal, but a district statement of resolution to comply with the law strengthens the position of school administrators in dealing with the community. The guidelines for the desegregation of school faculties included in the "Revised Statement of Policies for School Desegregation Plans Under Title VI of the Civil Rights Act of 1964" provide a model for school boards drafting their own policy statements. These guidelines are reproduced on a following page.

Adoption of the equal opportunity employment policy should not be construed to mean that the district is acting illegally if a campaign of increased minority hiring is instituted. To cover this contingency, the school board should include in its policy a statement similar to that in the New Assignments portion of the following example.

Guidelines for Desegregation of School Faculties

Desegregation of Staff—The racial composition of the professional staff of a school system, and of the schools in the system, must be considered in determining whether students are subjected to discrimination in educational programs. Each school system is responsible for correcting the effects of all past discriminatory practices in the assignment of teachers and other professional staff.

New Assignments—Race, color, or national origin may not be a factor in the hiring or assignment to schools or within schools of teachers and other professional staff, including student teachers and staff serving two or more schools, except to correct the effects of past discriminatory assignments.

Dismissals—Teachers and other professional staff may not be dismissed, demoted, or passed over for retention, promotion, or rehiring, on the ground of race, color, or national origin. In any instance where one or more teachers or other professional staff members are to be displaced as a result of desegregation, no staff vacancy in the school system may be filled through recruitment from outside the system unless the school officials can show that no such displaced staff member is qualified to fill the vacancy. If as a result of desegregation, there is to be a reduction in the total professional staff of the school system, the qualifications of all staff members in the system must be evaluated in selecting the staff members to be released.

Past Assignments—The pattern of assignment of teachers and other professional staff among the various schools of a system may not be such that schools are identifiable as intended for students of a particular race, color, or national origin, or such that teachers or other professional staff or a particular race are concentrated in those schools where all, or the majority of, the students are of that race. Each school system has a positive duty to make staff assignments and reassignments necessary to eliminate past discriminatory assignment patterns.

Source: "Revised Statement of Policies for School Desegregation Plans Under Title VI of the Civil Rights Act of 1964," as Amended for the School Year 1967–68, December 1966. (U.S. Department of Health, Education and Welfare, Office of Education), pp. 2–3. (Updated in a Memorandum of January 14, 1971, from the Director, Office for Civil Rights, to Chief State School Officers and School Superintendents.)

POLICY.   The superintendent should explicitly announce his personal
(D-3)   support of desegregation and the policies related to it.

The superintendent should relay the board's policies on desegregation to all school staff members in a way that expresses his personal support and his expectation that personnel will do their best to implement the policies. This statement of backing and encouragement is particularly important in those districts desegregating under court order. If opposition groups in the community have been particularly active or threatening, principals and teachers may be unclear as to whether they are really expected to make desegregation work.

The superintendent of Maryland's Montgomery County schools verbalized his support in the form of a challenge to his staff to accomplish what other segments of the community could not:

> "I know many times that most of us like to put a thing off, especially if it appears a little disagreeable or a little hard. Some of our citizens have done that, they like to shove it to one side; or say, 'I'm more or less set apart; I won't be affected. Well, all American citizens were affected by this thing, this proposal, this ruling. And for some reason or other, you know, I'm going to expect the leadership of this to come from school people. I think some people have criticized rather justly other organizations like churches and other community groups of perhaps not carrying their share of the load on this, and it comes to us directly and a whole lot is going to depend on the way we handle it."[17]

POLICY. The advice of principals and teachers should be sought in planning
(D-4)   for desegregation.

Because they must implement the desegregation plan on a daily basis, principals and teachers should be encouraged to participate in planning future changes. Particularly in the months following opening day, principals and teachers will know:

If additional staff members are needed for matters such as curriculum and guidance.

If the existing textbooks, or supplementary library materials, are adequate for the needs of the desegregated classroom.

If additional clerical help is needed to take care of routine matters.

How the in-service training can be improved.

If the administration should be considering new methods of grouping or other teaching measures.

This source of information and advice, which is based on in-school experience, should be sought on a regular basis.

POLICY. The principals should serve as examples of positive peer group
(D-5)   relations.

Principals meet and deal with parents, teachers and students of other racial and ethnic groups each day on highly personal bases. What happens during these meetings establishes the climate for inter-racial contact within the schools. Through daily reinforcement, this climate can eventually affect standard behavior in the school. Ideally, a principal's demeanor will be one of friendliness and acceptance of differences.

Suggested Techniques

1.   Sensitivity Training for Principals
     If principals are to supply guidance to teachers in intergroup relations, they should be given as much or more training as the teachers. The principals in a district should also have access to continuing professional help for handling difficult situations as they arise.

2.   Positive Public Pronouncements
     Statements on race relations within the school should be clear and to the point, and should avoid pointing an accusing finger at any particular group. This point is summarized in the following statement by a principal:

> "We've had black power and brown power and yellow power and white power and all other kinds of power here. The only kind of power we're going to have now is purple (ed. school colors) people power."[18]

3.   Evaluation of Performance
     Principals can suggest to the superintendent that evaluation of teachers' performances include consideration of their activities in promoting positive intergroup relations. Through the same channels, principals can suggest establishment of a system of recognition for teachers making an extra effort.

4.   Eliminating Racist Staff Members
     The desegregated classroom is no place for a consciously racist teacher of any race or ethnic group. Nor is the presence of such a person particularly conducive to establishing good relationships among staff members. If a principal discovers that a member of his staff is either unable or unwilling to promote positive intergroup relations, he should take the steps required by his district to remove that person from the classroom.

E. Revision of the Principal's Role

PROBLEM: Desegregation places new demands on a principal's time. In addition to administrative details, he must handle parent, teacher and student counselling when problems arise, and he must serve as a visible example of positive intergroup relations.
     The principal is the chief administrator of the individual school within the district, in terms of both insuring that system-wide policies are carried out and formulating policies unique to the school. With desegregation, he has to handle more planning, paperwork, meetings, etc. A principal who is tied to his desk by administrative matters, or who views himself primarily as an administrator

and prefers to stay at his desk, will not be available to discuss problems with staff and students and will not be visible on the school grounds.

POLICY.   The superintendent should recognize the need for reduced
 (E-1)   administrative demands on principals.

A survey of secondary school principals in which they were asked to list activities according to the amount of time consumed during a "typical" school year produced the following top five items in this order:

1.   Administrative planning alone and/or with subordinate administrators.
2.   Meetings with students on matters other than discipline.
3.   Work with individual teachers regarding their teaching proficiency.
4.   Meetings with teachers on matters of curriculum or instruction.
5.   Correspondence.[19]

The same survey revealed that over one-third of the principals wanted to move into more prestigious administrative positions than the ones they were filling.

Desegregation is not likely to produce any change in the priorities of principals unless the superintendent recognizes that change is needed and that principals will resist if they feel that their futures depend primarily on their ability to perform administrative tasks. Each superintendent should recognize that the principalship is a cluster of functions that are best realized through the efforts of several administrators and supervisors rather than only one person.[20]

Suggested Techniques

1.   Review of Principals' Duties
The superintendent should analyze the principalship in each school to identify those administrative tasks that must be performed only by the principal and those that could be performed just as easily and efficiently by someone else, such as a school secretary, a guidance counsellor, or an assistant principal. After this review, appropriate adjustment should be made in the assignment of tasks within the school.

2.   Policy Statement on Principals' Roles
There is evidence that a superintendent's expectations of principals, and principals' perceptions of those expectations, can be divergent.[21] It is therefore suggested that districts incorporate in their written policies a description of the role of a principal. Then individuals can act within well-defined specifications.

3.   Verbal Communication
Neither the hiring of additional personnel nor a definitive policy statement

should be assumed by the superintendent to take the place of close and regular
verbal communication. Personal conversations are the best means of discovering
problems of principals' use of available time after desegregation.

POLICY.   Principals should become more accessible to students, teachers
(E-2)   and parents.

A *New York Times* story on a troubled urban high school includes an
excellent description of an accessible principal:

> "He instituted a series of regular 'speakouts', during which he talked with
> students and teachers about the life of the school. He was, and is, often
> on the move—roaming the halls, chatting with students, sitting in on classes,
> talking to teachers.
> 'Time was,' he explained, 'when the principal was never seen by the
> teachers, let alone the kids. You've got to be a presence.' "[22]

All of the roles of the principal—as administrator, as educational leader, as
model for race relations, as chief disciplinarian—demand that he increase his
accessibility with desegregation. As top administrator and educational leader in
his school, he is the only institutionalized channel by which teachers and students can relay their needs to the district administration. As intergroup relations
example, he can hear and deal with individual problems before they become
school-wide problems. And simply the visibility of the principal, and the feeling
of students that they do not have to misbehave to be noticed, helps improve
discipline.

Suggested Techniques

1.   Participatory Management (Formal Access)
     The power to guide behavior through standards of reward and punishment
for specific acts is not the same as the power to influence people to spend
time and energy fulfilling school goals. When teachers and students can meet
with the principal and clearly have influence in setting and establishing standards,
they are more likely to follow them in ways that support school goals.[23]
     This type of access to the principal is formal, with contact taking place on
a regular basis. The "speakouts" referred to in the newspaper account cited
above probably resulted in adoption of policies recommended by student and/or
faculty participants. This exemplifies to students democratic, rather than purely
authoritarian, school administration.

2.   Open-Door Policy and Principal Visibility (Informal Access)
     The principal should establish certain hours of the day or "any time my
door is open" for students to visit. Many students "want only to know that
someone in authority is willing to take the time to listen to them"[24]
     Part of the success of the principal's policy of accessibility depends on his
visibility and how he conducts himself in public areas of the school. The follow-

ing two principals, described by a student in the first instance and by a newspaper reporter in the second, are undoubtedly very successful:

> "Yea, well our principal, I think he's really a good guy. You know, you really get the feeling that he's with it, he's really with the kids. You see him around everywhere in the halls, you know, he'll say hello to you. I don't think he knows everybody's name, but he gives the impression that he knows you. You sort of have that feeling about him. Like there's a . . . at our football games, there's a popcorn machine; and he could go to the head of the line and get it, you know, like he's the principal, but he just stands in line like everybody else and he waits his turn."[25]

> "McGee has another philosophy about running his school—a principal cannot stay in his office.
> " 'In an urban high school like ours you have to get out of the office,' he said. 'You can't be a desk principal in this school.'
> "And so he walks, nearly all the day. He strolls the halls, pops into classrooms, tours the sidewalks around the school and even eats his lunch in the middle of the cafeteria with students all around. From time to time, he has been seen doing a little dance if there is music to be heard.
> "On these tours, McGee carries a sheet of notebook paper in his pocket. Students continually run up to him with problems—an athlete never got a medal he won; a teacher ousted a student from class, a student is in trouble with the law."[26]

POLICY.   Principals should become stronger and more responsive educational
(E-3)   leaders.

The role of principals as educational leaders and the importance of their assuming stronger and more responsive stances during the process of desegregation is treated in the portion of this chapter on Teaching Techniques and Training.

POLICY.   Principals should adopt firm, clear rules for behavior and enforce
(E-4)   them fairly and impartially.

Policies for in-school behavior and discipline are discussed in the section of this chapter titled "Student Adaptation to Achieve Effective Desegregation". The recommendation is made there that students be allowed to participate in setting behavior standards for themselves. Methods of encouraging good behavior are also discussed.

NOTES

1. Robert T. Stout, "The Processes of Desegregation," paper prepared for Real Estate Research Corporation (July 1971).
2. A group called HOPE (Helping Our Public Education) that formed in Providence following the School Committee's decision to desegregate offers

a good example. The group formed for the purpose of preparing minority
students academically and socially for desegregation; the two schools with
which HOPE worked were the only two in the city whose children and
parents received preparation.

3. Sam W. King, *Organization and Effective Use of Advisory Committees,*
   Office of Education, Department of Health, Education and Welfare,
   OE 84009 (Washington, D.C.: U.S. Government Printing Office, 1960), p.20.

4. Edgar G. Epps, "Notes on Desegregation," paper prepared for Real Estate
   Research Corporation (July 1971).

5. Chester Gromacki, *A Study of Current Practices and Development of an
   Advisory Committee Handbook,* Department of Health, Education and
   Welfare, ERIC Reports (ED 014 950), p. 16.

6. James H. Bash and Thomas J. Morris, *Practices and Patterns of Faculty
   Desegregation, A Guidebook,* Office of Education, Department of Health,
   Education and Welfare, ERIC Reports (ED 020 277), p. 10.

7. In an interview with Real Estate Research Corporation personnel in May
   1971, the assistant superintendent of the Sacramento City Unified School
   District said that there was intense competition for black education
   majors. Cf. "How Are Negro Teachers Doing?" *Southern Education Report*
   (December 1968), pp. 25–27.

8. See n. 1 above.

9. Bash and Morris, p. 21

10. Robert L. Crain, *The Politics of School Desegregation* (Chicago: Aldine
    Publishing Company, 1968), p. 116.

11. Frederick Luther Dunn, Jr., *Programs and Procedures of Desegregation
    Developed by the Board of Education, Montgomery County, Maryland*
    (unpublished doctoral dissertation: University of Maryland, 1960), p. 49.

12. The following news item contains the announcement of the superintendent's
    closure of a school but also tells what action is being taken about the
    situation:

    "About 600 parents gathered at Hiram Johnson High School this morning
    to seek solutions to the racial violence which has plagued the southeast
    Sacramento campus this week. Yesterday at noon the sporadic incidents
    had mounted to such a degree of tension that the school was closed until
    Monday."

    "Parents Seek Cures for Johnson High Race Strife," *Sacramento Bee*
    (October 2, 1970).

13. H.S. Blanton, *The Relationship of Behavioral Patterns of Selected Superin-
    tendents to the Process of Public School Desegregation* (Unpublished
    doctoral dissertation, 1959), p. 9.

14. Frederick William Phillip Reuter, *An Administrator's Guide to Successful
    Desegregation of the Public Schools* (Unpublished doctoral dissertation:
    New York University, 1961), p. 95.

15. Mark Chesler, Carl Jorgensen and Phyllis Erenberg, *Planning Educational
    Change,* Volume III, *Integrating the Desegregated School* (Center for
    Research on Utilization of Scientific Knowledge, The University of

Michigan), Office of Education, Department of Health, Education and Welfare (OE 38016), p. 47.

16. John Egerton, "When Desegregation Comes, the Negro Principals Go," *Southern Education Report* (December 1967), pp. 8–11.

17. Dunn, p. 88.

18. "SHS Whirlwind. Principal Offers Fresh Approach," *Sacramento Bee* (February 7, 1971).

19. John K. Hemphill, James M. Richards and Richard E. Peterson, *Report of the Senior High School Principalship* (Washington, D.C.: National Association of Secondary-School Principals, 1965), p. 81.

20. AASA Committee on the Selection of School Principals, "The Right Principal for the Right Job" (Washington, D.C.: American Association of School Administrators, 1967), p. 23.

21. DeLars Funches, *The Superintendent's Expectations of the Negro High School Principal* (Unpublished doctoral dissertation, University of Oklahoma, 1961), p. 60.

22. "Washington High: From Riot to Hope," *The New York Times* (June 1, 1971).

23. Chesler, et al, p. 48.

24. Sacramento, California school principal's description of why he maintains an "open door" policy. Personal interview with Real Estate Research Corporation staff, May 1971.

25. Chesler, et al, p. 36.

26. "SHS Whirlwind. Principal Offers Fresh Approach," *Sacramento Bee* (February 7, 1971).

Bibliography

Allen, Jesse Lee. *The Effects of School Desegregation on the Employment Status of Negro Principals of North Carolina.* Unpublished Doctoral Dissertation, Duke University, 1969.

American Association of School Administrators and the National School Boards Association. *Selecting a School Superintendent.* Washington, D.C.: AASA, 1968.

American Association of School Administrators and Research Division. *Local School Boards: Size and Selection.* Educational Research Circular No. 2. Washington, D.C.: AASA, February 1964. (Out of print).

—. *Local School Boards: Status and Practices.* Educational Research Circular No. 6. Washington, D.C.: AASA, November 1967. (Out of print).

AASA Committee on the Selection of School Principals. *The Right Principal for the Right Job.* Washington, D.C.: AASA, 1967.

Bash, James H. and Thomas J. Morris. *Practices and Patterns of Faculty Desegregation, A Guidebook.* Office of Education, Department of Health, Education and Welfare, ERIC Reports (ED 020 277).

Blanton, Harry Smith. *The Relationship of Behavioral Patterns of Selected*

Superintendents to the Process of Public School Desegregation. Unpublished Doctoral Dissertation, 1959.

Cecil, Carl Edwin. *Levels of Involvement Needed to Key on Educational Desegregation.* Center for Intercultural Education, University of Alabama, 1969.

Chesler, Mark, Carl Jorgensen, and Phyllis Erenberg. *Planning Educational Change,* Volume III. *Integrating the Desegregated School.* (Center for Research on Utilization of Scientific Knowledge, The University of Michigan.) Office of Education, Department of Health, Education and Welfare (OE 38016).

Combs, Willie Everett. *The Principalship in the Negro Secondary Schools of Florida.* Unpublished Doctoral Dissertation, Indiana University, 1964.

Crain, Robert L. *The Politics of School Desegregation.* Chicago: Aldine Publishing Company, 1968.

Draper, Dorothy Watts. *The Status of the Elementary School Principalship in Negro Schools in Alabama.* Unpublished Doctoral Dissertation, University of Pittsburgh, 1958.

Dunn, Federick Luther, Jr. *Programs and Procedures of Desegregation Developed by the Board of Education, Montgomery County, Maryland.* Unpublished Doctoral Dissertation, University of Maryland, 1960.

Education U.S.A. Special Report. *School Boards in an Era of Conflict.* Highlights of the Cubberley Conference, School of Education, Stanford University, July 26–28, 1966.

Egerton, John. "When Desegregation Comes, the Negro Principals Go," *Southern Education Report,* December 1967, pp. 8–11.

Eye, Glen G. *The Influences and Controls Over Local School Systems.* Office of Education, Department of Health, Education and Welfare. ERIC Reports (ED 011 706), April 30, 1967.

Frady, Marshall. "Discovering One Another in a Georgia Town," *Life,* February 12, 1971.

Funches, De Lars. *The Superintendent's Expectations of the Negro High School Principal in Mississippi.* Unpublished Doctoral Dissertation, University of Oklahoma, 1961.

Gromacki, Chester. *A Study of Current Practices and Development of an Advisory Committee Handbook.* Department of Health, Education and Welfare, ERIC Reports (ED 014 950), June 1966.

Gunter, Pearl Kennedy. *Problems and Patterns of Staff Desegregation with Implications for Tennessee.* Unpublished Doctoral Dissertation, University of Tennessee, 1963.

Hamm, William Carson. *Changes in the Selection and Retention of Senior High Schools in Oklahoma, 1954 to 1964.* Unpublished Doctoral Dissertation, University of Kentucky, 1964.

Hemphill, John K., James M. Richards, Richard E. Peterson, *Report of the Senior High School Principalship.* Washington, D.C.: The National Association of Secondary School Principals, 1965.

Hickox, Edward S. *Power Structures, School Boards and Administrative Style.*

Office of Education, Department of Health, Education and Welfare. ERIC Reports (ED 012 510), February 1967.

Hooker, Robert W. *Displacement of Black Teachers in Eleven Southern States.* Race Relations Information Center, Nashville, Tennessee, December 1970.

"How are Negro Teachers Fairing?" *Southern Education Report,* December 1968, pp. 25-27.

Hulsey, John Adler, Jr. *A Study of Certain Aspects of Faculty Desegregation in Georgia.* Unpublished Doctoral Dissertation, University of Alabama, 1969.

Issues and Alternatives, A Report of the Fifth National NEA Professional Rights and Responsibilities Conference on Civil and Human Rights in Education. 1968 Theme: *Public School Personnel Policies.* Washington, D.C., February 14-16, 1968.

Kavina, George. *The Predisposition of School Board Members Toward Change.* Unpublished Doctoral Dissertation, University of Arizona, 1969.

King, Sam W. *Organization and Effective Use of Advisory Committees.* Office of Education, Department of Health, Education and Welfare, OE 84009 (Washington, D.C.: U.S. Government Printing Office, 1960).

Memorandum from the Director, Office for Civil Rights, to Chief State School Officers and School Superintendents, dated January 14, 1971.

Morris, Eddie W. *Factors Related to Faculty Desegregation in Public Schools.* Unpublished Doctoral Dissertation, University of Kentucky, 1965.

NEA Commission on Professional Rights and Responsibilities. *Fair Dismissal Standards.* February 1969.

NEA Commission on Professional Rights and Responsibilities. *Report of Task Force Survey of Teacher Displacement in Seventeen States.* Washington, D.C.: National Educational Association, December 1965.

NEA Professional Rights and Responsibilities Committee on Civil and Human Rights of Educators. *Faculty Desegregation.* Spring 1966 Conference. Washington, D.C.: NEA

NEA Research Division. *Recent School Board Action Related to De Facto Segregation of Pupils and to Integration of Employed Personnel.* NEA Research Memo 1964-9.

Office of Education, Department of Health, Education and Welfare. *Planning Educational Change.* Volume IV. "How Five School Systems Desegregated," Washington, D.C.: U.S. Government Printing Office No. FS 5.238:38013, 1969.

O'Reilly, Robert P., ed. *Racial and Social Class Isolation in the Schools: Implication for Educational Policy and Programs.* New York: Praeger Publishers, 1970.

"Parents Seek Cures for Johnson High Race Strife," *Sacramento Bee,* October 2, 1970.

Reuher, Frederick P. *An Administrator's Guide to Successful Desegregation of the Public Schools.* Unpublished Doctoral Dissertation, New York University, 1961.

"Revised Statement of Policies for School Desegregation Plans Under Title VI of the Civil Rights Act of 1964," as Amended for the School Year 1967-68,

December 1966. U.S. Department of Health, Education and Welfare, Office of Education.

Ryder, Jack McBride. *A Study of Personnel Practices and Policies with Relation to Utilization of Teachers from the Negro Minority Group in Certain Michigan Public School Districts.* Unpublished Doctoral Dissertation, Michigan State University, 1962.

School Administration in Newly Reorganized Districts. Washington, D.C.: American Association of School Administrators, 1965.

School Superintendents Conference on the Practical Problems of Public School Desegregation. August 5–7, 1963. Report Prepared Under the Direction of George B. Brain, Conference Chairman, Superintendent of Public Instruction, Baltimore City Public Schools.

"SHS Whirlwind. Principal Offers Fresh Approach," *Sacramento Bee,* February 7, 1971.

Smith, John Thomas. *Programs of Preparation for School Administration in Negro Graduate Schools.* Unpublished Doctoral Dissertation, University of Kentucky, 1961.

Stoff, S. *The Two-Way Street: Guideposts to Peaceful School Desegregation.* Indianapolis, Indiana: David-Stewart Publishing Company, 1967.

Taylor, Joseph H. *Summer Institute of Psychological-Sociological Problems of Desegregation. 80 School Administrators, Supervisors, Principals and Teachers in Ten Florida Counties.* Office of Education, Department of Health, Education and Welfare, ERIC Reports ED 023 730, March 28, 1968.

"Washington High: From Riot to Hope," *The New York Times,* June 1, 1971.

Wey, H.W. "Desegregation—It Works," *Phi Delta Kappan,* Volume 45, 1964, pp. 382–87.

**Teaching Techniques and Training to
Achieve Effective Desegregation**

Instruction In The Desegregated Classroom

Classroom instruction has two basic objectives—teaching and management. The primary role of the classroom teacher is to induce the student to learn. To accomplish this, the teacher works personally with students, directing them to undertake an activity or establishing situations that stimulate the student to learn. These objectives may be attained by working alone with individuals or collectively with groups of students.

A secondary role of the classroom teacher is to manage student behavior. To attain this objective, the teacher must interpret and diagnose the behavior of students; reinforce or correct it; and control the classroom by inducing students to act in a socially desirable manner. Provided that the function of management complements the teacher's primary objective—to induce learning—the instructional process will:

Motivate students by providing situations in which learning can occur.

Activate the student by directing his attention toward specific learning situations.

Give the student experience through practice.

Induce subsequent learning by reinforcing the student's interest in learning.

Develop the student's insight.

Guide the student toward appropriate objectives.

Contribute to healthy development of the student's personality.

Basic Problems Caused or Aggravated by Desegregation

1. In most schools, the instructional process is directed at teaching particular subjects. Classroom management is limited to the control of the student's surface behavior—particularly when it detracts from the teacher's ability to establish an "orderly" classroom. This approach to instruction tends to reward students who are able to work quietly by themselves with minimal direction or control from the teacher.

2. Many minority-group and disadvantaged students enter the desegregated school with feelings of self-doubt that make it difficult for them to adjust to the details of a subject-oriented curriculum. Often they withdraw or become frustrated if teachers give assignments that require them to study on their own and/or do not appear to "care" when the student exhibits exceptional behavior. This problem is magnified if teachers are not familiar with the student's parents or his performance in his previous school. Much of the teacher's ability to manage a class is dependent upon knowledge

of a) the student's past performance and behavior problems, and b) the degree to which parents are aware of problems and reinforce the teacher's decisions. Because teachers in newly desegregated schools are unfamiliar with their students' problems of adjustment, minor incidents in the classroom tend to increase significantly.

3. Members of minority groups and disadvantaged students tend to be more anxious about their ability to succeed in the desegregated school than are members of the dominant community. Unless opportunities are provided for the student to demonstrate his ability to interact or compete with his peers, the student is more likely to create minor disruptions in the classroom—rather than seek recognition through achievement in academic problems. Often, directive or authoritarian attempts on the part of teachers to "control" such behavior result in increased tension and hostility of the entire class toward the teacher.

4. Minority-group and disadvantaged children are often highly motivated to succeed but lack skills and knowledge in the "core curriculum" courses. Many desegregated schools have met this problem by increasing the level of ability grouping, remedial coursework and non-promotion. In view of the relative lack of success with compensatory programs, lack of clarity about the results of grouping among children of average intelligence, and a body of evidence against non-promotion, it appears that excessive use of these procedures over long periods of time is unwarranted—especially when the student's problem stems more from self-doubt and isolation than lack of ability or lack of motivation. In fact, excessive use of these procedures in many desegregated schools may be a measure of the district's desire to maintain the status quo.

5. The organization of many schools is highly bureaucratic. Teachers in such schools tend to spend less time interacting with students and often act only as information givers or disciplinarians. This occurs largely because they lack the support of the principal, or are evaluated on the basis of their ability to maintain order in the classroom. Desegregation may aggravate this problem if the teachers refuse to accept changes in the classroom, or do not make attempts at working with their peers. In some cases, this may cause the eventual resignation of principals and teachers. In almost all cases where it occurs, this reaction creates increased tension throughout the school.

Basic Objectives To Remedy These Problems

1. Schools must accept responsibility for the actions of their faculties—particularly if those actions aggravate problems attendant to desegregation. This responsibility should include development of professional standards of teacher conduct, training and reinforcement of teachers in their efforts to

improve human relations, adoption of new teaching procedures and materials, and establishment of democratically-organized classrooms.

2. Schools should provide training and reinforcement of teachers in their efforts to become good classroom managers. Often this will require the principal to reallocate a significant percentage of his time to pursuit of an "open-door policy" on discipline, remaining "visible" to the students and teachers, and conducting in-service training of teachers to reinforce his policies.

3. School supervisors or leaders with skills in improved classroom management and teaching need to be developed. Either they should come from among the present staff or new school positions should be created for this purpose. Such personnel should be capable of establishing, maintaining and evaluating good management and teaching techniques—particularly those that lead to the formation of democratically-organized classrooms.

4. Schools should attempt to develop new organizational techniques that give teachers more free time to work with individual students or small groups of students. These efforts should be intended to eliminate feelings of confusion and self-doubt among minority-group and disadvantaged children. They should also circumvent the need for excessive grouping of students who are highly motivated but lack certain skills required in the desegregated school.

Specific Problems, Policies, and Techniques

A. Improving Teacher Sensitivity to Diversity and to Impacts Upon Others

PROBLEM: Like all individuals, teachers often unconsciously assume that their own personal values are the only acceptable values, and therefore reject the values and behavior patterns of those unlike themselves. For those students who are "different," especially those who are poor, minority-group members, or culturally handicapped, rejection by their teachers can mean lasting damage to their self-images and alienation from the school institution.

Arthur Foshay speaks precisely to the problem confronting teachers and administrators of desegregated schools in the following quote: "As educators . . . we are required to tell the next generation, black and white, the ugly truth about [the racism] of their heritage, and to design a curriculum that will free them from it. We, who know no such freedom, are required to lead naive children to a knowledge we lack. The blind are required to lead the innocent."[1]

The problem facing most teachers and administrators is how to become less "blind". A major solution lies in the use within schools of in-service education in human relations and activities designed to promote sensitivity to all students and their needs.

POLICY.   All teachers should be exposed, as a matter of course, to some
 (A-1)   form of human relations training.

The difficulties that teachers of one race or ethnic group often have in
understanding, much less accepting, the values and behavior patterns of children
from another group often prevent them from fulfilling two primary objectives of
education: transmitting academic knowledge to their students, and promoting
the healthy personality development of those students. This difficulty also
inhibits the relationships between teachers and students of different races and/or
backgrounds, and sometimes causes the classroom to become merely a place
of discipline and "babysitting".

Thus, in-service education for school personnel in human relations becomes
critical if students are indeed to learn, and to live up to their academic potential.
The goals of human relations training are several:

1.   To understand the values and behavior patterns of all students.
2.   To understand the minority-group students' need for acceptance by others
     and for belief in self.
3.   To understand how all students perceive individuals as teachers and
     authority figures, and why.
4.   To understand what the minority-group student is sensitive to, and why.
5.   To understand the institutionalized racism in American society.
6.   To understand and recognize the basis and persistence of racial and/or
     ethnic stereotypes, and why they inhibit positive interaction.

School administrators have a responsibility to see that teachers and school
support staff develop positive approaches toward their interactions with all
students. They have a responsibility, where these positive approaches do not
currently exist, to develop programs in human relations training that will
contribute to a greater understanding of all students, and thus lead to meaningful
changes in the attitudes and behavior of all school personnel.

Suggested Techniques

1.   Small Group Workshops

A popular human relations training technique has been the small group
workshop with multi-racial and multi-ethnic participants. They meet over a
period of time to discuss common problems or to develop programs to meet
specific educational needs. Participants in these workshops can be drawn from a
variety of sources: representative community leaders, school administrators,
parents, school teachers, or students. The important aspect of these workshops
for desegregation is that they provide the participants with a structured opportunity to work out common solutions to a problem or to develop programs
to meet widely recognized needs. The relative intimacy of the small group

usually results in a broadened understanding of the various participants' values and personal merits. Descriptions of two workshops follow.

The presence of several conditions increases the likelihood of small group workshop experiences being meaningful. First, the group should have a stated purpose and be responsible for coming up with specific results; i.e., a program or a solution to a problem. Second, the administration, or those responsible for forming the group, should respect the results of that group. Third, each group should have a leader who believes in the concept of positive human relations and who is able to manipulate the group when necessary to achieve involvement of all members. The leader should have received special training in conducting such workshops, if possible.

2.   Sensitivity Training

The technique commonly known as sensitivity training has been widely used in desegregating school districts. Unlike small group workshops, which are oriented toward a specific outside goal, sensitivity training sessions have as their main purpose the sensitizing of people to one another. In sensitivity training, groups of eight to twelve participants are led by a trained psychologist (or a person specially trained for leadership of such a group) to learn about each other and to discover how they affect and are affected by other people.

School districts that do not have trained psychologists on their staffs should approach sensitivity training with caution. These sessions, because they deal primarily with the emotions of the participants, should always be led by trained professionals, preferably psychologists or psychiatrists. When handled carefully, the candor and the intimacy of these training sessions can uncover and discredit basic feelings of prejudice and therefore aid in the improvement of teacher sensitivity to diversity.

3.   Field Trips for Faculty Members

White teachers, even more than minority-group teachers, are hindered in their relationships with minority-group students because they have little comprehension of the physical and social background of those students. To overcome this problem, some school districts have initiated a program of field trips into minority-group neighborhoods for their teachers. Teachers "visiting" a minority-group neighborhood might meet with local clergy, have coffee in a parent's house, or just walk the streets.

4.   Faculty Meetings

Faculty meetings provide a logical opportunity for lectures and/or discussions on human relations. Subjects appropriate to human relations that can be discussed in faculty meetings include: language usage by white or black teachers that offends students of another race; facts about common misconceptions, such as a belief that minority students are inherently less intelligent than white

Two Examples of Small Group Workshops

To foster greater human relations understanding, the faculty of an integrated high school in Portland, Oregon, was organized into fifteen departments and into seven multidisciplinary units. Both types of units meet twice a month to talk about programs, problems, and solutions. A major purpose of the two different groupings is to promote better relations and sensitivity among all staff.

In New Albany, Mississippi, a three-week pre-service institute for the thirty-eight elementary teachers involved in complete desegregation of the elementary level students began with a one-week workshop to help teachers get to know each other and to reduce racial fears. To assist in this process, teachers were divided 1) into a primary and an intermediate group and 2) into groups representing the two schools to which they would be assigned. Thus, four groups of about ten participants each were formed. Each group was assigned specific tasks (sorting out student folders, assigning students to teams, reporting anecdotes about specific children, etc.). At the end of the first week; "Apprehension regarding integration of faculty was beginning to lessen. Communication between the races was becoming more open."

One Example of Sensitivity Training

In 1970, a Portland, Oregon, high school held three, three-day weekend retreats for faculty and students on a volunteer basis. During each weekend, the seventy-five to one hundred participants were divided into groups of fifteen persons, each section being led by a psychologist. This sensitivity program was deemed successful by most of its participants.

Sources: Description of programs at Jefferson High School, Portland, Oregon; and New Albany Municipal School District, *Annual Report 1968–69, A Title IV Project,* New Albany, Mississippi, pp. 17–19.

students; problems in student discipline and differences in discipline practices by white and minority teachers, etc.

5.   Supervision of Teacher Classroom Behavior

Many of the difficulties in teacher-student interaction arise from the fact that behavior patterns are often unconscious and therefore not easily observed by the one committing them. Thus, teachers frequently need someone who can objectively point out practices that may reflect insensitivity to students of a different background from their own. Examples of such behavior are not referring to children of another race by name, not calling on them in class, treating them differently than their classmates, or avoiding physical contact.[2]

Techniques of supervision are discussed later in this section.

6. Faculty Exchange of Student Information

In many school systems, the occasion of school desegregation will mean that teachers will have children in their classrooms about whom they have no knowledge and with whom they have had no previous experience. The fact that the teachers may even be unfamiliar with the general backgrounds of their new students will compound the difficulties of effective interaction with them. To meet this problem, it is suggested that teachers make a point of meeting with the former teachers of new students to obtain factual and anecdotal information. Such an exchange of information could take place at a meeting of all faculty involved in school desegregation. This meeting should occur prior to opening day but after both students and teachers have received their new assignments.

Overall Effect of Techniques. Past use of these different types of human relations programs has not shown any one to be consistently more successful than the others. However, in those school districts where the most progress has been made, these programs have frequently been used in combination with each other. Experience has demonstrated that a number of factors contribute to the success of a program and should be built into whatever type of program is utilized. Among these factors are the following:

Consistent leadership and support for the objectives of human relations programs by school administrators (from the superintendent to the principal);

Candor in discussion;

Required attendance;

Released time for participants, or stipends;

Small group discussions as well as large group discussions;

Some participation by minority parents and students;

At least the initial meetings led by persons trained in human relations;

Involvement of minority and majority community leaders;

Training of existing school staff to conduct on-going meetings or programs;

Introduction of instructional techniques and classroom arrangements that teachers can use in pursuing their new ideas; and

Follow-up services provided by school administrators or teachers with extra human relations training to periodically review classroom progress.

It is important to note that one key characteristic of the successful program is that it is on-going in nature, rather than a one-time meeting. Attitudes developed over many years cannot be changed overnight. Successful programs are those that occur over a period of time—such as two-hour meetings once a week

for six weeks—and are accompanied by follow-up services after the official
program has been completed. In addition, successful programs not only present
the rationale for attitude changes, but also present techniques that can be used
by the teacher in carrying out new ideas. Many of these techniques will be
discussed in the following section.

POLICY.   School administrators should encourage greater formal and
(A-2)   informal peer group relations among teachers.

Teachers usually do not have enough opportunities for peer group interaction within their schools to develop the type of interracial relationships that
help make desegregation really effective. Relatively autonomous within their
classrooms, their contacts with other teachers are often limited to social
conversation. This type of contact is desirable, but it rarely provides an adequate
forum for serious discussion of common goals, problems, or successful teaching
experiences. Opportunities for such discussions need to be created, particularly in
desegregated schools. Honest interaction and understanding between white and
minority-group teachers will assist teachers in understanding students of
backgrounds unlike their own.

Small group workshops and faculty subcommittees are examples of
structured opportunities for greater teacher interaction. Additional discussion
of these sorts of techniques is presented in the section of this chapter titled
"Administrative Measures to Achieve Effective Desegregation".

Much of the informal interaction among teachers is strongly influenced by
seemingly trivial factors. Examples are whether they have breaks at the same
time, or whether their rooms are adjacent, or whether they frequent the same
coffee room. Principals wishing to encourage greater interracial contacts among
teachers should take these physical proximity factors into account. Even
relatively casual opportunities for contacts, if repeated every day over a whole
year, can significantly contribute to better understanding and closer relationships.

POLICY.   School administrations should develop explicit standards of
(A-3)   evaluation and student discipline that recognize the diversity of
               the school population.

A common problem in desegregated schools is the confusion existing over
methods and standards of student discipline and evaluations. Both black and
white teachers are hesitant to severely discipline students of another race,
fearing charges of prejudice. They also wish to avoid charges of favoritism. In
some cases, black and white teachers have used different methods of discipline
in the past. Moreover, the children in a single school room may have been
exposed to many different styles of discipline at home; hence it is difficult to
know how they may react to whatever method a teacher employs.

It is therefore extremely important that teachers be made aware of differences in methods and, even more important, that they be explicitly instructed
concerning common techniques to be used throughout the school. It is vital that
all children and their parents clearly understand what the rules of discipline are
and precisely what behavior is expected of them.

Suggested Techniques

1. Policy Statements
    Perhaps the first task of school administrators in facing this problem is to develop and to write down school policies on discipline and evaluation. These policies should be straight forward and, while not being inflexible, should provide clear guidelines for teachers to follow in almost every situation. The policies should be presented to teachers and discussed thoroughly early in the school year. Teachers should have the opportunity to react to the policies in faculty meetings or individual conferences, but they should be encouraged to adhere closely to the announced policies to avoid any inconsistencies of treatment.

2. Supervision
    School administrators should watch carefully to see that school guidelines are being followed. For example, if a parent reports that a child has been hit by a teacher—against school policy—the administrator should immediately discuss and evaluate the incident with the teacher.

3. Discipline Records
    Teachers should keep a daily discipline record listing students who have been singled out for special punishment, such as detention. If the administration in charge notices any patterns of punishment, such as students of one race being punished more frequently or severely, he should discuss the matter with the teacher. One advantage of the discipline record for the teacher is that it serves as a reminder of who has been punished and how, and what form of punishment is given for particular misdemeanors.

4. In-Service Education
    Confusion over matters of discipline and evaluation provides a good opportunity for in-service education to help teachers. Several faculty meetings could well be devoted to hearing a consultant explain and demonstrate new techniques of evaluation and discipline. Films and special classroom observations would be appropriate. Other techniques are described in the portion of this chapter titled "Student Adaptation to Achieve Effective Desegregation".
    POLICY.   School administrators should ensure that teachers provide clear
    (A-4)   channels of communication with all their students' parents or
                     guardians.
    The ability of teachers to understand and be sensitive to their students will in part depend on the teachers' knowledge of their students' families and home environments. Further, students will obtain more motivation and support for their in-school efforts from their homes when parents are aware of, and involved in, the school program.

Suggested Techniques

1. Parent-Teacher Conferences

Traditionally, teachers have met with parents through the parent-teacher conference. Such conferences usually occur in the school, after school hours but before nightfall. Often teachers only meet with parents when a student is doing badly in school. However, school desegregation demands a new emphasis on, and more flexible format for, the parent-teacher conference. First, teachers could meet with all parents or guardians at least twice a year. If a child's parents cannot attend a daytime meeting, Saturday or evening meetings could be arranged. The teacher could take the initiative in providing for such meetings.

2. "Open House" Policy

White and minority-group parents are certain to be curious or have fears about school desegregation when it first occurs. Schools could adopt an "open house" policy whereby the classrooms are open to parents for observation at certain times each week throughout the school year. All parents should be encouraged to come and "observe".

3. Parent Volunteers

An increasingly utilized technique for involving parents in schools is to develop a parent volunteer program. One afternoon or morning a week, a parent aide could assist the teacher in classroom administrative duties, special tutoring, reading to children, assisting teachers with field trips, and helping to keep order in the cafeteria and the halls, and on the playground. A description of such a program follows. Using parents as aides is an especially helpful way of involving the minority-group parent who may have "given up" on the school system. If money is available, paid parent aides who can devote more time than volunteers are of even greater assistance in freeing teachers for other tasks or in providing individual help to students.

4. Home Visits

Some schools require each teacher to visit the home of each student in his or her class once a year. This gives the teacher a chance to see what the home environment of the student is really like, and to make contact with those parents or guardians who take little interest in attending events held in the school.

B. Using New Classroom Management Techniques

PROBLEM: Most teachers have traditionally used subject-centered methods of instruction almost exclusively. As indicated in the general introduction to this section, this emphasis can produce negative results, especially for disadvantaged children or others who are not used to working quietly on assigned subjects. Resulting discipline problems can create tensions between teacher and students, and in the classroom generally. The more a teacher's activities must be centered on discipline, the more difficult it is for all students either to acquire academic knowledge or to develop healthy personalities. Therefore, it is desirable for teachers in desegregated schools to introduce other techniques of class management than subject-centered instruction by a single teacher. Certainly these will not replace that dominant mode altogether in any school system, but they may provide important alternative channels of development of great benefit to children who are not well-suited to the traditionally predominant approach.

POLICY.   Teachers should be taught the concepts and techniques pertaining
(B-1)   to individualized instruction, and practice them where possible.

The development of classroom techniques to individualize instruction assists in solving one of the major problems accompanying school desegregation: the wide range of student achievement levels in each classroom. Techniques to individualize instruction allow the teacher to spend more time with those who most need assistance, without lowering the amount of instruction given to other students.

Suggested Techniques

1. Individual Student Plan Books
    Some teachers have difficulty seeing their students as *individuals,* as opposed to members of a *group.* The first step toward individualizing instruction is to view each child as an individual with unique academic, emotional, and social characteristics. Teachers could be instructed to prepare individual plan books for each student, books that could be updated at least once a month. These booklets might include the teacher's goals for the child (i.e., "John will learn to write a compound sentence," or "John will participate more in class discussion"), as well as anecdotal accounts of what the student may or may not have achieved during the previous period.

2. Teacher's Aide Program
    Teachers often feel too occupied by the responsibility of leading the whole class at once to devote much attention to individuals who need extra help, or who are ready for more advanced work. Teacher's aides—volunteer or professional—can be extremely useful in this situation. They are able either to work with most of the class (reading a story, showing a film), or to work with one or two students while the teacher leads the rest of the group.
    Teachers participating in an aide program should receive guidance from the administration as to how this assistance can best be used.

Example of a Teacher Aide Program

The Objectives:

This project in Colorado Springs, Colorado, is designed to employ thirty parents and train them for full-time employment as teacher aides in four schools with a priority need to provide more individual assistance to children with learning difficulties. It is fully intended that these aides serve as a link between the school and other parents in the community to improve communications and relations between the school and the home. A specific task of these aides will be to assist the school staff in identifying and planning ways of involving other parents in programs to develop a fuller understanding of the mutual roles in the home-school partnership and to raise the level of aspiration for the family as a whole.

Teacher aides will be employed and trained to carry out, or assist in carrying out, the activities planned in the succeeding objectives:

a. Aides will be parents of children who are attending, or will attend, one of the four participating schools.

b. Aides will be assigned to the four target schools on the basis of one for every two teachers in grades two through six. The exact number cannot be determined until enrollment data is available; however, it is estimated that thirty aides will be needed.

c. Aides will be paid on an hourly basis to permit greater flexibility in their work schedule. This will enable the working mother with preschool or school children to see to the special needs of their children (lunches, doctor appointments, arranging for baby sitter care, etc.). Aides will be paid at the rate of two dollars per hour during the work day.

d. Aides must agree to participate in the preservice orientation program and the in-service training program described below.

e. Aides will devote no less than 75 percent of their time working directly with children. All work will be under the direction and supervision of the regular classroom teacher. The aide's role will include the following general functions:

To reinforce instruction presented by the classroom teacher.

To provide a greater measure of individual help and personal attention to children having problems.

To conduct large-group activities while the classroom teacher gives special instruction to individuals or small groups.

To share non-instructional duties with the classroom teacher.

To assist the classroom teacher in communicating with parents.

To participate in the planning of classroom activities to develop a necessary understanding of the purposes of such activities.

In-Service Training

Teacher aides will receive a minimum of sixty hours of training throughout the school year. The training program will be presented in two phases: preservice orientation and in-service training.

a. Preservice Orientation. About fifteen hours of orientation will precede beginning work in the classroom. Most of this phase will consist of formal classes
conducted by either the University of Colorado Extension Division or the El
Paso Community College, Colorado Springs, Colorado. Arrangements will be
made to either pay the tuition for the aides or negotiate a contract for the
least cost. Project funds will bear this expense. Although the details of the
content to be included in the formal orientation program will not be worked
out until project approval is obtained, preliminary planning suggests that the
following topics will be covered:
   Child growth and development.
   Role of the public school in the community and society.
   Employee ethics and responsibilities.
   Personal appearance and grooming.
   Considerations in working with small children.
   Parent-child relationships.
   Basic clerical skills (telephoning, typewriting, duplicating, etc.).
   In addition to the formal orientation classes, a preservice workshop will be
provided by the District. It will be organized by the Project Coordinator with the
assistance of district educational specialists, the four school principals, and class-
room teachers. It will include the following:
   Getting acquainted with the school staff with whom the aides will be
   working.
   Familiarization with the school building in which the aides will be working.
   Explanation of the goals of the Colorado Springs Public Schools and an
   overview of the K-12 instructional program.
   Explanation of the grade level program in which the aide will be working.
   Explanation of the duties and responsibilities of the aide and her relationship with other members of the school staff.
   Introduction to the materials and equipment with which the aides will be
   working. (Specific training will be provided during the in-service phase.)
   Introduction to school policies and regulations.
b. In-service Training. This phase will consist of on-the-job training conducted
by the teachers and a series of workshops to be held periodically throughout
the school year. The Project Coordinator will establish a Professional Growth
Committee for Parent Aides to assist in the planning of specific in-service
training activities. Committee membership will include a teacher and an aide
from each participating school, a principal, and a member of the central instructional staff. Each workshop will be devoted to a specific topic, such as:
   The preparation of aids to instruction.
   Techniques in using specific instructional materials, such as games, work-
   books, drill exercises, and various kits (SRA, *Sights and Sounds, Pace-
   maker, Peabody,* Kottmeyer, etc.).
   The operation of specific items of equipment (tape recorder, record player,
   controlled reader, listening stations, various projectors, etc.).

(continued)

Example of a Teacher Aide Program
(Continued)

> Procedures for ordering audiovisual materials from the district Instructional Materials Center.
> Nutrition and personal hygiene.
> Community services available to the needy.

c. In recognition of the substantial investment to be made in the training of these aides, every effort will be made to encourage and make it possible for aides to develop greater competence and higher levels of skill in classroom work with children. Professional workshops, adult education courses, college level courses, and committee assignments will be extended to aides whenever such participation will enhance the professional growth of the aide.

> Source: El Paso County, District No. 11, Colorado Springs, *Project Description: Parent/ Teacher/Pupil Aid Project,* funded under the Colorado Department of Education, The Educational Achievement Act, 1970. excerpts.

---

3. Student Tutors

Some schools have successfully used student tutors to assist in classrooms. These tutors can be older students who come especially to provide tutoring help, or students within the classroom who have mastered a problem and are able to help a peer. In either case, the student tutor usually benefits from the experience at least as much as the student being assisted. A tutoring program is discussed on the following page.

4. Independent Study

In an independent study program, each student develops and carries out a project with the guidance of a teacher. This approach is applicable to students at almost all levels. Supervisors and curriculum specialists could assist teachers in developing ideas for independent work, particularly in the elementary grades where the concept is not common. Teachers using this approach should set aside time each day, or week, for students to work on their projects—and for teachers to work with each student. Five or ten minutes of a teacher's undivided personal attention can be highly beneficial to any student, particularly one in a desegregated school who may not normally feel accepted.

5. Team Teaching

Experiments with team teaching are being conducted all over the country. There are several types of team arrangements, some of which definitely assist a teacher to individualize instruction, although that is not their primary purpose or advantage. In one type, two or more teachers share responsibility for a

Example of a Student Tutor Program

The Student Tutor and Assistant Teacher Program at Jefferson High School in Portland, Oregon, involves 380 students in activities ranging from tutoring and teaching to typing and other clerical duties. Over 50 students travel to area elementary schools to tutor grade school youngsters. A servicar bus has been leased to provide transportation for them.

Other students work with Jefferson students in the tutoring center while still others work in the classrooms helping the teacher in many ways. Over 100 other students are assigned to do mainly clerical work—typing, dittoing, filing, etc.

Source: Description of programs at Jefferson High School, Portland, Oregon.

large group of children. The teachers may or may not have subject specialties. In any case, it is possible for one teacher to lead most of the class while the other holds individual or small-group student conferences.

Team teaching, however, requires practice and considerable planning to be successful. Team leaders must be experienced in group dynamics, and members need to share objectives and goals.

Despite its challenging aspects, teachers at a high school experimenting for the first time with team teaching, concluded that:

a. Teams provided a wider variety of experiences and input in lessons and problem solving.
b. Teams provided wider perspective on approaching a problem.
c. Team teaching was seen as better for teacher growth.
d. Trainees were offered a wider variety of experience in different teacher methods and styles.
e. Teaming required a greater amount of teacher self-discipline, which was valuable.
f. Working more extensively with adult colleagues in the same room, as well as in planning, was seen as valuable.
g. Teams provided the opportunity to interact and learn from one another.[3]

To date, there has been no conclusive evidence that team teaching increases or decreases levels of student achievement. Team teaching is discussed further in Part D of this section.

6. Modular Scheduling
Modular scheduling differs from traditional scheduling in the organizational

structure of the school day. The day is divided into small segments, called mods, and these segments of time can be combined in various ways to meet specific instructional needs. Modular scheduling can be seen as a tool designed to provide students with a maximum of individualized learning experience.[4]

Successful use of modular scheduling necessitates complex programming of all student activities. Teachers will probably need detailed instruction in its use in order to take full advantage of it.

Two characteristics of modular scheduling are relevant to school desegregation. First, each student has more free time, and thus must have developed self-discipline in order to use free time well (resource centers, laboratories). Second, students are apt to attend a wide variety of different types of classes each day and most of these with different groups of students. This requires that the students be adaptable to many situations. Low achievers and minority-group students may have special difficulty meeting the requirements of self-discipline and adaptability. In order, then, for modular scheduling to be effective when low achievers and minority-group members make up a large portion of the student body, special attention will have to be paid to the needs of these students. Structured "free" time, close guidance of a tutor, and efforts to provide for some peer group continuity may be necessary.

A specific example of modular scheduling is set forth in the section of this chapter on Curriculum Adaptation.

7.   "Teaching Machines," Programmed Instruction, and Other Innovative
     Materials

In the recent past, the educational industry has produced a variety of resources oriented toward individualizing instruction. Programmed texts and booklets are probably the simplest; mathematics labs using computer technology are the most complex. Intermediate are reading laboratories, tape recording centers, and audio-visual centers. Too frequently, in schools where such books and new equipment have been introduced, they lie unused for want of teachers capable of using them. Clearly, schools that make the capital commitment involved in such purchases should be willing to provide in-service education so that their investments can pay off in improved instruction.

8.   Observation and Exchange Programs

The final technique for individualized instruction to be discussed is one of the most useful: observation by teachers of other teachers who have mastered the art of individualizing instruction. Observation may occur within the school, or by visits to other schools. Where physical observation is not practical, films and discussions by experts are essential. In any case, schools should have resource persons available to assist teachers in their efforts to individualize instruction. Teacher exchange is discussed on the following page.

POLICY.   Teachers should be instructed in group interaction techniques,
 (B-2)   group dynamics, and means of perceiving and managing group
             behavior.

Example of a Teacher Exchange and
Observation Program

In October 1968, eight New Albany, Miss., teachers, black and white, spent a week at the Laboratory School in Evanston, Illinois. A month later, eight more teachers had the same experience. The purpose of the visit was to allow close identification of local problems with similar problems in the Evanston school, as well as to provide practical evidence as to the solution of these problems by the visitation of the New Albany teachers in Evanston. The visiting teachers were assigned to teams where they observed, taught, sat in on planning sessions, attended faculty meetings, and in general became a part of the faculty for the week.

Seven months after the exchange, eight of the teachers who were participating in the curriculum writing workshop were asked to recall their experiences by responding to a set of questions. The questions and responses are paraphrased below:

Question 1: What did you see of interest?

The enormous amount of material and equipment in each classroom, its use in many new ways by children, aides, and teachers, and how the resource center served as the hub for all things; the open space rooms, how the teachers creatively used them to motivate kids, and the team organization and utilization of teams and the creative approach to the many disciplines in a new structure, especially art, science, and language arts; the work of aides; and the sophistication, independence, and behavior of kids.

Question 2: In what ways did you participate?

Discussed new methods with teachers; observed team teaching; participated in team planning; and taught classes. Thrilled with the amount of instructional materials available in remedial reading, math, and language arts—even wrote Halloween stories dictated by the children.

Question 3: What materials did you bring back to New Albany, and what did you use?

Materials ranging from science, social studies, language arts, math and remedial reading units to booklets and pencils of the President; notes on class activities; work sheets; and catalogs of continuous progress materials. Many of these items were used.

Question 4: What changes took place in your team as a result of the Evanston trip?

No changes were made; many changes took place, relationships took on deeper meaning; team was reorganized from back-to-back teaching to each teacher working in every subject; revamped language arts program to include reading, grammar, and spelling; alternated social studies and science units rather than teaching them all the time; tried new ways of individualization; better correlated social studies and language arts; and team meetings became more profitable, resulting in changes benefiting children.

(continued)

Example of a Teacher Exchange and
Observation Program (Continued)

Question 5: What recommendations would you make if other teachers were
considering such a trip?

Teachers should watch the classroom instruction, going with an open mind,
willing to assess the program in terms of what can be done in their own school,
and avoiding the attitude, "it won't work for us"; concentrate on seeing how the
resource center operates or the kindergarten and first grade or how the reading
is taught and materials used; and actually do some teaching and planning.

Question 6: How did you feel about your week in Evanston?

Enjoyable, inspirational, a rich experience making me a better teacher with
more self confidence; we saw it working (team teaching, individualized instruction, and continuous progress); and the exchange of teachers is one of the best
features of our program.

Source: New Albany Municipal School District, *Annual Report 1968–69: A Title IV
Project,* New Albany, Mississippi, pp. 46–48.

The phenomenon of group interaction has been increasingly managed or
organized in classrooms to foster positive attitudes toward both learning and self-
respect. Through the careful management of classroom dynamics, teachers can
better cope with the wide range of social and cultural backgrounds in many
desegregated classrooms. Group interaction techniques can also result in greater
achievement than is possible in the traditional classroom, especially for students
whose primary orientation is toward approval by their peers rather than by
their teacher.

Suggested Techniques

1. Charting Interaction

Charting the interaction of their students is an extremely useful exercise for
teachers. The charting process can be relatively simple (such as noting student
seating patterns in a free-seating arrangement) or quite complex. An example of
the latter is the interaction analysis technique developed by Ned Flanders of the
University of Michigan. The purpose of charting is to make teachers more
aware of "what's going on" within their classrooms, and help them to recognize
how individual students affect, and are affected by, others. This is a necessary
first step in trying to use group dynamics to influence classroom behavior.

The paper presented in the following example lists the variety of questions
that can be asked of any group. Few teachers are likely to be able to observe
all facets of group interaction without considerable technical assistance. The

Example of How to Chart Interaction
"What to Look for in Groups," by
Philip G. Hanson, Ph.D.

In all human interactions there are two major ingredients: content and process. The first deals with subject matter or the task upon which the group is working. In most interactions, the focus of attention of all persons is on the content. The second ingredient, process, is concerned with what is happening between and to group members while the group is working. Group process or dynamics deals with such items as morale, feeling tone, atmosphere, competition, cooperation, etc. In most interactions, very little attention is paid to process, even when it is the major cause of ineffective group action. Sensitivity to group process will better enable one to diagnose group problems early and deal with them more effectively. Since these processes are present in all groups, awareness of them will enhance a person's worth to a group and enable him to be a more effective group participant. Below are some observation guidelines to help one analyze group behavior.

Participation.   One indication of involvement is verbal participation. Look for differences in the amount of participation among members.
1.   Who are the high participators?
2.   Who are the low participators?
3.   Do you see any shift in participation, e.g., highs become quiet; lows suddenly become talkative. Do you see any possible reason for this in the group's interaction?
4.   How are the silent people treated? How is their silence interpreted? Consent? Disagreement? Disinterest? Fear? etc.
5.   Who talks to whom? Do you see any reason for this in the group's interactions?
6.   Who keeps the ball rolling? Why? Do you see any reason for this in the group's interactions?

Influence.   Influence and participation are not the same. Some people may speak very little, yet they capture the attention of the whole group. Others may talk a lot but are generally not listened to by other members.
7.   Which members are high in influence? That is, when they talk, others seem to listen.
8.   Which members are low in influence? Others do not listen to or follow them. Is there any shifting in influence? Who shifts?
9.   Do you see any rivalry in the group? Is there a struggle for leadership? What effect does it have on other group members?

Styles of Influence.   Influence can take many forms. It can be positive or negative, it can enlist the support or cooperation of others or alienate them.

(continued)

Example of How to Chart Interaction
"What to Look for in Groups,"
by Philip G. Hanson, Ph.D. (Continued)

HOW a person attempts to influence another may be the crucial factor in determining how open or closed the other will be toward being influenced. Items 10 through 13 are suggestive of four styles that frequently emerge in groups.

10. Autocratic—Does anyone attempt to impose his will or values on other group members; tries to push them to support his decision? Who evaluates or passes judgment on other group members? Do any members block action when it is not moving in the direction they desire? Who pushes to "get the group organized"?

11. Peacemaker—Who eagerly supports other group member's decision? Does anyone consistently try to avoid conflict or unpleasant feelings from being expressed by pouring oil on the troubled waters? Is any member typically deferential toward other group members—gives them power? Do any members appear to avoid giving negative feedback, i.e., who will level only when they have positive feedback to give.

12. Laissez faire—Are any group members getting attention by their apparent lack of involvement in the group? Does any group member go along with group decisions without seeming to commit himself one way or the other? Who seems to be withdrawn and uninvolved; does not initiate activity— participates mechanically and only in response to another member's question?

13. Democratic—Does anyone try to include everyone in a group decision or discussion? Who express his feelings and opinions openly and directly without evaluating or judging others? Who appears to be open to feedback and criticisms from others? When feelings run high and tension mounts, which members attempt to deal with the conflict in a problem-solving way?

Decision Making Procedures. Many kinds of decisions are made in groups without considering the effects of these decisions on other members. Some people try to impose their own decisions on the group, while others want all members to participate or share in the decisions that are made.

14. Does anyone make a decision and carry it out without checking with other group members? (Self Authorized) For example, he decides on the topic to be discussed and starts right in to talk about it. What effect does this have on other group members?

15. Does the group drift from topic to topic? Who topic jumps? Do you see any reason for this in the group's interactions?

16. Who supports other member's suggestions or decisions? Does this support result in the two members deciding the topic or activity for the group? (Handclasp) How does this affect other group members?

17. Is there any evidence of a majority pushing a decision through over other members' objections? Do they call for a vote? (Majority Support)

18.   Is there any attempt to get all members participating in a decision? (Consensus) What effect does this seem to have on the group?
19.   Does anyone make any contributions which do not receive any kind of response or recognition (plot)? What effect does this have on the member?

Task Functions.   These functions illustrate behaviors that are concerned with getting the job done, or accomplishing the task that the group has before them.
20.   Does anyone ask for or make suggestions as to the best way to proceed or tackle a problem?
21.   Does anyone attempt to summarize what has been covered or what has been going on in the group?
22.   Is there any giving or asking for facts, ideas, opinions, feelings, feedback, or searching for alternatives?
23.   Who keeps the group on target? Prevents topic jumping or going off on tangents.

Maintenance Functions.   These functions are important to the morale of the group. They maintain good and harmonious working relationships among the members and create a group atmosphere which enables each member to contribute maximally. They insure smooth and effective work within the group.
24.   Who helps others get into the discussion (gate openers)?
25.   Who cuts off others or interrupts them (gate closers)?
26.   How well are members getting their ideas across? Are some members preoccupied and not listening? Are there any attempts by group members to help others clarify their ideas?
27.   How are ideas rejected? How do members react when their ideas are not accepted? Do members attempt to support others when they reject their ideas?

Group Atmosphere.   Something about the way a group works creates an atmosphere which in turn is revealed in a general impression. In addition, people may differ in the kind of atmosphere they like in a group. Insight can be gained into the atmosphere characteristic of a group by finding words which describe the general impressions held by group members.
28.   Who seems to prefer a friendly congenial atmosphere? Is there any attempt to suppress conflict or unpleasant feelings?
29.   Who seems to prefer an atmosphere of conflict and disagreement? Do any members provoke or annoy others?
30.   Do people seem involved and interested? Is the atmosphere one of work, play, satisfaction, taking flight, sluggish, etc.?

Membership.   A major concern for group members is the degree of acceptance or inclusion in the group. Different patterns of interaction may develop in the group which gives clues to the degree and kind of membership.

(continued)

Example of How to Chart Interaction
"What to Look for in Groups,"
by Philip G. Hanson, Ph.D. (Continued)

31.   Is there any sub-grouping? Sometimes two or three members may consis-
      tently agree and support each other or consistently disagree and oppose
      one another.
32.   Do some people seem to be "outside" the group? Do some members seem
      to be most "in"? How are those "outside" treated?
33.   Do some members move in and out of the group, e.g., lean forward or
      backward in chair or move chair in and out? Under what conditions do
      they come in or move out?

   Feelings.   During any group discussion feelings are frequently generated by
the interactions between members. These feelings, however, are seldom talked
about. Observers may have to make guesses based on tone of voice, facial expressions, gestures and many other forms of non-verbal cues.

34.   What signs of feelings do you observe in group members? Anger, irritation,
      frustration, warmth, affection, excitement, boredom, defensiveness, com-
      petitiveness, etc.
35.   Do you see any attempts by group members to block the expression of
      feelings, particularly negative feelings? How is this done? Does anyone do
      this consistently?

   Norms.   Standards or ground rules may develop in a group that control the
behavior of its members. Norms usually express the beliefs or desires of the
majority of the group members as to what behaviors should or should not take
place in the group. These norms may be clear to all members (explicit), known
or sensed by only a few (implicit) or operating completely below the level of
awareness of any group members. Some norms facilitate group progress and some
hinder it.

36.   Are certain areas avoided in the group (e.g., sex, religion, talk about present
      feelings in group, discussing leader's behavior, etc.)? Who seems to rein-
      force this avoidance? How do they do it?
37.   Are group members overly nice or polite to each other? Are only positive
      feelings expressed? What happens when members disagree?
38.   Do you see norms operating about participation or the kinds of questions
      that are allowed? (e.g., "If I talk you must talk," "If I tell my problems
      you have to tell your problems") Do members feel free to probe each
      other about their feelings? Do questions tend to be restricted to intellectual
      topics or events outside of the group?

   Source: Prepared at the Veteran's Administration Hospital in Houston, Texas.

charting process, however, will begin to awaken the teacher's senses to the classroom group. (Specific exercises for teachers to assist in charting classroom interactions are discussed in the section on "Student Adaptation to Achieve Effective Desegregation").

2.   Academic Courses in Group Psychology

Theories of group dynamics are based upon the study of psychology and sociology. In school districts convenient to a university or other higher educational institution, efforts could be made to make courses in group psychology available to teachers. Teachers who do attend and complete such courses might be given salary credits and, when possible, free tuition or scholarships to attend the courses.

3.   Greater Teacher-Teacher Interchange

Many teachers have intuitively developed skills in managing their classrooms based on principles of group dynamics. School administrators attempting to introduce group dynamics methods of teaching could encourage their faculties to exchange ideas, opinions and methods.

One method of doing this would be to show a film that demonstrated use of group dynamics, and to follow-up that film with discussion by the teachers. An experienced educational psychologist would be valuable as a discussion leader.

Further discussion of group dynamics and classroom interaction focused upon using these techniques for classroom management is found in the section on "Student Adaptation".

C. Using New Curriculum Materials and Instructional Techniques for Minority-Group and Disadvantaged Students

PROBLEM: The traditional subject matter of the classroom may not be suitable for all children. Too frequently it derogates or ignores some students, uses concepts and words unfamiliar to others, or assumes certain experiences not common to all.

The widespread occurrence of school desegregation, the recognition of the educational poverty of many of the nation's urban slum schools, and awakening insight into the special needs of the learning disabled have led to the rapid development of new curriculum materials and the advocacy of new instructional techniques. The following section is aimed primarily at racial and ethnic minorities, and the culturally deprived.

School administrators, curriculum specialists, and teachers are today the recipients of a multitude of new teaching "packages" designed to provide multi-racial and multi-ethnic educational experiences for their students. Teaching packages are also being developed to make the school experience more relevant to the culturally deprived child, be he a white or minority student. In-service education is an essential prerequisite to making this barrage of new materials and techniques meaningful to the classroom teacher and to other school personnel.

POLICY.   Schools should adapt to the needs of their disadvantaged stu-
(C-1)   dents by introducing new or revised curriculum materials.

Techniques are discussed in the section on "Curriculum Adaptation to Achieve Effective Desegregation".

POLICY.   Teachers should be instructed in the content and use of new or
(C-2)   revised curriculum materials.

In-service education in new curriculum materials and teaching techniques responds to a basic problem facing teachers who try to use new materials without adequate preparation: the absence of pre-service education regarding minority-group or disadvantaged students and their special needs. Six objectives of in-service education to meet this problem are listed below:

New Curriculum Materials

To transmit to teachers academic information about minority-group histories.

To introduce to teachers primary source literature about and by minority-group members, and assist them in understanding it.

To introduce teachers to multi-racial curriculum material and demonstrate its use and to assist in the development of curriculum guides.

To explain how standard texts can be amplified to include more materials on minorities' contributions.

New Instructional Techniques

To explain the conceptual basis for individualized learning, group inter-action, and diagnostic teaching techniques.

To demonstrate "new" techniques and provide assistance in their use.

Described below are a number of in-service techniques designed to provide education for teachers in the use of new curriculum materials.

Suggested Techniques

1.   Academic Courses
New curriculum emphases following school desegregation frequently involve minority histories (i.e., black studies, Spanish-American history) and sociological material relevant to the culture and psychology of minority or ethnic groups. Relatively few teachers have any academic background in these areas. Therefore, in order to teach them adequately, they need training.

Many school districts have utilized the resources and/or course offerings at neighboring educational institutions to provide the necessary teacher prepara-

*Example of Academic Courses
for In-Service Education*

The In-Service Education Component of the Sacramento City Unified School District's 1969–70 ESEA, Title I project was designed to provide in-service education programs for all personnel in the target elementary and Project Aspiration receiving schools. The programs of this component were broad in scope, and were planned to complement the compensatory education activities provided through the other components.

The primary purposes of the In-Service Education Component were to offer teachers, counselors, administrators and supportive, non-certificated personnel opportunities to acquire deeper understandings of the problems facing socially disadvantaged children and techniques that might be employed in assisting these children to reach their maximum potential. A variety of techniques and approaches were used to disseminate such information and understandings. Release time and salary schedule credit were features of a number of the in-service education activities. Among the in-service education courses and programs offered were:

1. English as a Second Language—Two in-service education courses on the teaching of English as a second language were conducted during the 1969–70 school year. One course was conducted during the fall semester and one course was conducted during the spring semester. These in-service education courses were designed to present theory, methods, techniques, and materials for use by specialist teachers, classroom teachers, and teacher assistants working with non-English speaking pupils of all native language backgrounds. They were also designed to provide guidance and direction to teachers receiving pupils who speak little or no English.

2. History and Contributions of the Negro in America—An in-service education course on the history and contributions of the Negro in America was conducted during the 1969–70 school year. This course was conducted during the fall semester. This in-service education course was designed to present the history of the Negro and his relationship to the total American story. It was designed to assist teachers in giving a more balanced classroom presentation of United States history. Additional goals of this program were to aid teachers in gaining a better understanding of the Negro American today and to aid teachers in gaining skill in promoting intergroup understanding and respect.

3. History and Culture of the Mexican-American—An in-service education course on the history and culture of the Mexican-American was conducted during the 1969–70 school year. This course was conducted during the fall semester. This in-service education course was designed to help teachers develop a better understanding of the Mexican-American. The most significant goals of this program were to aid teachers in gaining an understanding of the history of Spain as it relates to the Mexican-American; to aid teachers in

(continued)

Example of Academic Courses
for In-Service Education (Continued)

gaining an understanding of the history of North America as it relates to the
Mexican-American; to aid teachers in gaining an understanding of the culture
of the Mexican-American; and to aid teachers in gaining an understanding of
the educational disadvantage common to many Mexican-Americans.

4. Seminar in Contemporary Urban Social Problems and Educational Strategies—
During the spring semester of the 1969–70 school year, a seminar in contemporary urban social problems and educational strategies was conducted by the
district's Intergroup Relations staff for teachers and administrators. The
purpose of the seminar was to help teachers and administrators acquire more
knowledge, skill and insight needed to deal with the multiplicity of social
problems prevalent in an urban school district with various ethnic minority
and socio-economic groups. Seminar activities included lectures, group discussions, guest speakers, home and community visitations and written reports.
The seminar met for two hours weekly for fifteen weeks during the spring
semester. Participants were expected to complete approximately sixty-six
hours of outside preparation and were granted two units of salary advance-
ment credit upon successful completion of the semester.

Source: Sacramento City Unified School District, E.S.E.A. *Programs and Services for
the Educationally Disadvantaged, Evaluation Report, 1969–70,* Sacramento, California,
1970.

tion. Some large school districts have hired college teachers to provide courses
specially designed for the elementary and secondary teachers of their school
system.

School districts might provide certain incentives to their teachers for
attending these courses. Such incentives could include:

Salary credits
Credits toward a higher degree
Released time for attendance
Stipends
Tuition

All teachers should be encouraged to take at least some of these courses, but
social studies teachers should be required to complete a certain number of them.

The preceding example is taken from the Sacramento, California in-service
education program. The courses described were sponsored by the school district.

2.   In-Service Programs
     When outside academic courses are not widely available, school districts

might conduct in-school programs that provide teachers with a general introduction to a subject area (such as Indian History and culture), lectures by consultants, films, and a bibliography for futher study. School desegregation consulting centers, funded under Title IV of the Civil Rights Act of 1964, often can provide "packaged programs" for school districts. The following example contains excerpts from a program package developed by the Consultative Center for Equal Educational Opportunity at the University of Oklahoma.

---

*An Example of an In-School Program
for Ethnic or Cultural Differences*

The following in-service program is designed specifically for classroom teachers who wish to broaden their knowledge about children from ethnic and minority groups. This packaged program is a flexible guide which should be useful in helping teachers to clear up many misconceptions and to gain new knowledge about minority group children. The basic plan requires approximately fourteen clock hours:

1. A one or two-hour planning session with teachers representing all grade levels or subject areas that the program intends to serve.
2. An intensive training session for group leaders, recorders, etc.
3. Four three-hour meetings—preferably one each week for four consecutive weeks. If possible, these meetings should be scheduled during the regular school day on released time. Four consecutive Saturdays would be acceptable as an alternative.

Consultative services should be determined by the planning groups. Ample suggestions appear with each "program." Although the package is rather specific in suggestions concerning outside consultants, feel free to request services from the Consultative Center during any phase of the program.

Part I—General Planning Session(s)

A.   This planning should be done several weeks prior to the opening of the in-service effort.
B.   Form a committee of appropriate Central Office personnel, principals, classroom teachers, outside consultants, etc. Example: (1) Director of Curriculum/area supervisor, (2) four or five key teachers, (3) community resource person if such is available and (4) Consultative Center consultants.
C.   Determine most pressing concerns of teachers who will be involved. For example:
1. Black's attitude toward authority.
2. Indian's lack of competitive spirit.
3. Mexican-American customs.
These concerns may be determined through informal surveys, observations, previous evaluations of problems, etc.

(continued)

An Example of an In-School Program
for Ethnic or Cultural Differences
(Continued)

D.   Determine in-service mechanics: dates, time, location, selections of participants, selections of consultants/committee, and arrangements for materials/special equipment.

Part II—Training Group Leaders

A.   Group dynamics.

B.   Provide with lists of questions and special materials. These people should be provided appropriate questions and reading material prior to each in-service effort.

Consultants

Bill Waltman, Consultative Center
William Carmack, Speech Department, University of Oklahoma

Bibliography

Bales, R.F., E.F. Borgatta. "Size as a Factor in the Interaction Profile," In A.P. Hare, E.F. Borgatta, and R.F. Bales (eds.). *Small Groups: Studies in Social Interaction.* New York: Knopf, 1955.

Barnlund, Dean C., and Franklyn S. Haiman. *The Dynamic of Discussion.* Boston: Houghton Mifflin Co., 1960.

Cartwright, D., and A. Zander (ed.). *Group Dynamics: Research and Theory.* Evanston, III.: Row, Peterson, 1960, 2nd edition.

Haiman, F.S. *Group Leadership and Democratic Action.* Boston: Houghton Mifflin, 1951.

Jackson, Vic. "Leadership Training: A Focal Point for Nurturing the Individuality Climate in Secondary School Speed Programs," 15pp.

"Leadership Tasks in Small Groups." Discussion Guide.

Southwest Center for Human Relations Studies. "Task Group Problem Solving Method Incorporating Concepts of Dual Leadership," 7 pp.

(Most of the reading materials are available in handout form and may be secured from the Consultative Center offices.)

Session One

1:00–1:15	*Overview* of Program
1:15–1:45	*Presentation*: "Cultural Groups in the U.S."
	"The Dynamics of Culture"
	A minority group speaker and/or film
1:45–2:15	Break
2:30–3:30	Small group discussions—six to ten people with leader and consultant
3:30–4:00	Discussion of group reports

Suggestions for next program
Evaluation
Reading materials

Suggested Speakers and Consultants

1. George Henderson, University of Oklahoma
2. Joe Hill, Evanston
3. Clayton Feaver, University of Oklahoma
4. Walter Mason, OBU
5. Boyce Timmons, University of Oklahoma
6. Robert L. Boobi, Norman
7. Gertrude Noar, ADL

Bibliography

American Home Economic Association. "Working with Low Income Families."

Benedict, Ruth. *1934 Patterns of Culture.* Boston: Houghton Mifflin, paperback, 1961.

Bernstine, Basil. "Social Class and Linguistic Development: A Theory of Social Learning," in A.H. Halsey, J. Fland, and A. Anderson (eds.), *Economy, Education and Society,* New York: Harcourt, Brace and World, 1961, pp. 288–313.

Bloom, Benjamin Samuel. *Compensatory Education for Cultural Deprivation.* New York: Holt, Rinehart and Winston, 1965.

Darnerell, Reginald G. *Triumph in a White Suburb.* New York: William Marrow and Co.

Deutch, Martin. (ed) *Social Class, Race, and Psychological Development.* New York: Holt, Rinehart and Winston, 1965.

Harrington, M. *The Other Americans.* Baltimore: Penguin, 1962.

Kraeher, Alfred L. *The Nature of Culture.* Chicago: University of Chicago Press, 1952.

Kraeher, A.L., and Clyde Kluckhohn. *Culture: A Critical Review of Concepts and Definitions.* Cambridge, Mass.: Harvard University, Peabody Museum of American Archaeology and Ethnology Papers, Vol. 47, No. 1 (1952) paperback, 1963, Vintage Books.

Meissner, Hanna H. (ed.). *Poverty in the Affluent Society.* New York: Harper and Row, 1966.

Murdock, George P. *Social Structure.* New York: Macmillan, 1949, paperback—Free Press, 1965.

Peary, R.B. *General Theory of Value: Its Meaning and Basic Principles Construed in Terms of Interest.* Cambridge, Mass.: Harvard University Press, 1951.

Taylor, Edward B. *Primitive Culture: Research Into the Development of Mythology, Philosophy, Religion, Art and Customs.* Gloucester, Mass.: Smith, 1958.

Eliot, T.S. *Notes Toward the Definition of Culture.* New York: Harcourt, 1949.

Audio-Visual Materials

1. "Black Guardians of Freedom"—Record and Filmstrip, Coca Cola
2. "The Forgotten American"—film, Carousel Films
3. "Exiles"—Contemporary Films
4. "Lay My Burden Down"—Indian University Audio-Visual Center
5. "Our Country, Too"—IU Audio Visual Center
6. "Our Race Problem"—(Parts I, II) IU Audio Visual Center
7. "The Poor Pay More"—IU Audio Visual Center
8. "Beyond These Hills"

(continued)

An Example of an In-School Program
for Ethnic or Cultural Differences
(Continued)

Session Two

1:00–2:15   Unstructured Question and Answer Period with consultant. Focus:
             "Do Differences Really Exist?"
2:15–2:30   Break
2:30–3:45   Small group study of specific questions with prepared materials
             Film strips and records available and/or simulated game—|
             Beacon Hill High School
3:45–4:00   Group Assembly
             Discuss Session Three Bibliography
             Brief progress reports
             Suggestions for next week
             Organize group projects to be completed by end of Fourth Session
             Evaluation

Consultants and Speakers

1.   George Henderson, University of Oklahoma
2.   Dan Selakowich, Oklahoma State University
3.   Ruth Tibbs, Tulsa
4.   David W. Levy, History, Univ. of Oklahoma
5.   Joe Hill, Evanston
6.   Boyce Timmons, University of Oklahoma
7.   Bob Miller, University of Oklahoma
8.   The Consultative Center Staff
9.   Katharine Boobi, Norman
10. Freddie Cudjoe, Oklahoma City
11. Pauline Owens, Central State College
12. Addie Herbert, Muskogee
13. Clara Luper, Oklahoma City

Session Three

1:00–2:30   *Presentation*: (Black or Indian)
             "The Black Sub-Culture"
             "The Cultures of Various Indian Tribes" (and/or a particular
             tribe)
2:30–2:45   Break
2:45–3:45   Discussion
             List of questions
3:45–4:00   Large assembly
             Brief summary
             Announcement of participant panel for Session Four

Other Suggested Topics

"The Cultural Patterns of Negroes in American Society"
"The Cultural Patterns of American Indians"
"The Cultural Patterns of Low Economic Status White Americans"
"The Cultural Patterns of Mexican-Americans"
"Conflicting Cultural Patterns"

Suggested Consultants and Speakers

Indians
Overton James, State Department
Robert L. Goobi, Norman
Mrs. Katharine Goobi, Norman
Bob Randquist, Carnegie
Boyce Timmons, OU
Bob Miller, OU

Blacks
George Henderson, OU
Ruth Tibbs, Tulsa
Freddie Cudjoe, Oklahoma City
  Public Schools
David W. Levy, OU
Walter Mason, OBU
Ada Lois Fisher, Langston U.
Joe Hill, Evanston

Bibliography

Indians

   A Guide for Teachers of Indian Children. Boise: Department of Education, 1968.

   Bureau of Indian Affairs. *Answers to Your Questions About American Indians.* Washington: U.S. Government Printing Office, 1968.

   Bureau of Indian Affairs. *Indians of the Central Plains.* Washington: U.S. Government Printing Office.

   Bureau of Indian Affairs. *Indians of Oklahoma.* Washington: U.S. Government Printing Office.

   Coffey, Ivy, and Allan W. Crowley. "The Red Man's Crisis," *The Daily Oklahoman,* September 17, 1966.

   Cameron, Harold. "Problems of Oklahoma Youth from Traditional Indian Homes."

   Dumont, Robert V. "Cherokee Children and the Teacher," *Social Education* (January 1969), pp. 70-72.

   Idaho State Department of Education. *Books About Indians and Reference Material.* Boise: Department of Education, 1968.

   Idaho State Department of Education. *There's An Indian in Your Classroom.* Boise: Department of Education, 1968.

   Indian Education Division, Southwest Center for Human Relations Studies, University of Oklahoma. *Directory for Indian Resources in Oklahoma* (October 1968).

   Owen, Roger C., James J.F. Deetz, and Anthony D. Fisher. *The North American Indians, A Sourcebook.* New York: The Macmillan Company, 1967.

   Vogt, Evan L. "The Acculturation of American Indians," *Annals of the American Academy of Political and Social Sciences,* 311 (1957), pp. 137-146.

Blacks

   Dunbar, Ernest. "The Negro in America Today," *Look* (April 10, 1967).

   Grier, William H. and Price M. Cobb. *Black Race.* New York: Basic Books, Inc., 1968.

   Harrison, Charles H. "The Negro in America," *The Education Digest* (January 1969).

   Hughes, Langston and Milton Meltzer. *A Pictoral History of the Negro in America.* New York: Crown Publishers, Inc., 1967.

(continued)

An Example of an In-School Program
for Ethnic or Cultural Differences
(Continued)

Morais, Herbert M. *The History of the Negro in Medicine.* New York: Publishers Company, Inc., 1967.

Patterson, Lindsay. *Anthology of the American Negro in the Theatre, A Critical Approach.* New York: Publishers Company, Inc., 1967.

Patterson, Lindsay. *The Negro in Music and Art.* New York: Publishers Company, Inc., 1967.

Pettigrew, Thomas. "Negro American Intelligence," Excerpt from *A Profile of the Negro American.* New York: ADL

Rose, Arnold. *Social Change and the Negro Problem.* New York: ADL, 1968.

Rustin, Bayard. *Three Essays by Bayard Rustin.* New York: A. Philip Randolph Institute, 1969.

Saunders, Doris E. et al, eds. *The Kennedy Years and the Negro.* Chicago: Johnson Publishing Company, Inc., 1964.

Schary, Dave. "The Ordeal of American Negroes," *The ADL Bulletin,* May 1963.

The Negro Family. Washington: U.S. Government Printing Office, 1968.

Walker, Margaret. *Bibliography: Negro Life and History.* Atlanta: Georgia State Department of Education, 1970.

Wesley, Charles A. and Patricia A. Romero. *Negro Americans in the Civil War from Slavery to Citizenship.* New York: Publishers Company, Inc., 1967.

Wynes, Charles E. (ed.). *The Negro in the South Since 1865.* University of Alabama: University of Alabama Press, 1967.

Session Four

1:00–1:30	Participant Panel: Four people and panel leader
	A. Cultural Differences vs Cultural Similarities
	B. Black Culture
	C. Indian Culture
	D. Majority Group Culture
	E. Low Socio-economic Whites
1:30–2:00	Interaction
2:00–2:30	Break
2.30–3:00	Task Groups-Recommendations
3:00–4:00	Report on Projects (see Session Two)
	Presentation of Recommendations
	Evaluation

Panel: The panel should include minority group members if available in the system. If not, use outside minority group members. Also, in order to get maximum interaction and new ideas, consider asking a white to discuss black culture, a black to discuss Indian culture, etc. Theoretically, all of the teachers have been exposed to the same information; therefore, any member of the group should be able to handle any phase of the program. This may be a form of evaluation.

Additional Discussion Problems

1. Special agencies that deal with particular groups in your community.
2. Cultural differences vs racial differences.
3. Class differences.
4. Life styles of: Blacks, Indians, Mexican-Americans; compare and contrast.
5. The effects of poverty.
6. Value differences.
7. The self-concept.
8. What effect do experiential deficiencies have on minority group members?
9. Are there really many cultural differences?

Source: Consultative Center for Equal Educational Opportunity, Ethnic or Cultural Differences, preliminary draft, University of Oklahoma, Norman, Oklahoma, 1970.

---

3.   Short-Term Training Institutes

Still another method of introducing teachers to new curriculum materials is through the short-term training institute. These sessions are often conducted at a central location such as a university, in order to serve a number of school districts. They usually run for three to five days, and are attended by teachers and school administrators. Participants may receive stipends.

Training institutes are concentrated learning experiences. Sponsored generally by universities with federal funding under Title IV of the Civil Rights Act of 1964, they are oriented toward lectures and group discussions. Because training institutes are short-term, however, experience with them has demonstrated that, unless followed up within the separate schools, their impact may be of short duration. If districts conduct programs in their own schools with teachers and students, the effects will be longer lasting.

4.   District or Countywide Conferences

District or countywide conferences are frequently held prior to school desegregation. Usually one or two days in length and involving all teachers and administrators, their purpose is primarily to introduce participants to the concepts of desegregated education and to answer any questions about desegregation that the participants may have.

Subsequent conferences may deal with questions and problems raised during the school year, and also serve to introduce new teachers to local programs.

5.   Demonstrations

New curriculum materials and teaching techniques can be introduced to teachers through the use of demonstrations. These can be put on by specially

trained in-house teachers, by the developers of new material, or by outside
consultants. Because of the rapid advance in the technology of education, in-
service education in this area is essential. The two following examples, taken
from the Sacramento, California in-service education program, illustrate two
methods of assisting teachers in utilizing new materials.

---

*Two Examples of Training in Use of New
Materials*

Demonstration Teacher Program. The In-Service Education Component
has included a demonstration teacher program, during each of the last three and
one-half years. The 1969–70 ESEA, Title I project provided funding for three
and one-fourth demonstration teacher positions. The teachers who were assigned
to these positions were not considered supervisors, but primarily served the
function of teachers helping other teachers. They became involved with individual classroom teachers only when their services were requested by the classroom teacher or his/her principal. The demonstration teachers provided help for
teachers in improving instructional techniques, identifying instructional needs,
assisting in curriculum innovations, and assisting in the selection and development of appropriate materials. In addition, they conducted classroom demonstrations and small group in-service education sessions, and assisted in the
development and operation of other in-service programs.

Preparation and Utilization of Audio-Visual Materials. Two in-service
education courses on the preparation and utilization of audio-visual materials
were conducted during the 1969–70 school year. One course was conducted
during the fall semester and one course was conducted during the spring
semester. These in-service education courses were developed to assist teachers
who were interested in opportunities to become better acquainted with the
basic principles of effective utilization and preparation of audio-visual materials of instruction in the elementary school.

Source: Sacramento City Unified School District, *E.S.E.A. Programs and Services for
the Educationally Disadvantaged, Evaluation Report 1969–70,* Sacramento, California, 1970.

---

6.   School Resources
     Schools and/or school districts expanding their range of curriculum
materials to deal with the educational needs incident to desegregation could
develop an in-house capability in the use of these new materials. A specially prepared core staff can disseminate information and techniques to other teachers,

and insure its proper and full use. Resource staff preparation can be achieved by designating certain teachers for this role, and by sending them to training institutes, or educational conferences, or on teacher exchange programs.

7. Consultants
    Many desegregating school districts have utilized the services of full or part-time consultants to assist with in-service education. University consulting centers and the field offices of the Office of Education maintain lists of educational consultants and school desegregation efforts. Use of consultants for school desegregation is more fully discussed in the section of this chapter on Administrative Measures.

Overall Effect of Techniques.   Regarding all forms of in-service training, experience with different types of programs has not shown any of them to be consistently superior. Experience has, however, provided insight into various factors that are likely to contribute to the success of any program. Some of the primary characteristics of successful programs are described below.

1. Programs should preferably occur over a period of time, rather than occurring only once—as in a two-day institute.
2. All programs, whether short- or long-term, should be followed up within the classroom—teachers should have assistance available as they try out new techniques or materials.
3. School administrators, and particularly school principals, should actively support training programs and follow-up activities.
4. Whenever possible, in-service education programs should provide released time for teachers, stipends, or credit toward salary advances.
5. Positive efforts should be made to encourage participation by all teachers, and introductory programs should be mandatory.
6. Efforts should be made to train in-house personnel so that activities continue after consultants complete their share in programs.
7. Innovations of all types should be accompanied by persons capable of acting as resource staff.

In conclusion, successful in-service education programs should leave the teacher familiar with the new subject matter or technique, able to apply it consistently and willingly, and provided with back-up resources and references.

D. Improving Teacher Performance Through New Supervisory Arrangements
PROBLEM: Teachers faced with new situations and required to use methods and materials with which they are not familiar need to have constant advice and reinforcement, not just one-time training programs. School principals, however, are often too concerned

with administrative goals to provide such assistance, and school
systems are too often lacking in supervisory personnel. However,
without continuing support, school administrators will find
their teachers quickly returning to former methods.

POLICY.   School administrations should develop new types of supervisory
(D-1)   arrangements so that all teachers have continual reinforcement
                and assistance available to them as they attempt to use new
                materials and methods.

Throughout the preceding discussions of in-service education, references
have been made to the need for supervisors or resource teachers who can
provide continuing support for improved education. J. Minor Gwynn [6] has
identified three kinds of responsibilities that should be assumed by supervisors:

To give individual help to teachers.

To coordinate the instructional services of the school and make them more
available to all personnel.

To act as a resource person for the superintendent and other administrative
personnel, as a special agent in training teachers in service, and as an
interpreter for the school personnel and to the public.

The supervisory position need not be restricted to individuals whose
responsibility is solely that of supervising classroom teachers. In many schools,
particularly those in small districts, the principal—by delegating most of his
purely administrative functions—can and should assume a supervisory role.
Another method of providing supervisory positions could be to appoint master
or resource teachers, remove some or all of their teaching responsibilities, and
have them use that time to aid other teachers. The technique used is not
critical as long as the objective is clear: an emphasis on educational (rather than
administrative) goals and the provision of continual in-service support and
training to achieve these goals.

George W. Denemark summarizes the current trend as follows:

"One of the most exciting and important things that has happened to the
concept of teaching in many years—perhaps in a half-century or more—has
been the current departure from the image of the teacher as an isolated
adult working in lonely professional solitude with a standard size group of
children. The impossible demands upon the classroom teacher—demands
ranging all the way from the most complex and sophisticated professional
diagnoses to a host of routine clerical and custodial burdens—have convinced many thoughtful educators and school board members of the validity
of the concepts of a supportive staff for the classroom teacher and of
differentiated roles for classroom instructional personnel. In an age of
growing demands upon the school for an expanding range of urgent social
and economic objectives, demands which the school has often been unable
to meet adequately, it is more apparent than ever that we must abandon
the concept of the 'omnicapable' teacher. Instead, we must view teaching

as participation in an instructional team including a broad range of properly coordinated professional and paraprofessional workers."[7]

The above quotation by George W. Denemark serves as a summary to the growing interest in, and practice of, team teaching, differentiated staffing, and new forms of supervision. School districts throughout the country are instituting team teaching on an experimental and full-time basis. Some have done so for the reasons cited above. Others, particularly in the Southern and border states, have used team teaching as they desegregate school faculties. In whatever case, the concept of team teaching, together with differentiated staffing, provides new opportunities for continual in-service education for the teaching staff, and continual support and supervision for all teachers.

Suggested Techniques

1.   The Master Teacher Concept
     The master teacher concept applies to the designation of an experienced classroom teacher as a resource person for other teachers. The title *master teacher* can be used interchangeably with senior teacher, supervisory teacher, or resource teacher (except when resource teacher refers to a teacher in charge of library materials, or serving a specialized function). A master teacher program is valuable to schools trying to meet the educational needs occasioned by desegregation. The master teacher, who retains a teaching function, is provided released time for the purpose of assisting other teachers. Generally, each master teacher is "assigned" to a number of regular teachers and maintains daily contact with them. Master teachers should be provided with special training in needed areas so that they will be able to meaningfully disseminate new materials and techniques to other teachers. The system of master teachers is especially useful in large schools or wherever special training for all teachers is not practical. Another advantage of a master teacher program is that especially good teachers can be rewarded with supervisory functions without being lost to the teaching profession.
     Depending upon the particular needs of each school, the master teacher can fulfill a variety of responsibilities. These might include:

Classroom observation
Classroom experimentation
Demonstration teaching
Curriculum development
Liaison between school teachers and administration
Guidance of beginning teachers

The following example illustrates a master teacher program developed in a Louisiana school district. This program is eligible for funding under Title IV of the Civil Rights Act of 1964.

An Example of a Master Teacher Program

Objectives of the Program

1. To provide for an in-service program with continuing effect to lessen the problems of school desegregation.
2. To retrain inexperienced teachers in teaching techniques to help students with special needs arising from the process of desegregation.
3. To assist the older teachers in adjusting personally and professionally to the techniques necessary for effective teaching in an integrated school system.
4. To provide general assistance in adjusting to the requirements of discipline and control in integrated classes.
5. To provide assistance in handling controversial issues that arise in the classroom including race relations.
6. To promote communication between teachers, teachers-to-students, and student-to-student in an integrated school situation.
7. To help in the selection and use of the kinds of material that will assist in a smooth transition from learning in a non-integrated to learning in an integrated classroom setting.

Procedures.   The initial step to implement a plan to meet the goals listed above is the selection of the persons to be trained as master teachers. Since so much of the effectiveness of this program is dependent on these people, their careful selection is of great concern. From within the ranks of the teaching staff, six persons will be selected. The basic qualifications to be used in the selection are listed below. Qualified teachers of both races are being considered and will be chosen solely on the basis of qualifications.

At least a masters degree in education.

At least 12 years successful teaching experience.

Previous experience in working with others in a supervisory situation.

Stable and contributing members of the community.

An ability to adjust to new situations constructively.

Experience in working with children of both races.

A history of creative teaching.

Teaching experience in a field critical to the students' total growth.

Genuine concern for the student as a maturing person and his relationship to the school and society.

Four of these teachers will be in the field of reading and language arts and one each from the fields of mathematics and social studies.

Three permanent supervisors already on the staff will have the responsibility of direct supervision of the master teachers. The elementary supervisor and the reading supervisor will supervise the master teachers in the fields of reading and language arts, and the high school supervisor will supervise the master teachers who are to specialize in mathematics and social studies. These supervisors will be consulted in the selection of the master teachers.

After the selection of these, a two-week training program will be presented. This program will be conducted by the staff and will consist of twenty three-hour periods with time devoted to the following areas:

1. Teaching in non-graded integrated school.
2. Teaching as one of a team.
3. Requirements for teaching in a bi-racial classroom.
4. The use of standard tests and devices of measurement.
5. The preparation of teacher-made devices of measurement.
6. The maximum use of related materials with special emphasis on requirements of an integrated classroom.
7. Television as a classroom tool.
8. Providing for the slow learner in the classroom.
9. Providing for maximum growth for all students.
10. The discussion of controversial subjects in the classroom.
11. Developing communication skills required to effectively teach in racially mixed classes.

After the two-week session with the master teachers, the classroom teachers who represent the target for this activity will be brought in for one week of orientation. At that time, they will have an opportunity to meet and work with the master teacher and supervisor who will be assigned to work with them. The subject matter will be identical to that presented to the master teachers, except, of course, in an abbreviated form. There will be approximately sixty classroom teachers involved, selected from all of the schools on the basis of need.

With the beginning of school, each master teacher will move from one of the teachers assigned to him to another throughout the school day every day. He will provide materials, advice, criticism or support as needed. This will be done under the direction of the supervisor assigned to that particular teacher. The master teachers will be full time in this work with no other classroom assignments. It will be their function to provide on-the-spot leadership for the target teachers.

As the school year progresses, periodic meetings will be held with all of the participants coming together to review the program and to suggest possible alterations. This, coupled with monthly meetings held by the master teacher and the teachers in her charge, and with weekly meetings between the supervisors and the master teachers, should provide the necessary lines of communication between groups.

It will be the responsibility of the director of the program to coordinate the efforts of all involved and to furnish personal supervision of the program in action. He will meet with the various groups and keep acquainted with the progress of the program.

Source: Obtained from Region VII, Office of Education, Dallas, Texas.

2.   A New Role for the School Principal

School principals could take an active role in the support and reinforcement of new teaching techniques and curriculum methods. This would require
delegating purely administrative functions to others and arranging time to over-
see and guide curriculum development and improvement of the quality of
teaching.

In small schools the principal could probably become the equivalent of a
master teacher, maintaining close contact with the school faculty. In a larger
school, he might maintain a good working relationship with master teachers and
with department chairmen. He could assume the responsibility for initiating
curriculum development and for programs designed to improve teaching methods.

3.   Team Teaching

Team teaching can provide a framework for continued supervision and
reinforcement of teaching efforts. Each team should have a leader—usually an
experienced teacher—who may be responsible for lesson coordination, planning,
and curriculum development.

When teaching teams are formed and each teacher has a different role and
responsibility, the following advantages accrue:

Beginning teachers assigned to an instructional team have the advantage of
the experience of senior teachers continually available to them.

By assigning excellent teachers a leadership role in a team situation, rather
than a central supervisory or administrative role, these teachers are not
"lost" to the teaching profession.

The assignment of some teachers to a supervisory role within the team
diminishes the distance between the supervisor and the teacher, and increases the supervisory time that can be made available to each teacher.

Coordinating or leader team teachers can be responsible, on a continuing
basis, for curriculum development and in-service education for both professional teachers, and para-professional aides.

4.   Differentiated Staffing

One of the major problems facing the teaching profession has been the fact
that all teachers have essentially the same responsibilities, and except for
credits added by tenure, the same salaries. Thus, when a teacher wants to advance
himself professionally in the education field, or earn more money, he must
leave teaching and enter school administration.

Differentiated staffing is an idea recently developed in education to reduce
this problem. In differentiated staffing, there are several levels of teachers, each
with unique functions. Salaries increase as the level increases, and not necessarily according to tenure. Raises in levels are based on excellence, rather than
longevity.

The top teachers under the differentiated staffing arrangement generally
spend part of their time supervising other teachers or becoming involved in cur-

riculum development. Differentiated staffing thus provides each school with its own cadre of supervisors, without losing these people as teachers.

5.   In-Service Training Provided by Special Personnel

Many schools have personnel specializing in areas of speech, learning disabilities, music, physical education, art and guidance. These people can perform some training and consulting services for teachers as well. Usually such specialists welcome an opportunity to explain their roles and to obtain cooperation from classroom teachers. They should be allowed to do this formally during a meeting and they can invite teachers to ask for their help in casual daily contacts. These people might also be asked to present special programs. For example, the school nurse can give teachers a talk on drugs, and a guidance counselor can train teachers to give and interpret standardized tests.

A Sample In-Service Education Program

In-service education for teachers and other school personnel is not routine in many schools today. Because of this, the development of in-service programs to assist school personnel to adequately meet social and educational problems resulting from school desegregation will not be an easy task. Suggestions for the development of a comprehensive in-service program are listed below.

A.   Prior to actual desegregation of the school system if possible, the superintendent of schools should meet with the principals of schools to be desegregated and central office personnel. The purpose of this and subsequent meetings should be to form an initial committee to develop objectives for an in-service program, obtain commitment to these objectives, and plan the initial program. The meetings of this core committee should include presentations by outside consultants on school desegregation, as well as by people who have been involved in other school desegregation-related efforts in that region.

B.   During the summer an intensive training session in human relations, curriculum, and instructional techniques should be conducted for all principals, system supervisors, curriculum developers, and for each school's master (or senior) teachers. (Principals should designate master teachers for this purpose.)

This training program should probably be a week in duration, with stipends offered the teachers selected for participation. Its objectives are two-fold: one, to introduce and train participants to deal with the situations they will be meeting; and, two, to refine the in-service program developed for all school staff. The participants in this program will have on-going responsibilities during the year to work with individual school faculties on the problems incident to desegregation.

C. Prior to opening day, the entire school faculty of each school in the system should conduct meetings to introduce each teacher to the coming program. The functions of the master teachers would be explained, and each teacher would be assigned to work with a master teacher. The principals and the master teachers would impress upon all teachers their responsibility for making school desegregation work. (A similar meeting should be held for school support staff: bus drivers, cafeteria workers, secretarial help.)

D. The first year's in-service education program should emphasize human relations and instructional techniques. A specific time should be set aside at least every two weeks for all-school faculty meetings. Although the agenda should remain flexible, a variety of subjects should be covered and a variety of techniques used. Discipline, grading, social studies, and curriculum are likely subjects; films, consultant lectures and demonstrations are likely techniques.

Each master teacher should have a schedule that provides time to assist other teachers during the school day. The principal, as the chief instructor and supervisor, should ascertain that the master teacher program functions well.

E. The central system staff should assign somebody the responsibility of exploring and publicizing available courses relevant to desegregation at nearby colleges or universities. The central office staff should direct to each school experts and consultants in school desegregation, and make films and literature available. They should also ascertain that each school is carrying out their in-service programs in good faith.

F. During the years following initial desegregation, in-service programs should not be abandoned. All teachers new to the system should participate in a general training program prior to the start of school. Early in the school year the school faculties should determine their in-service needs for the coming year, and programs should be developed accordingly. Emphasis may be shifted at this time from human relations training to education in instructional devices and curriculum. Again, outside courses should be made available.

The figure on the following page represents the major components of an in-service training program undertaken (and prepared) by the New Albany, Mississippi school district. This program differs from the recommended program presented above (it does not emphasize the use of in-school supervisors or master teachers), but it represents a thorough program. Of special interest is the Pre-Service Institute for elementary teachers held prior to integration of the elementary schools. This was a three-week institute that included a pilot school program to provide teachers with practical experience in integrated education prior to the official opening of the schools. New Albany's program was funded under Title IV of the Civil Rights Act of 1964.

Example of a Program for
Desegregation and Improvement of Instruction

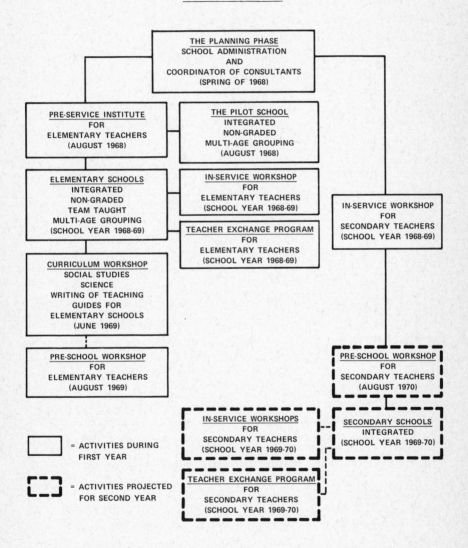

DESIGN OF OPERATIONS

THE PLANNING PHASE
SCHOOL ADMINISTRATION
AND
COORDINATOR OF CONSULTANTS
(SPRING OF 1968)

PRE-SERVICE INSTITUTE
FOR
ELEMENTARY TEACHERS
(AUGUST 1968)

THE PILOT SCHOOL
INTEGRATED
NON-GRADED
MULTI-AGE GROUPING
(AUGUST 1968)

ELEMENTARY SCHOOLS
INTEGRATED
NON-GRADED
TEAM TAUGHT
MULTI-AGE GROUPING
(SCHOOL YEAR 1968-69)

IN-SERVICE WORKSHOP
FOR
ELEMENTARY TEACHERS
(SCHOOL YEAR 1968-69)

IN-SERVICE WORKSHOP
FOR
SECONDARY TEACHERS
(SCHOOL YEAR 1968-69)

TEACHER EXCHANGE PROGRAM
FOR
ELEMENTARY TEACHERS
(SCHOOL YEAR 1968-69)

CURRICULUM WORKSHOP
SOCIAL STUDIES
SCIENCE
WRITING OF TEACHING
GUIDES FOR
ELEMENTARY SCHOOLS
(JUNE 1969)

PRE-SCHOOL WORKSHOP
FOR
ELEMENTARY TEACHERS
(AUGUST 1969)

PRE-SCHOOL WORKSHOP
FOR
SECONDARY TEACHERS
(AUGUST 1970)

☐ = ACTIVITIES DURING
FIRST YEAR

IN-SERVICE WORKSHOPS
FOR
SECONDARY TEACHERS
(SCHOOL YEAR 1969-70)

SECONDARY SCHOOLS
INTEGRATED
(SCHOOL YEAR 1969-70)

⬚ = ACTIVITIES PROJECTED
FOR SECOND YEAR

TEACHER EXCHANGE PROGRAM
FOR
SECONDARY TEACHERS
(SCHOOL YEAR 1969-70)

Source: New Albany Municipal School District, Annual Report 1968–69, A Title IV
Project, New Albany, Mississippi.

Conclusions: Implications of Improved In-
Service Education for the Teacher and Other
School Personnel

The need for increased levels and varieties of in-service education in public
schools has been amply demonstrated. The widespread occurrence of school
desegregation has not created this need, but has magnified and clarified it. However, before individual schools and school districts will be able to undertake
sophisticated in-service education for the purpose of making school desegregation
a success, several things must occur:

A.   There must be a positive attitude on the part of all school personnel toward
     school desegregation. To be effective, school desegregation cannot be seen
     as a one-time act of mixing minority with majority children. It must instead
     be seen as a continual effort to achieve meaningful social and academic
     interaction among children of different social, cultural, and racial back-
     grounds.

B.   School boards and superintendents must be prepared financially, and with
     central staff resources, to widen the available opportunities for in-service
     education.

     School budgets must include teacher education as well as student education.

     Opportunities for extension courses or credit courses relevant to the needs
     occasioned by desegregation must be explored and publicized.

     Consultants and other resource personnel need to be made available.

     School policy should be oriented toward providing released time, salary
     credits, or stipends for teachers participating in in-service education.

     The use of volunteer teacher's aides and/or paraprofessionals should be
     encouraged within the schools.

C.   Principals need once more to become instructional leaders, or chief super-
     visors, within their schools. Many administrative duties should be delegated
     to others.

D.   Teachers must be willing to lose some of their classroom autonomy, to open
     their teaching behavior to constructive comments by supervisors, and to
     work closely with their peers.

If these things do occur, supervision and in-service education for teachers
will assume the importance in public education that they deserve. Clearly, their
occurrence will have implications for the roles traditionally assumed by school
personnel. The building principal, for example, will become more an educational

leader, and less an administrator. Ideally, he will work more closely with the school faculty, and make fewer solo decisions. Supervisors, curriculum developers, and resource teachers will become a more important hierarchy within the school, and their concerns will at least be given equal consideration with purely administrative concerns. Teachers will become less autonomous and more likely to work within teams, or to work more closely with resource specialists and guidance counselors. Volunteer aides and paraprofessionals will come more commonly into use, and their assumption of many teaching chores will free teachers for advancing their own knowledge, developing curriculum, and working with individuals.

Ideally, schools should provide a link by which students are able to enter the mainstream of American society. This theoretical function can only become a reality when school personnel can treat each child as a worthwhile individual, and respect each child for what he can contribute to his current classmates, and to his future friends and partners in work. The perpetuation of flagrant discrimination is no longer tolerated in the public educational system. Likewise, if the goals of the schools are to be achieved, subtle forms of prejudice must be dismantled. Positive acceptance of cultural diversity can be learned. Schools have a responsibility to do everything in their power to teach it to both teachers and students. In-service education, as the vehicle for such learning, must be common and continuous. It is a vital ingredient in making public education more meaningful to all students, regardless of race or social background.

Notes

1. Arthur W. Foshay, "Shaping Curriculum: The Decade Ahead," *Influences in Curriculum Change,* Glenys G. Unruh and Robert R. Leeper, eds. (Association for Supervision and Curriculum Development, National Education Association, Washington, D.C., 1968), pp. 8–9.
2. Gertrude Noar, *The Teacher and Integregation* (Washington, D.C.: National Education Association, 1966).
3. John Adams High School, *First Year Report 1969-70* (Portland, Oregon, September 1970), p. 39.
4. *Mitchell High School Student Handbook, 1970-71* (Colorado Springs, Colorado), pp. 9–11.
5. Ned A. Flanders, "Interaction Analysis and In-Service Training," *Journal of Experimental Education,* Vol. 37, No. 1 (Fall 1968), pp. 126–133.
6. *Theory and Practice of Supervision* (New York: Dodd, Mead and Co., 1970), p. 27.
7. "Coordinating the Team," *The Supervisor: New Demands, New Dimensions* (Washington, D.C.: Association for Supervision and Curriculum Development, National Education Association, 1969), p. 62

Bibliography

"Administrative Leadership in Theory and Practice," *The Bulletin of the National Association of Secondary School Principals*, No. 322 (November 1967).

Association of Classroom Teachers, National Education Association. *Classroom Teachers Speak on Differentiated Teaching Assignments*. Washington, D.C., 1969.

Association for Supervision and Curriculum Development, National Education Association. *The Supervisor: Agent for Change in Teaching*. Washington, D.C., 1966.

ASCD, NEA. *The Supervisor: New Demands, New Dimensions*. Washington, D.C., 1969.

ASCD, NEA. *Supervisor: Perspectives and Propositions*. Washington, D.C., 1967.

ASCD, NEA. *Theories of Instruction*. Washington, D.C., 1965.

ASCD, NEA. *Toward Professional Maturity of Supervisors and Curriculum Workers*. Washington, D.C., 1967.

ASCD, NEA. *The Unstudied Curriculum: Its Impact on Children*. Washington, D.C., 1970.

Chesler, Mark, Carl Jorgenson, and Phyllis Erenberg. *Planning Educational Change*. Volume III: *Integrating the Desegregated School*. U.S. Department of Health, Education, and Welfare, Office of Education.

Dentler, R.A., B. Mackler, M.E. Warshauer. ed. *The Urban R's: Race Relations as the Problem in Urban Education*. New York: Published for the Center for Urban Education, Frederick A. Praeger, 1967.

Department of Classroom Teachers, National Education Association, *The Classroom Teacher Speaks on His Supportive Staff*. Washington, D.C., 1967.

Department of Elementary-Kindergarten-Nursery Education, National Education Association. *Prevention of Failure*. Washington, D.C., 1965.

Educational Policies Commission, National Education Association and the American Association of School Administrators. *The Unique Role of the Superintendent of Schools*. Washington, D.C., 1965.

Education and Urban Society, Vol. 1, No. 2 (February 1969).

Gwynee, J. Monor. *Theory and Practice of Supervision*. New York: Dodd, Mead and Company, 1970.

Hillway, Tyrus. *Education in American Society, an Introduction to the Study of Education*. Boston: Houghton Mifflin Company, 1961.

Hudgins, Bryce B. *The Instructured Process*. Chicago: Rand McNally & Company, 1971.

Kuhleen, R.G. and G.C. Thompson. ed. *Psychological Studies of Human Development*. New York: Appleton-Century-Crofts, 1963.

Loretan, Joseph O. and Shelley Umans, *Teaching the Disadvantaged*. New York: Teachers College Press, Teachers College, Columbia University, 1966.

Noar, Gertrude. *The Teacher and Integration*. Washington, D.C.: Student National Education Association, 1966.

Passow, A. Harry, ed. *Education in Depressed Areas*. New York: Teachers College Press, Teachers College, Columbia University, 1968.

Silberman, Charles E. *Crisis in the Classroom*. New York: Random House, 1970.

Street, David, ed. *Innovation in Mass Education*. New York: John Wiley & Sons, 1969.

Trubowitz, Sidney. *A Handbook for Teaching in the Ghetto School*. Chicago: Quadrangle Books, 1968.

Weinstein, Gerald and Mario D. Fantini. ed. *Toward Humanistic Education: A Curriculum of Affect*. New York: Published for the Ford Foundation by Praeger Publishers, 1970.

Wrightstone, J. Wayne. *Class Organization for Instruction*. What Research Says to the Teacher, No. 13, Association of Classroom Teachers, National Education Association. Washington, D.C., 1969.

Community Relations to Achieve Effective Desegregation

The Function of School-Community Relations

The school is a social institution that was established to prepare students for participation in community life. To accomplish this task, schools develop and implement policies on organization, methods and content of education.

Teaching requires specialized skills and knowledge. For this reason, the community allows the school to operate independently in matters of academic freedom; but in turn, the school must assume responsibility for communication of the results of educational activities to the public. In meeting this responsibility, the school should:

1. Establish and maintain public confidence in education.
2. Inform parents about their children's progress in school.
3. Promote the health and welfare of students.
4. Provide information about the community.
5. Inform the community about the school.

Basic Problems Caused or Aggravated by School Desegregation

1. The faith that education should be independent of community influence has fostered the belief that the school is autonomous. Yet the school's policies are often influenced by the values of persons who are felt to represent leadership in the community. Often these policies do not adequately reflect the values and needs of the total community. In other cases, the intent of the policies is not properly communicated to community leaders or the public.

2. School desegregation is not purely educational in nature. In most communities, it necessitates major social changes. Failure of school officials to inform all members of the community of the intentions of desegregation creates uncertainty and differing expectations.

3. Because desegregation is imposed upon community leaders and school officials, it is often difficult for them to make needed policy changes. Such changes often require the school to ask leaders from all aspects of community life to participate in the decision-making process. Without the support of a united minority community and patterns of minority leadership that reassure the entire community, school officials will be unable to accomplish an effective desegregation plan.

4. Because school officials usually maintain only limited contact with the community, most residents of a district do not understand the process of education. For this reason, formal communication devices that make use of the

media and the public meeting do not adequately prepare the community for desegregation.

Basic Objectives in Desegregation to Remedy These Problems

1. School officials should inform the community that desegregation is inevitable and establish definite policies on the manner in which the process will occur. This action should be taken as a means of maintaining their authority and reducing uncertainty about the effects of desegregation within the community.

2. The school district should involve leaders from all aspects of community life in planning for desegregation. Where possible, school officials should press community leaders to establish common objectives and policies affecting the performance of school functions.

3. School personnel should take the initiative in reducing isolation both between and among leaders and residents of the community. Formal and informal methods of communicating school policies and objectives should be employed.

4. Attempts should be made to increase involvement of community residents in the schools' activities. Close cooperation and continuing contact between the schools and local public and private agencies should be established.

Specific Problems, Policies and Techniques

A. Reducing Community Uncertainty About Desegregation Issues

PROBLEM: Many school boards fail to keep their communities informed about their stand on school desegregation issues. School boards that do not inform their communities, either that they are considering the adoption of school desegregation policies or that they are developing school desegregation plans, will probably generate anxieties and frustrations within the community. Similarly, discussion of potential actions with only the community elite will raise suspicions by the non-elite that their feelings are not being considered.

POLICY.   School boards should determine early in the process of school
(A-1)   desegregation that they will adopt firm desegregation policies. The decision to adopt policies, and the policies themselves, should be clearly communicated to the public.

School board members must decide among themselves that they will stand firm as a unified body and clearly communicate their decision to the community. Resolution on matters of school policy, procedures and plans is almost always a necessary prerequisite to the gathering of community support and the eventual implementation of decisions. Agreement on support of board decisions must be reached by the board members prior to any actual decision making.

POLICY.   School boards should inform their communities that they are
(A-2)   considering the implementation of school desegregation.

This is not a formal announcement to the community of school board policy with regard to school desegregation. It is a preparatory statement initiated in an attempt to make the community aware that the board seeks support and understanding as it considers school desegregation. By issuing a general statement, the board adequately informs the community of the possibility of impending school desegregation. This announcement should be made well in advance of any formal statements on school desegregation policy that would emanate from the board. The most likely medium for conveyance of this announcement would be the community newspaper, but radio and television coverage should also be encouraged. It is very important that an explanatory memorandum be distributed to all administrative, teaching and support staff throughout the school system.

Exceptions to this policy occur when desegregation is involuntary, and when the community is involved in a court order. If desegregation is voluntary, the school board should initiate a thorough community dialogue in order to generate consensus and support. If desegregation is involuntary, the board might be advised to bypass "consideration" of desegregation, and announce instead the decision to desegregate.

POLICY.   The school board's policy announcing its decision to desegregate
(A-3)   should be clearly expressed, in writing, and disseminated to the
          community. The policy should include faculty as well as student
          desegregation. The school board should stand solidly behind
          the policy statement.

School board members should adopt a resolution that, in effect, establishes a base for their commitment and continued interest in bringing about school desegregation. Such a resolution must be the board's first order of business in the desegregation process and is crucial under all school desegregation circumstances. It is designed in part to foster unity among board members and thereby use the prestige of members to engender favorable reactions in the community for school desegregation efforts. In order to bring about this board resolve, it is often useful to seek the advice and guidance of the superintendent as a professional. The board can then produce a resolution defining school desegregation policy (see section on Administrative Measures), as well as a resolution commiting them to open communication with the public throughout the school desegregation process.

Arrangements should be made with all local newspapers to have the text of this resolution publicized. Radio and television can announce the resolution and indicate specific locations where copies of the text may be secured; e.g., neighborhood school offices, banks, etc. Copies of the document can also be sent home with students for their parents' information.

POLICY.   School boards should inform their communities about the process
(A-4)   of developing a desegregation plan. Under most circumstances,
               except when the community is unalterably opposed, there
               should be a strong element of community participation in plan
               preparation.

In developing the plan, or initiating the planning process, school boards
should clearly state that they will consider both liberal and conservative
viewpoints. In cases where communities are strongly polarized, participation in
the planning process should probably be limited to a few key leaders; but even
so, they should represent all views. Public forums at this stage might cause
further polarization in a divided community.

Suggested Techniques

1.   Support of Business and Civic Organizations
     An example of a public announcement of business support for school
desegregation is shown on the following page. This type of policy statement
by community leaders aids in amelioration of local uncertainty and reinforces
the position of school officials.

For other techniques related to this policy, see the discussion on citizen
advisory boards in the section of this chapter titled Administrative Measures to
Achieve Effective Desegregation.

POLICY.   Upon completion of the desegregation plan, the school board
(A-5)   should make a presentation to the public, and make the plan
               publicly available in written form.

The school board's announcement of the completed school desegregation
plan should be a formal and detailed presentation to the community. It would
also be desirable at this time for the board to reiterate its commitment to the
concept of school desegregation. The board's firm support of the plan and its
implementation should be explicit. It is important that the announcement of the
details of the plan occur only after the final product has been completed.
Piecemeal presentation confuses and distorts the community's initial encounter
with school desegregation.

The board should provide newspapers and other media (i.e., radio and
television), with the salient aspects of the plan. Enough facts should be given so
that readers and listeners will have a clear picture of what the plan entails.

POLICY.   The school board should continue to issue public policy state-
(A-6)   ments throughout the desegregation process.

The school board should periodically issue policy statements that reaffirm
the board's resolve with regard to school desegregation, its backing of the
adopted plan, and its continuing interest in the future of desegregation efforts in
the community. As the formal political representative of the community, the
board is responsible for this function. A firm policy statement of this kind
should come from the board just before opening day. Optimally, repetition of

Example of Business Leaders' Policy
Statement on School Desegregation

"Within recent years there have been sweeping changes in our social and political attitudes. Those in position of authority have been caught up in these changes and are criticized, often for reasons beyond their control, by all factions involved in the change. School Boards have especially been involved in the controversies over school desegregation as it has been planned and carried out by our constitutionally appointed representatives. The Rocky Mount City School Board has not been an exception to this controversy. The School Board has had to operate under extreme pressure and undue criticism from the community at large in what has been a thankless and unrewarding job.

"At the present time, it appears uncertain as to what specific plans for desegregation will be established for our city schools. Regardless of the program ultimately approved and implemented, it is especially important that the community rally to the support of our School Board as it attempts to resolve its problems within the framework of the law.

"The Rocky Mount Chamber of Commerce supports the efforts of the Rocky Mount City School Board to comply with Title IV of the 1964 Civil Rights Act.

"Furthermore, the Rocky Mount Chamber encourages all citizens to support its School Board in these efforts, to give constructive suggestions and criticisms that are free of prejudice, and to refrain from actions or words that would tend to deteriorate the confidence the community has in its public schools."

Source: Rocky Mount Chamber of Commerce, March 4, 1969. From: *Hearings,* Select Senate Committee on Equal Educational Opportunity (91st Congress, Second Session, June 18, 22, 23, 24; July 8, 1970), p. 1369.

the board's position could occur about half way through the academic year, at the end of the first school year, and before the second opening day. More important than such formal statements, though, are continuing endorsements of the actions of district administrators and school staffs.

Suggested Technique

1. Incorporation of Desegregation Policy into Districtwide Educational Goals
   One means of reassuring the community about the quality of the schools continuing—and improving—after desegregation is to issue a statement of educational goals for the school system. These goals should be formulated with the assistance of community members and teachers. A detailed example of one such goal statement is presented on the following pages.

Example of Statement of Educational
Goals for a School System

Self-Realization.   The purpose of the school is:

To encourage and assist in the development of a desire for knowledge and self-improvement;

To develop appreciation and respect for thought and knowledge;

To inspire respect for intellectual freedom and creative thought;

To develop the basic skills of reading, writing, mathematics, and speech as aids to the acquiring of knowledge for the purpose of self-expression and communication;

To develop individual initiative, good study habits, the ability to think clearly and reason objectively; to recognize honest differences of opinion; and to develop a sense of judgment and confidence in one's own abilities;

To develop the basic elements of character, such as integrity, truthfulness, kindliness, courage, tolerance, and gratitude;

To teach students to recognize and appreciate the physical self, its requirements, its protection against disease and accident, its limitations, and its constant dependence upon the good health of others; to recognize and learn to live with one's own mental and physical limitations so that a failure of effort will not result in mental or physical distress sufficient to harm or retard good mental or physical well-being;

To help students to understand basic scientific facts concerning the nature of the universe and of men, the methods of science, and the gathering of scientific information; to recognize the importance of these facts and their influence upon human progress; to develop an interest in the promotion of science for the betterment of all;

To encourage and aid the development of purely personal interests which afford mental and physical satisfaction such as an appreciation of the arts, the intelligent use of one's own leisure time, and the enjoyment of, and participation in, sports and hobbies;

To teach a recognition of, and an ability to adapt to, ever-changing economic, social, political, and scientific conditions and patterns.

Economic Evaluation and Realization.   The purpose of the school is:

To furnish guidance and information so as to assist individuals in the selection of a suitable and desirable occupation;

To develop natural aptitudes and abilities along particular lines of economic endeavor;

To provide all educational prerequisites necessary for educational experience;

To furnish certain basic courses in trades and commercial subjects;

To help students learn basic economic theories and principles and to recognize the interrelation of all economic endeavor;

(continued)

*Example of Statement of Educational
Goals for a School System (Continued)*

To help students appreciate the economic importance of, and recognize the need
   for, conservation of our natural resources including wildlife;
To develop consideration of one's personal economic demands, requirements,
   and limitations, the need for economic planning, and the acquisition of good
   saving, buying, and spending habits.

Political Integration.   The purpose of the school is:
To teach respect for the laws and a general knowledge of how they are made and
   enforced;
To impart an understanding of the basic principles underlying the developments
   of the American system of government and the basic rights and privileges
   guaranteed by our Constitution;
To impart a general knowledge of the Constitution of the United States, the
   Constitution of the State of Illinois, the doctrine of separation of powers,
   the Australian ballot system, and the important documents in our history;
To develop a clear understanding of the history of the United States, the reasons
   for its growth, and its position in the community of the world;
To impart a knowledge of various types of government and an ability to compare
   and evaluate their principal characteristics;
To develop a loyalty to, and appreciation for, democratic ideals and a determination to protect them, preserve them, and assume personal responsibility
   for them.

Social Attitudes.   The purpose of the school is:
To develop a thoughtful consideration for the welfare of all members of a
   society; to recognize the equality of all people, the equality of rights and
   duties of all members of the community, and the right to benefit com-
   mensurate with one's contribution, whether individual initiative, capital,
   skill, or labor;
To develop a charitable attitude and a sense of obligation to aid in the correction
   of social inequalities and relieve human misery and want;
To develop personality for a full social life, the friendship of others, and the
   ability to cooperate with others at work and at play;
To help students learn and respect the rules of social behavior and common
   courtesy;
To develop a recognition of the family as a vitally necessary social institution,
   and to prepare the student to be a contributor to its welfare and to accept
   its responsibilities.

   Source: The Citizens Survey Committee, *A Survey of the Elgin Public Schools* (Elgin,
Illinois, 1956).

B. Implementation of a Positive Communications Program

PROBLEM: School system officials do not normally engage in active communication with the residents of the school district. Traditionally,
communication channels are limited to members of the community elite—business leaders, church leaders, and other prominent citizens. The absence of communication with a broad
spectrum of the district residents leads to rumors, uncertainties,
and diverse expectations.

POLICY.   School boards should establish a media policy and instruct school
(B-1)   administrators to adhere to it and to use the local press.

The development of solid relationships with the education editors and other
staff of the local newspapers, and with broadcasters of local radio and television
stations, will provide a base for continuing utilization of the media as communication channels to the public.

Suggested Techniques

1.   Development of a Board Communication Policy

Some school boards adopt specific resolutions on communication with the
community, including enumeration of the subjects that will be made public.
An example of an explicit policy statement on open communications appears on
the following page.

2.   Background Meetings of School Board Officials and Editors and Publishers

It is extremely important that the media in the local community report all
news on desegregation in a straightforward but positive manner, avoiding
sensationalism. In order to achieve this result, the head of the school board
should meet informally with the publishers and editors of all the leading newspapers, television stations, and radio stations serving the district. He should talk
to only a few at a time if there are many, and could invite several other school
board members and the superintendent to be present. The purpose of such
meetings is to gain the solid support of the media for carrying out desegregation
harmoniously and effectively, and to establish a reporting style concerning
desegregation that will not increase community conflict. Therefore, these meetings should occur as soon as the board begins thinking about desegregating,
perhaps even before it has formally decided to desegregate. Eventually, after
initial understandings about basic policy have been reached, the school officials
might ask the press to work out a way to handle any possible "incidents"
connected with desegregation in a manner fully consistent with reporting
integrity, but not likely to inflame local passions.

Example of Board Resolution on Open
Communication with the Public

WHEREAS, by law and tradition, all aspects of a public school system's operations are of public interest and concern, and the board of education welcomes and encourages the active participation of citizens in planning for the highest excellence of their public schools; and

WHEREAS, the community must have full access to information if its involvement in the schools is to be effective, responsible and useful; and

WHEREAS, full disclosure of information must undergird all the activities now carried on by the board of education and the staff to effect cooperation between the schools and the communities they serve; and

WHEREAS, local school boards, which are the main liaison between the board of education and the local communities, parent and parent-teacher associations, and other citizens, must be properly informed if their essential assistance in seeking continued improvement of the school is to be achieved; and

WHEREAS, the effectiveness of programs, experiments, and demonstrations are a matter of concern to the whole professional staff and to the parents and other citizens of the city; and

WHEREAS, effective communication between the school system and the public includes also the receipt and consideration of community attitudes, reactions, and proposals; be it, therefore

RESOLVED, that the board of education adopts the following policy with regard to communication between the schools and the public, for continued implementation by the superintendent of schools and his staff in schools, districts, and central offices:

1. The school system—central headquarters, district offices and schools— will inform local school boards, parent and parent-teacher associations, and the general public about the administration and operation of the schools frankly and completely, by every possible medium.

2. All reports of evaluations of experimental, demonstration, and on-going programs in the school system will be submitted by the superintendent of schools to the board of education and are to be made public immediately after the superintendent and the board have had an opportunity to read and discuss them. All new programs, demonstrations, and experiments are to have evaluation procedures built into them prior to adoption by the board of education.

3. Results of standardized tests of pupil achievement and other pertinent measures of performance will be made available to local school boards, parent and parent-teacher associations, and the general public.

4. The school system will use every possible means to ascertain public attitudes and invite constructive suggestions about all phases of its operation for consideration in the planning of policies and procedures.

5. Every employee of the school system has a role in the improvement of communication between the schools and the public. The superintendent of schools will develop a comprehensive and continuing program of in-service training in school-community relations for the professional and administrative staffs of schools, districts, and central offices.

Source: New York City resolution from: National Education Association, Educational Research Service Circular, *The Administration of Public Relations Programs in Local School Systems, 1966–1967* (Washington, D.C., 1967), p. 44.

---

3. Consistent Format in Press Relations

To assure an effective continuing relationship with the working press, school district officials should establish a format for news conferences, press releases and more informal dealings with reporters. The components of a program for press relations are listed on the following page.

Statements prepared for use by the media should be brief and simply stated. In order to avoid misunderstanding within the community, announcements of school policies and actions should be stated in a manner that will be clear to the differing segments of the community. The news release style recommended by the National Education Association is presented on an accompanying page.

4. Use of Media to Report Meetings on School Desegregation

School districts often do not keep communities adequately informed about meetings on school desegregation. The media should be made aware of when and where meetings are to be held so that they can be covered and reported. A Director of School-Community Relations could act as a liaison with the media and assist them by interpreting and providing relevant information so that factual, newsworthy stories are printed in newspapers and announced on radio and television.

5. Packaged Background Material on School Segregation and Desegregation

Some school districts have distributed general information on quality education and school desegregation to the media and to the community at large. Such documents point out the injuries caused by segregation and the benefits of desegregation. Among the elements included in publications of this type are the following:

Factual information and results of material research on academic performance by black and white students in desegregated settings.

Statements from teachers who have taught in desegregated schools and can speak on the varying achievement levels in the classroom.

Narrative descriptions of past efforts by the school district to improve

Guidelines for Press Relations

1. One person from the central administrative offices of the school district should be designated to deal with the press. This could be a Director of School-Community Relations.
2. Although messages are conveyed to the media by a Director of School-Community Relations, the official spokesman should be the chairman of the school board or the district superintendent. Press releases should cite the official spokesman.
3. A list should be prepared of the daily and weekly newspapers that circulate in the school district, and the local radio and television stations. Any large newspapers or radio or television stations in nearby cities that cover activities in the local community should also be listed.
4. A list should be prepared of the newsmen who represent the local media. The reporters should be asked about the meeting times that would be most convenient for them with respect to their daily or weekly deadlines.
5. In-person meetings with media representatives should be carefully scheduled, and they should be brief but allow time for questions.
6. Before a meeting with the media, a fact sheet should be prepared. The full name, title and school address of the person submitting the news release should be included, along with his home address and telephone number.
7. Press conferences should be announced several days in advance, if possible, and each newspaper and broadcasting station should be contacted.

Guidelines for Press Release Preparation

1. Copy should be composed of short words, short sentences, and short paragraphs. A newspaper column ranges from 1-3/4" to 2" and a five-minute radio newscast, even without a commercial announcement, can accommodate only six-hundred words of news, on a number of different stories.
2. News copy should be double-spaced and preferably one page, seldom more than two.
3. A story should not use words that would not be used in everyday conversation. If technical or professional terms must be used— such as *negotiation*—the sentences should be brief. In some communities, *contract talks* will carry much more meaning than *negotiation*.
4. Exact dates are needed: "April 3" rather than "next Thursday" or "tomorrow"; "March," not "next month." Every date and day of the week must be checked on the calendar.
5. Assuming the reader knows a particular piece of information, such as an address, can lead to confusion. It must be noted, as well as the name of the meeting place.

6. Adjectives aren't needed when writing a news story. If the meeting was *outstanding* or a speaker *dynamic*, a factual description will indicate these qualities. Editorial comments or opinions should be omitted.

7. Figures in a news story should be consistent. As a general rule, numbers are spelled out from one to nine; numerals are used from 10 on. A number beginning a sentence is spelled out. The Associated Press stylebook is a good reference and is available at most newspaper offices.

8. Consistency is also needed in terminology and style. Is it *inservice* or *in-service, dropout* or *drop-out, preschool* or *pre-school, counselor* or *counsellor*? A decision based on observation, examining the style of newspapers, and the editor's opinion should be followed regularly.

9. Above all: honesty and accuracy. When handing a story to an editor or broadcast newsman, the association's news media chairman in effect becomes a part-time member of the reporting staff. If newsmen find the copy accurate, it is likely that it will be published or broadcast. Misinformation or careless mistakes will appear in print or be heard by thousands of people. Newsmen will quickly lose confidence and stop using association information. The truth must be told—even if it hurts. That is the way to win the solid confidence of newsmen.

10. When a news story is finished, it should be read over. All unnecessary adjectives and other words that frequently are unnecessary—the, an, a, etc.—should be deleted.

Source: National Education Association, *Press, Radio and TV Tips* (Washington, D.C., 1969), pp. 7–8.

---

substandard achievement levels and educational performances of disadvantaged students.

Narrative descriptions of ways in which the school district is working with teachers to deal better with differing achievement levels in the same classroom.

Suggestions of ways in which parents and citizens can augment the work of the schools, be supportive of efforts to provide a quality education for every child, and assist teachers in a voluntary capacity.

Pictorial evidence of school desegregation can also be supplied by the school district. Human interest pictures of parent teacher association picnics, activities of student interest clubs, teachers using new classroom techniques, etc., can be given to local newspapers. Pictures of members of community bi-racial advisory committees on school desegregation can also be released. Film strips or photographs suitable for use in television news programs can be prepared as well.

Parents and others in the community can participate with the schools in developing this material. Assistance could be provided in research, typing, collating and distribution. Some types of information in leaflet or flyer form could be distributed in banks, theaters, downtown squares or other public gathering places.

6.   Teacher Checklists of Newsworthy Items
       After schools have been physically desegregated, district administrators could ask teachers to cooperate in spotting newsworthy items in the classroom. A checklist of suggested topics—such as new teaching techniques being employed in the classroom—could be distributed to all teachers. When they were returned, the administrators could follow-up and gather the details to develop a news story. An example of such a checklist appears below.

---

*Example of Teacher Checklist
for Newsworthy Ideas*

Fellow Teacher:
       Take one minute to look over this checklist of possible news feature ideas. Do you have a situation like any of these in your school?
       Just check the one that applies and return the form to me in the interschool mail. I'll call you for details.
                                   Many thanks!

                                   Joe Blaze
                                   News Media Chairman, OEA
                                   Mill Elementary

_____

_____Success story of a student or grad
_____Accomplishment of an individual student who
             overcame a handicap
_____Student who has done unusually well through
             exceptional effort
_____Awards, honors, citations to a student or students
             (no long lists, please)
_____Interesting method of instruction
_____Instructional project being carried out in unusual or
             exceptional fashion
_____Resource person from the community making a
             presentation to a class
_____Results of a new instructional idea in comparison
             with the old way
_____Professional meeting attendance by a teacher, pro-
             gram participation by a teacher

_____Professional honors, awards, grants, scholarships
awarded a teacher

_____Unusual part-time or summer job or travel experience
of a teacher

Reporter_____School_____

Source: National Education Association, *Press, Radio and TV Tips* (Washington, D.C., 1969), p. 13.

7.   Multi-Racial and Ethnic Educational Television Programs

Local broadcasting of multi-racial and ethnic television programs can aid community understanding of desegregation. These programs are usually prepared for students, but they can also be shown publicly. Such programs emphasize the social and economic contributions made by members of minority groups and are influential in reducing misconceptions on the part of non-minority-group students and parents. Examples are given on an accompanying page of programs produced for student and community viewing by WVIZ, a metropolitan educational broadcasting station in Cleveland, Ohio, and the Ohio State Department of Education. In addition to the two programs described in the example, WVIZ is currently planning a series titled, "Other Families and Other Friends." Each of the programs in this series will feature the heritage of one of the ethnic groups in the Cleveland metropolitan area.

8.   Radio and Television Discussions and Documentaries

A personal level of communication is reached by presenting interviews, lectures or round-table discussions on radio or television. A school district could also prepare a documentary on the development of school desegregation in the community for viewing on local television. Such a documentary should make reference to other desegregated activities and schools elsewhere in the country.

POLICY.   School administrators should explain the desegregation process to
(B-2)   district residents in public meetings held at schools or other convenient locations. In cases where community feelings are highly polarized, smaller meetings should be held with representative community leaders.

Suggested Techniques.   There are two types of meetings that can be held— large public meetings and personal encounters with key community leaders. The choice of which type to focus upon usually depends on the overall attitude in the community, as discussed below.

1.   Large Public Meetings

Community meetings coordinated by district administrators and/or bi-

Examples of Ethnic Educational Television Series

The History of Black Americans

1. Ancient African Kingdoms—Part I
2. Ancient African Kingdoms—Part II
3. Slavery and the Slave Trade
4. Conditions Before the Civil War
5. Blacks in the Civil War
6. Presidential Reconstruction
7. Congressional Reconstruction
8. Jim Crow and the Populist Movement
9. Political and Social Renaissánce
10. Renaissance in the Arts
11. The Depression and World War II
12. The Start of Protest: Black Nations South of the Border
13. Protests Before the Civil War
14. Protest Movements, Organizations
15. The Civil Rights Movement
16. The Militant Movement

    Reflection in Black
1. Early Folk Literature
2. Early Black Writers
3. The Folk Literature of Paul Laurence Dunbar and James Weldon Johnson
4. The Negro Renaissance
5. Langston Hughes
6. Contemporary Writers

    Source: Ohio State Department of Education and WVIZ-TV, *A Teacher's Guide to History of Black Americans: A Television Series for Secondary School Students* (Cleveland, Ohio).

---

racial advisory committees can serve a number of purposes. They allow the community members to ask direct questions on the specific impacts that a desegregation plan will have on the community and individual neighborhoods. Two-way communication occurs between the general public and administrators, which enables identification of possible problem areas. Local area leaders who support the concept of school desegregation should be encouraged to attend such gatherings so that the community can identify with these individuals. The following guidelines cover techniques that can be employed for these community assemblies:

A series of informational meetings at schools (both formerly all-white and formerly all-black schools) throughout the district should be scheduled after the Initial Plan for desegregation has been completed.

These meetings should be open to the public and should be held in the evening.

Advisory committee members should be designated to attend these meetings to assist administrators in explaining the district's plan and to make the community aware of the work of the committee. Emphasis should be placed on the way in which the school desegregation plan will be implemented in the specific school or area where the meeting is held.

The times and locations of such meetings should be well publicized in advance.

There should be ample opportunity for dialogue between school district representatives and members of the audience.

Maps and other visual aids should be used.

It would be desirable for one or more of the recognized leaders of the area (minister, PTA officer, political leader, etc.) to be included in a leadership capacity in the meeting (moderator, participant on a panel, etc.)

Consideration should be given to having a lawyer present at the community meetings to answer questions on school desegregation law and any federal administrative requirements that apply to the school district.

It would be beneficial to have at the meetings education and school desegregation experts recruited from either within or without the community.

Community meetings of the type described above should be held in most desegregating districts. The exception is areas with strong and large opposing factions. In these districts, the focus should be upon smaller meetings such as are described below.

2.   Small Meetings with Community Leaders
        Where the community is highly polarized, the board, superintendent or bi-racial advisory committee members should meet only with the community's leadership to discuss school desegregation. These meetings may occur at a school or at an office of one of the community leaders. The purpose of the meetings is to win the support of the community leadership so they will work with their respective groups to bring about more favorable opinion for school desegregation throughout the community. Examples of contacts that might be made by district administrators include: ministerial associations, Lions Club, Rotary, NAACP, Kiwanis, Boy Scout Leaders, League of Women Voters, PTA Council and local presidents, law enforcement associations, YWCA, YMCA, Business and Professional Women's Club, United Fund, Common Council, and Chamber of Commerce.

POLICY.   School administrations should make school records concerning
(B-3)   achievement test data, health information, teacher qualifications,
               and attendance available to the public.

The purpose of making public this kind of information is to allay possible
fears that student achievement decreases as a result of desegregation, or that
minority (or majority) teachers are less qualified than others. Schools dis-
seminating this information must be careful, however, not to damage the reputation of any one individual or small groups of individuals.

Suggested Techniques

1.   Coordinated Data Collection and Distribution

Release of information on student achievement, health and teacher
qualifications will bring about better community understanding and usually
increase confidence in the desegregation process. Where the faculty in a school
system has been desegregated, for example, white parents may be concerned
about the abilities of black teachers. The qualifications of black instructors
should then be published. Black parents may feel that their children will not
have an opportunity to participate fully in student activities, and pictures
and reports of intergroup activities in the desegregated school could be used to
reassure them. White parents may believe that black students have poor attendance records and that this will in some way influence white student attendance.
It has been found that black student attendance is often more regular than
that of whites and, where necessary, this information should be made available
to the public.

POLICY.   School administrations should establish and continually use
(B-4)   informal channels of communication to inform district residents
               about desegregation and about general education goals and
               problems and to listen to their views.

Informal communication is a necessary supplement to formal communication established by public meetings and media reporting. Informal communication, whether through individual conferences or social events like neighborhood
"coffees," provides both school personnel and residents the opportunity to
discuss hopes, fears and plans concerning school desegregation. Informal communications should be used extensively to encourage person-to-person contact
and discussion. Examples are given on the following page of the kinds of
activities that afford opportunities for informal association and communication
during the school desegregation process.

POLICY.   School administrators should establish, and maintain, contact with
(B-5)   both opponents and allies of school desegregation.

If school desegregation is to be effective, it is necessary for school board
members, district administrators or bi-racial advisory committee members to
answer all complaints and comments from opponents. It is also necessary to

Examples of Informal Communication
Techniques in School-Community Relations

Informal teas
Field trips and excursions
Father's nights
Informal parent group meetings with principal
Informal picnics, barbecues or box lunch dinners with parents
Open houses in the schools
Special musical programs, art or other exhibits in the schools
Athletic events
Convocations
School-sponsored parent-child camping programs
Vocational nights
Special assemblies and lectures
School plays
Teacher home visits
Weekly visiting days (invite small group of parents to school)
Home visits by school nurses
Meetings between guidance personnel, students and parents
Room mothers or teacher aides
Meetings of fraternal organizations
Parades
School-sponsored bazaars
Pre-school teacher, parent and child meetings
Special programs during National Education Week
Sermons on education delivered at various places of worship
Dedications at schools
Activities welcoming new students or teachers
School-sponsored films open to the public
Adult education programs
School-sponsored parent dances

identify community leaders who can be allies with the schools in desegregation efforts. Techniques for identifying and communicating with opponents and allies are presented below.

Suggested Techniques
1.   Identification of Allies and Opponents by Mutual Choice
       School administrators can identify and define the roles of opponents and allies by contacting key community members and tabulating the number of times that a person is identified as being a community leader and either an ally

or an opponent of school desegregation efforts. By comparing the totals, a
school official can determine the relative values of involving different individuals
in the school desegregation process.

2.   Identification of Allies Through Personal Contact

    The Director of the American Friends Service Committee's South
Carolina Community Relations Program, M. Hayes Mizell, suggests that advisory
committees make personal contact with the leadership of many community
organizations. By discussing desegregation with these groups, the advisory committee can determine where its support lies, and what issues are of genuine
concern in the community. These personal contacts can often provide the
schools with ideas that are helpful in planning and implementing school
desegregation.[1]

    Mizell also mentions goals to be achieved by a bi-racial advisory committee
identifying and communicating with opponents:

> Advisory committee identifies potential problem areas, groups, and
> personalities.
>
> Opposition groups and individuals do not feel that, because of their views,
> political affiliation, class, economic level, ideology, etc., they have been
> "written off" by the advisory committee as persons whose views are
> inconsequential.
>
> Opposition groups better understand the purpose of the advisory committee
> and the nature of the desegregation plan, and the committee is "personal-
> ized" rather than being seen as merely some tool of the Establishment.
>
> Advisory committee establishes some rapport with opposition, and com-
> munication deters hardening of positions.[2]

C. Gaining Community Participation in the School Desegregation Process

PROBLEM: A surprising number of parents and other residents have very
            little direct contact with the schools in their community.
            Although they are not normally concerned with their schools,
            school desegregation is likely to awaken their attention because
            of its communitywide social implications. However, limited
            prior experience will hinder their ability to understand both the
            meaning of desegregation and the impact it will have on the
            quality of education. Such people are likely to be suspicious of
            school desegregation, and unwilling to give it their support.

POLICY.   School administrators should attempt to actively involve as many
(C-1)   people as possible in the school desegregation process.

    The process of meaningful involvement by community members—for
example, in staffing rumor centers, assisting on school playgrounds, or chaperon-

ing field trips—often produces support for the schools and for what they are trying to accomplish. Such support is essential for the achievement of effective desegregation.

Suggested Techniques

1.   Bi-Racial Advisory Committee
     A bi-racial advisory committee to represent the community and to assist district administrators should usually be established when the decision to desegregate is made, if the decision is involuntary, or even earlier—when desegregation is first considered—if the decision is voluntary. A selection method for such a committee is described in the following paragraphs:

> "Great care must be taken in selecting and appointing members of the committee . . . many factors must be considered. Responsibility, concern for and dedication to the general welfare, sensitivity to the interest and feelings of all people—especially the least articulate and least fortunate—and prestige that is founded upon trust and confidence, are most important.
>
> "Prestige founded upon wealth, ancestry or power has little value unless the person is conversant with the problems and sensitive to the needs and feelings of both the inarticulate and the dissident.
>
> "The [committee] must be bi-racial and as representative as possible of the religious, ethnic, business, labor and civic groups in the community. Getting the broadest possible representation from the dissident or ideologically opposed elements of the community has value, but the value may be diminished if such representatives are uncompromising in pressing the interests only of their own adherents, white or Negro. It is less important that the opposing elements be represented on the [committee] than that the [committee] demonstrate that it will hear all groups and give fair consideration to all complaints, suggestions and demands, providing they are consistent with the general welfare.
>
> "The preceding statement should not be interpreted as being critical of the vigorous and uncompromising leader of a civil rights organization. Such persons play vital roles in our society. However, it is rare that such a person can function effectively in the dual roles of protest leader and as a member of an official [committee] that is trying to bridge the gulfs between the several groups within the larger community."[3]

2.   Rumor Center
     Many school districts have found rumor centers useful techniques for reducing alarm during desegregation. Such centers are generally staffed by citizen volunteers who are capable of intelligently answering inquiries about the school desegregation process and about specific actions and incidents. A short guide for establishing a rumor center is presented on the following page; the model for the description was in Greenville, South Carolina.

Guidelines for Establishing
A Rumor Center

1. Establish an Information Center in the central administrative office of the school system. Access to information and knowledge is often readily available here when required.
2. The Center should be staffed by volunteers who are identified as being allies of school desegregation. Volunteers might be solicited from churches, parent-teacher organizations, or other civic groups.
3. The Center should have special telephone numbers that are frequently publicized in the newspapers and over radio and television.
4. The Center should be staffed throughout the entire working day and on weekends. It should remain open and available for telephone or other inquiries until late in the evening (e.g., 10 p.m., 11 p.m.).
5. Volunteer staff should receive a briefing that is adequate but not so extensive that it wards off volunteers. These briefings might include such information as the following:

Details of the district's desegregation plan.

Maps and statistical data showing projected black and white enrollment for each school.

Data on the extent of bussing, if any, for black and white students for past, present and future grade structure for each school.

Details of the history of school desegregation for the particular district and for the nation.

Details of the history of relations with HEW's Office for Civil Rights and Office of Education, including litigation, involvement in administrative proceedings, etc.

Details of schools that have high dropout rates, large numbers of children from low-income families, large numbers of students with poor academic records and tested achievement levels, high and low numbers of graduating seniors going on to college, and other indicators of which schools are considered "good" and which ones are viewed as "bad".

Source: M. Hayes Mizell, *Recommendations for Action to be Taken by the Advisory Committee* (Columbia, S.C.), p. 4.

3.   Speakers Bureau

Another technique for furthering school-community relations is for the school district to make speakers available to local groups. If the district is small, key administrators should be designated to accept evening speaking engagements. If the district serves a medium-sized or large community, the public relations office of the school system or the bi-racial advisory committee should establish a speakers bureau. A conscious effort should be made to send well-advised and articulate speakers to describe the district's position on desegregation to members of community organizations.

Among the types of groups that could be contacted to offer speakers would be: church groups, fraternal organizations, unions, boards of trade, bar associations and other professional organizations, parent teacher associations, OEO-funded local groups, etc. Basic guidelines for operating a speaker's bureau are provided below.

Guidelines for Operating a Speakers Bureau

1. Request the media to inform the community of the bureau's existence.
2. Develop a list of topics for presentation or ask various local groups what specific topics on school desegregation they are particularly interested in.
3. Send formal announcements of the bureau's services to community organizations. Follow-up this announcement by making appointments with officials of the organizations to arrange speaking engagements.
4. Provide bi-racial teams. Two speakers should appear at each engagement—one black and one white. The speech should be divided into two segments so each has the opportunity to address the audience.
5. Allow an opportunity for open discussion and a question-and-answer period after each speech.
6. Attempt to have each speaking engagement covered by a newspaper reporter or other media representatives.

---

4.   Volunteer Teachers Aide Corps

Development of a voluntary teachers aide corps is an excellent means of involving parents in the classroom. For discussion of this technique, see the portion of this chapter on Teaching Techniques and Training to Achieve Effective Desegregation.

5.   Volunteer Homeroom Mothers

A variation on the teachers aide corps technique is the use of students' mothers for voluntary service in making arrangements for field trips, chaperoning activities, and performing various other supportive tasks. These so-called "homeroom mothers" are usually obtained through the parent teacher associations, which may make phone calls to parents to solicit their assistance. The roles of the parents in the schools will depend, of course, upon their own interests and the needs of the schools. Some of the activities in which homeroom mothers can be effective are:

Helping to arrange and chaperone field trips and excursions.

Helping to arrange and chaperone classroom parties (e.g., Valentine's Day, Christmas, Easter, Columbus Day, etc.).

Assisting with and chaperoning school plays and picnics.

Handling communications with parents on class activities.

Marshalling playground activities.

Serving and preparing food in the cafeteria.

Monitoring halls.

Typing or providing nursing aid if parents have these special skills.

6.   Community Forums
     The City of Portland, Oregon, has established a program of community forums as a means of advising parents of matters pertaining to school desegregation and student instruction, and as a means of eliciting parental responses. The program is described below:

> "As an attempt to insure that parent opinion would be reflected in policy regarding the instruction of students, a series of Community Forums was established. The first was held during the summer before school opened, and was followed by four others during the school year. Forum topics included the General Education program, issues of student freedom and responsibility, college entrance, and vocational education. The meetings were enthusiastically attended. The usual format was a progress report by the principal, or a presentation by guest speakers, followed by questions and discussion from the floor. Then parents usually met with the Curriculum Associate and teachers from the House [subschool] of which their children were members, for small group discussion."[4]

7.   Parent Advisory Groups
     As a result of the Community Forums discussed above, the Portland schools also established parent advisory groups, which are more limited in size. These advisory groups are closely tied to the "house" system developed in the Portland schools. Each school is divided into racially heterogeneous Houses; there are usually four such groups in a school. A description of the parent advisory groups follows:

> "The parents and teachers from each of the Houses met in a series of evening meetings, usually bi-weekly, which were arranged independently, House by House. These served as a valuable opportunity for exchange of views, conferences around specific problems, and better communication between parents and teachers. In many cases the House curriculum was directly affected by parental wishes and advice. These Parent groups supplanted the schoolwide meetings, and to a large extent also supplanted the schoolwide PTSA" (Parent, Teacher, Student Association).[5]

8. Parental Visitation Program

One high school in Portland set up a program where counsellors visited, or at least contacted by telephone, parents of students that were being transferred to the school as a result of desegregation. When visits were made to homes or arranged at a local public library, two counsellors were involved in each meeting with parents. Usually the man and woman who would be the sophomore counsellors the next year worked together, as did the two who would be the freshman counsellors. The program was conducted on an experimental basis in 1960, and it was judged successful. Most parents expressed appreciation for the school's efforts to inform them personally of the plans for their children.

9. Business Support for School-Community Activities

Local businesses may be willing to help sponsor school-community social events, such as barbecues, picnics, open house teas, etc. A supermarket may be willing to donate a limited amount of foodstuffs for such an activity. Other businesses (e.g. real estate brokers, insurance and banking institutions, or large area employers) may wish to make donations to help defray the costs of these events. Civic organizations, such as the League of Women Voters, fraternal groups, etc., should be contacted for volunteer assistance in the preparation and execution of school-community social functions.

10. Discussion Sessions in Homes

If asked, prominent citizens will often set up or host group discussions in their homes to allow school officials to talk with small groups of parents. The following techniques should be considered in establishing such a program:

> School administrators, with the assistance of the bi-racial advisory committee, should contact community leaders who support school desegregation.

> These leaders would be asked to contact other prominent individuals in the community in an attempt to arrange a meeting at a private home, where a small group of influential citizens could discuss school desegregation.

> Pamphlets of information on the benefits of desegregated education should be prepared for these gatherings.

> Superintendents, principals, teachers, law enforcement officials, speakers bureau personnel, etc., should be contacted and requested to attend and participate.

> Written invitations should be sent out to the expected participants.

POLICY.   Representative planning committees should be established at
(C-2)   various levels of the desegregation process.

Citizens, students and teachers all have a stake in the effectiveness of school desegregation. All will suffer if desegregation becomes a hostile and self-defeating process, so each of these groups should be given a formal role in the development and implementation of school desegregation. Specific planning functions of teachers and students were discussed in Chapter 3, and the roles of advisory groups are discussed elsewhere in this chapter (see Administrative Measures and Student Adaptation).

It is also possible for the community advisory group to cooperate with teachers and to give them assistance. The bi-racial advisory committee can work directly with faculty members or establish a sub-committee to do so. The goals for such an advisory group would be:

To indicate to teachers that the community supports them and is willing to provide aid in the transition period of early desegregation.

To identify specific ways in which the community can help teachers.

To encourage teachers to view the community as a resource that can be used to support and augment the process of education.

Some of the needs of teachers that could come to light as a result of this kind of communication are:

A desire for teacher aides of the opposite race to assist in classrooms during the first few weeks or months of desegregation.

A desire for information and assistance in determining the home backgrounds of new students.

A desire to work during summer months with groups of students or citizens in smoothing the transition from segregated to desegregated schools.

D. Obtaining the Cooperation of Other Public Agencies

PROBLEM: Many schools maintain an organization and structure unrelated to and relatively isolated from such other public agencies as health and law enforcement. Therefore, these schools generally do not include other agencies in their planning for school desegregation. The result is that potentially valuable assistance and support is not available or well co ordinated when it is most needed.

POLICY.   School administrators should develop a close relationship with
(D-1)   law enforcement officials prior to, and throughout, school desegregation.

The support of police officials and patrolmen can be critical in situations where school desegregation has caused racial tension. Especially in cases where mass picketing or boycotting is occurring, calm and decisive action on the part of both school officials and law enforcers is essential to relieve the tension.

Suggested Techniques

1. Joint Policy Statement
    In the early stages of school desegregation planning, a policy statement should be prepared on law enforcement procedures. Community leaders, including the mayor, should be consulted when this statement is being prepared. An example of guidelines for police executive conduct with respect to school desegregation appears on the following page. From guidelines like these, a policy statement could be prepared. Public statements on this subject should be clear and firm; and if incidents occur, law enforcement should be in accordance with the determined policy.

2. Specific Plans
    School district and police officials should develop specific action plans in anticipation of incidents. This planning must be done well in advance of opening day and take into consideration possible tension in the early months after desegregation has taken place.

POLICY.   School administrators should establish good working relation-
(D-2)   ships with social and welfare workers.

    Cooperative working arrangements between the schools and the public social and welfare workers can serve a number of purposes. One is to explain to white and middle-class parents that lower-class students will not be a health danger to their children. Another is to make arrangements so that teachers who suspect that a student may be undernourished or have physical disabilities (such as poor hearing) can contact social workers for referral for corrective action. Such contact between school personnel and the social agencies helps teachers and school administrators to understand the home environments of students. It also provides the social worker with a person capable of observing the child and possibly helping him to receive necessary medical attention.

Suggested Techniques

1. School-Community Worker Program
    Throughout the school desegregation process, it is likely that some students will be confronted with problems in the school, home and/or community. Social workers can play critical roles in offering help to these students. A School-Community Worker Program undertaken in a Colorado public school system with Title I funds is described on a following page.

2. Family Helper Centers
    The city of Lansing, Michigan currently uses a program, funded through the state, that provides in-home assistance for disadvantaged families so that children

Example of Guidelines for Police Conduct
Related to School Desegregation

1. It is the obligation of the law enforcement officer to lawfully protect life and property, peace and order in his community. He should extend to all a consistent interpretation of the law and equal treatment and protection under the law. Every person acting in the community has an obligation to assist in this function and to shape his conduct so as to minimize unnecessary interference with the achievement of this obligation.

2. In matters relating to desegregation, the police executive should assert leadership towards, and accept responsibility for, a consistent and proper policy and its execution.

3. The police executive should attempt to maintain full and honest communication with the leaders of organizations acting for or against segregation in his community. Complaints of improper police conduct from any group should be freely accepted and fully investigated.

4. Non-violent demonstrators should be expected to establish communication with law enforcement to determine what are the pertinent laws and administrative regulations and to clearly state their immediate anticipated course of action. They should follow agreements mutually made with the police and at least those police regulations which would be considered reasonable for any group engaging in a similar though not desegregation related activity.

5. Mass demonstrations have long been held as subject to reasonable police regulation. When there is rejection of such regulation, as would be considered proper for any other group using the same roadways, it should be recognized that there is an element of illegality not present in many desegregation tactics which may or may not be illegal on other grounds.

6. The public and public information media should be given the maximum possible information about desegregation related events with particular emphasis on clarifying police policy and action.

7. Police personnel should be of high quality, well trained, adequately directed and supervised strictly to enable them to carry out actions consistent with the general provisions previously enumerated.

8. Police executives should—within the bounds of proper conduct—cooperate with lawful and reputable agencies or institutions working to maintain or establish the peace of the community and should expect similar cooperation in return.

9. Unlawful force or violence by any person or group is seriously prejudicial to the welfare of the community and the professional reputation of its law enforcement agency. It should be clearly and unequivocally forbidden, and if it does arise, met with all proper force.

Source: Southern Regional Council, *Statement of Recommended Police Policy Resulting from the New York University Graduate School of Public Administration Conference on "The Challenge of Desegregation for the American Police Executive,"* (Atlanta, Georgia, 1962), pp. 1-2.

Example of School-Community
Worker Program

This Title I effort was initiated in the Spring of 1968 with the assignment of a school-community worker to South Jr. High School. The following fall, a second worker was assigned to West Jr. High School. The program was further expanded in the Spring of 1969 with a third worker assuming duties at Lowell Elementary School. In December 1970 a full-time worker and a half-time worker were assigned to the Palmer area.

The workers seek to assist children experiencing problems at school, at home, or in the community. They have been selected on the basis of their interest in and concern for youngsters, their ability to work well with people, and their knowledge of the area which they serve. These qualifications allow them to approach all problems, social, academic, or health, with special understanding. The workers are able to solve many problems by improving communication and cooperation between home and school and by enlisting aid, when necessary, from those community agencies best equipped to assist with a particular problem. The workers also use their knowledge of home, school and community in a preventive role, to meet needs before problems develop.

Source: Board of Education, *Facts About ESEA Title I Programs* (Colorado Springs, Colorado), pp. 1–2.

can go to school and learn. Medical, dental and psychological examination and treatment are available for entire families. An experimental project under this grant provides teachers for very disturbed students in secondary schools.

3.   Federal and State Aid Programs

Many federal, state and foundation programs can be used by school systems undergoing desegregation. Title I funds are available, for example, for special educational programs for disadvantaged students. An example is a reading improvement project that annually assists 1,200 to 1,500 first to third grade students in Cleveland schools. Compensatory education programs in some areas have provided supplemental nutrition to disadvantaged children.

By working with social agencies, school districts can identify community problems that affect the learning ability of students and then develop compensatory programs. All avenues should be examined for funding of projects to aid students from disadvantaged homes.

Notes

1. M. Hayes Mizell, *Recommendations to be Taken by the Advisory Committee* (Columbia, S.C.), p. 1.

2. *Ibid.*, p. 2.
3. George Shermer, *Guidelines: A Manual for Bi-Racial Committees* (Anti-Defamation League of B'nai B'rith), p. 23.
4. John Adams High School, *First Year Report, 1969–70* (Portland, Oregon, 1970), p. 12.
5. *Ibid.*, p. 13.

Bibliography

American Association of School Administrators. *Public Relations for America's Schools.* Twenty-Eighth Yearbook. Washington, D.C.: National Education Association, 1950.

Bash, James H. and Thomas J. Morris. *Utilizing Community Resources to Implement School Desegregation.* Bloomington, Indiana: Phi Delta Kappa, Winter 1967–68.

Campbell, Roald F. and John A. Ramseyer. *The Dynamics of School-Community Relationships.* Boston: Allyn and Bacon, 1955.

Carter, Richard F. and William R. Odell. *The Structure and Process of School-Community Relations: A Summary.* Institute for Communication Research and School of Education, Stanford University, 1966.

Crain, Robert L. *The Politics of School Desegregation: Comparative Case Studies of Community Structure and Policy Making.* Chicago: Aldine Publishing Company, 1968.

Department of Elementary School Principals. *Parents and the Schools.* Thirty-Sixth Yearbook. Washington, D.C.: National Education Association, September 1957.

Fine, Benjamin. *Educational Publicity.* New York: Harper and Row, 1951.

Fisher, Paul L. and Ralph L. Lowenstein. *Race and the News Media.* Washington, D.C.: Anti-Defamation League of B'nai B'rith, 1967.

Fusco, Gene C. *Improving Your School-Community Relations Program.* Englewood Cliffs, New Jersey: Prentice-Hall, Inc., 1967.

——. *Citizens Committees for Better Schools.* Office of Education—20065. Washington, D.C.: U.S. Government Printing Office, 1964.

Gittell, Marilyn and T. Edward Hollander. *Six Urban School Districts: A Comparative Study of Institutional Response.* New York: Frederick A. Praeger, 1968.

Grinnell, J.E. and Raymond Young. *The School and the Community.* New York: The Ronald Press Company, 1955.

Hamlin, Herbert M. *Citizen Committees in the Public Schools.* Danville, Illinois: Interstate Printers and Publishers, Inc., 1952.

Hymes, James L., Jr. *Effective Home-School Relations.* New York: Prentice-Hall, Inc., 1953.

Kindred, Leslie. *School Public Relations.* Englewood Cliffs, New Jersey: Prentice-Hall, Inc., 1957.

——. *How To Tell The School Story.* Englewood Cliffs, New Jersey: Prentice-Hall, Inc., 1960.

Levin, Henry M., ed. *Community Control of Schools.* Washington, D.C.: The Brookings Institution, 1970.

McCloskey, Gordon. *Education and Public Understanding.* New York: Harper and Brothers, 1959.

The National Advisory Commission on Civil Disorders. *Report of the National Advisory Commission on Civil Disorders.* Washington, D.C.: U.S. Government Printing Office, 1968.

National Education Association. "A Primer in Publicity," *Public Relations Bookshelf Series.* PR Bookshelf No. 6. Washington, D.C.: N.E.A., 1969.

——. "Tips for the Public Relations Chairman," *Public Relations Bookshelf Series.* PR Bookshelf No. 2. Washington, D.C.: N.E.A., 1969.

——. "Community Decision-Making," *Public Relations Bookshelf Series.* PR Bookshelf No. 10. Washington, D.C.: N.E.A., 1969.

——. "Press, Radio, and TV Tips," *Public Relations Bookshelf Series.* PR Bookshelf No. 9. Washington, D.C.: N.E.A., 1969.

——. "Publishing a Newsletter," *Public Relations Bookshelf Series.* PR Bookshelf No. 5. Washington, D.C.: N.E.A., 1969.

Schermer, George. *Guidelines: A Manual for Bi-Racial Committees.* Washington, D.C.: Anti-Defamation League of B'nai B'rith, 1964.

Stearns, Harry. *Community Relations and the Public Schools.* Englewood Cliffs, New Jersey: Prentice-Hall, Inc., 1955.

Sumption, Merle R. and Yvonne Engstrom. *School-Community Relations: A New Approach.* New York: McGraw-Hill Book Company, 1966.

Thayer, V.T. and Martin Levit. *The Role of the School in American Society.* 2nd ed. New York: Dodd, Mead and Co., 1969.

**Student Adaptation to Achieve Effective
Desegregation**

The School's Responsibility for the Student

Schools attempt to reach their objectives primarily by conveying knowledge
and developing academic skills. However, schools must also accept some responsibility for the student's personality development and psychological adjustment.
If students are to learn to function in society, they need to experience working
and playing in group situations. To realize their potentials, they must be allowed
to develop healthy personalities, be encouraged to practice social skills and be
exposed to a wide variety of opportunities and experiences. To be prepared for
an adult vocational role, students must acquire adequate social experience as
well as academic expertise.

Educators have learned that the manner in which schools carry out their
academic program has a profound effect on the mental hygiene of students.
There are differing points of view on the extent of the school's responsibility in
this area. But there is agreement on the fact that if students are required by law
to attend school, then they have a right to an experience that is not psychologically damaging. Also, because public schools must accept and attempt to
educate all children under sixteen years of age (the state of Mississippi is the
only state that does not require compulsory attendance to age sixteen), they
must develop ways of coping with students whose behavior and personality
adjustment interfere with their own and other students' ability to learn.

Although the goals of education are expressed in many ways, most people
would agree that they include:

Teaching children to function effectively in a democratic society.
Helping every individual realize his or her maximum potential.
Preparing students for adult social and occupational roles.

Basic Problems Caused or Aggravated by Desegregation.   Many schools are
Many schools are limited in their ability to meet ideal educational goals.
As a result, desegregation tends to exaggerate old problems and create new ones.
An individual cannot realize his full potential when his social status in the
community demonstrates to him that he will not be allowed to take part in
broader society and reap its rewards. Nor can students who receive only college
preparatory educations be prepared for all, or even most, occupational roles.

The purpose of effective desegregation is not merely to achieve physical
redistribution of students in the schools. Rather, the purpose is to improve
the quality of education for all students by providing an opportunity for them
to learn about, and interact with, people who are often different from themselves. If resegregation occurs and if prejudiced treatment continues, many
students will experience psychological damage. Some may even be provoked to

misbehave or protest. If they are unable to participate fully in school activities, they will miss group experiences that are important to personality development and acquisition of social skills. The mere fact that such a great change occurs creates new adjustment and behavior problems. One of the greatest challenges is the need to teach individuals at their own instructional levels while keeping grouping and tracking at a minimum to allow full social interaction.

Basic Objectives in Desegregation to Remedy These Problems

1. Schools should establish fair and democratic school policies. In carrying them out, they should be sure students perceive them as being fair and democratic. This includes providing written rules so students know exactly what their rights and responsibilities are.
2. Schools should modify the curriculum to improve the teaching of all the skills and knowledge required for good citizenship.
3. Schools should provide opportunities for students to operate in democratic groups.
4. Students should be given opportunities to participate in making decisions that affect them, particularly those involving sensitive issues in desegregation.
5. School officials and teachers should understand the relationship between students' participation in activities and their self-images, achievement, and ability to interact socially.
6. Schools should encourage maximum participation in student activities.
7. Schools should modify their curricula and teaching techniques to give special attention to the following conditions concerning student motivation:

> Children have a need for genuine success.
>
> Students need to save face in front of their peers.
>
> Students need evaluation procedures that are realistic but not too discouraging.
>
> Students need learning tasks that are relevant to their present lives and their future aspirations.
>
> Students need to be taught on their own grade levels.
>
> Students need to be spared the frustration of performing tasks that are too difficult.
>
> Students want to avoid boredom.
>
> Minority-group students need to maintain their identities.

8. When desegregation occurs, schools should start performing some unique guidance services, and perform the common ones more meticulously.
9. Schools should consider substituting the term "behavior control" for "discipline," and treating it as a positive and preventative function of the school.
10. Schools should modify old approaches to behavior control and group management.

Specific Problems, Policies and Techniques

A. Forming Democratic School Structures and Policies

PROBLEM: Students basically believe in American democracy; so they expect
            the equality and opportunity they hear about to be provided
            for them in the total school situation. Many students feel that a
            good education is the only way to achieve dignity and equality
            for themselvčs and their race. When a student's last hope—
            education—offers nothing but frustration and failure, he becomes
            bitter and discouraged. Sheviakov and Redl say, "Persons who
            are dealt with in disparaging or humiliating ways . . . fail to
            develop the cooperative skills needed to realize ideals of our
            democracy."[1]

Prejudicial feelings and actions by fellow students and teachers are diffucult
to legislate or control. Nevertheless, the structures and policies of educational
institutions that are run by the government can and must be fair and democratic.
The basic structure of the educational system will reflect the true intent of the
school system: either to be fair and impartial, or to continue prejudicial treatment of a minority group.

POLICY.   Schools should establish fair, democratic policies. In carrying out
  (A-1)   those policies, they should be sure students can perceive them
            as being both fair and democratic.

Suggested Techniques

1. Fair Bussing Practices
    Bussing was used as a tool to segregate students; so it symbolizes unfair or
prejudicial treatment. Schools should avoid using illogical bussing patterns, with
black students traveling farther and/or at less convenient times (very early in
the morning or very late in the day), or with more blacks than whites being
bussed.

    Redistribution of students in schools should reflect common sense and
objectivity. For example, all the brightest black students should not be bussed a
long distance to provide token integration at the most fashionable white
school.

2. Use of Formerly Black Schools
    When possible, formerly all-black schools should be used when a district is
desegregated. If such facilities are closed, the implication is that, though they
were adequate for blacks, they are not suitable for whites. Fumigating or
excessively remodeling formerly black schools has the same effect.

3.   Written, Fair Rules
Consistency and fairness will be assured if students are provided with written information on attendance regulations, dress codes, disciplinary procedures and the like. These policies should be explicit enough to avoid misinterpretation by students or teachers. Subtly discriminatory rules should be avoided (e.g., dress codes that prevent students from wearing distinctive hair styles or clothing). All established regulations should be enforced fairly and consistently so that students clearly understand what is allowed and not allowed.

4.   Democratic Representation
Insofar as possible, students should be allowed to experience representation and self-determination. These are vital aspects of democracy that can be inculcated in the schools. On the high school level, student participation in desegregation planning will serve this purpose, so long as student recommendations are heeded. It should be remembered that students will not be satisfied with partial or ineffectual representation.

5.   Avoidance of Resegregation
Even though some are considered to be educationally sound, techniques that resegregate should be avoided. These include tracking, ability grouping, excessive fees for equipment and uniforms for school activities, grade average requirements for participation in extracurricular groups, etc.

6.   New Grading System
In an effort to resolve the problem that students in separate schools have been operating under different academic standards, desegregated school systems can institute new systems of testing, grading and promoting students. This could involve a complete change in the marking system—for example, A, B, C, D changed to Good, Satisfactory and Unsatisfactory. Or a new layout could be devised for report cards to include instructional levels, effort and improvement.
If some change is not introduced, higher standards at a new school might be viewed as prejudicial to minority-group students. Lower standards, on the other hand, might be interpreted as proof that the quality of education is lowered by the desegregation process.

7.   Fair Faculty and Staff Desegregation
The effects upon students should be considered in the redistribution, demotion and promotion of faculty and staff members. Observance of equal opportunity employment practices will demonstrate to students that members of all races, religions and nationalities can work together at all types of jobs.

B. Teaching Skills and Knowledge Required for Good Citizenship

PROBLEM: The school board is responsible for creating a democratic framework for the process of education, but the responsibility of
the school extends far beyond this. Schools are entrusted with
the task of teaching all of the academic and social skills, as
well as the knowledge, required for good citizenship. Some
schools have neglected to teach these skills completely or
accurately.

In order to prepare students for effective citizenship, schools should
provide: reading skills that will enable students to become accurately informed;
ability to think critically so that they can make wise decisions and fully exercise
the use of their votes; knowledge of governmental structures; and appreciation
of historical perspective, so as to promote patriotism and understanding. In
compliance with the Supreme Court ruling on desegregation, schools should
accept the responsibility of teaching students to appreciate and respect people
of different ethnic and religious backgrounds.

POLICY.   Schools should modify their curricula to improve the teaching of
 (B-1)   skills and knowledge required for good citizenship.

Techniques for achieving this policy are discussed in the section of this
chapter on Curriculum Adaptation. Nonetheless, key points can be cited here.

1. Students should be taught to respect the opinions of others and also to
    feel confident that they will not be rejected or ridiculed for expressing
    opinions that vary from those of their teachers or peers.
2. Facts and logical thought processes should be stressed in the classroom, but
    students should also be shown that there are often logical arguments for
    conflicting points of view.
3. Legal rights and responsibilities should be conveyed to students, with special
    attention given to those rights that are commonly denied passively because
    information is withheld or selectively disseminated.
4. Curricula should include material on minority and ethnic cultures and
    contributions to society made by members of such groups.
5. Compensatory and remedial education should be provided for disadvantaged
    students.

C. Practice of Democracy in All Phases of School Life

PROBLEM: The academic teaching of democracy achieves meaning only when
its principles are practiced regularly by the administration,
teachers and students. Many schools have used autocratic or
authoritarian methods to control students. As a result, a large
number of students lack the self-discipline and social skills

required for successful participation in democratically functioning groups.

The importance of allowing students to practice democracy in school is expressed by Sheviakov and Redl in the following way:

> Two important insights are back of this insistence that every member of a democracy has a part to play in arriving at decisions which affect him. One emerges from our experience that group decisions are often more trustworthy than individual decisions because the base of judgment and intelligence is broadened. Another principle is that as we share in making choices we learn to accept a responsible part in carrying out decisions or in changing them if they prove wrong. As a prelude to citizenship, children too must have practice making decisions of meaning to them. Responsible citizens of a democracy cannot be developed through living childhood years in small autocracies at home and school.[2]

Many children have experienced small autocracies at home and school. In general, lower-class parents are more authoritarian and use more corporal punishment than those in the middle class. The lower-class Negro child, in particular, experiences strict authoritarian control in the home.[3] In the South this authoritarianism in the home is often reinforced at school; Northern schools more often emphasize self-discipline. Many students, therefore, are not experienced in democratic decision-making.

POLICY.   Schools should provide opportunities for students to operate in
(C-1)   democratic groups.

If students are to be encouraged to participate in democratic groups, principals and teachers will need guidance and suggestions on developing techniques that emphasize democratic leadership. Also, they will need a basic understanding of the ways in which groups function. In this regard, the studies of Lewin, Lippitt and White [4] are useful. After studying three types of group leadership, they reported the following experiences:

Autocratic Leadership—The autocratic leader told group members exactly what to do, step by step, without giving a reason or explaining how their work fit into a total picture. He exerted rigid control. The group was productive, but when the leader was absent the group broke down; work stopped; and behavior became hostile and aggressive and there was a great deal of scapegoating.

Laissez-faire Leadership—The leader told group members what task was to be done and sat back to watch without offering help or participating. The members soon lost interest and turned to aimless non-constructive activity, whether the leader was absent or present.

Democratic Leadership—The leader explained the general plan, accepted suggestions, and led group members in deciding upon the steps to be taken. The quality and quantity of the work was high, and interest and constructive behavior continued in the absence of the leader.

The above findings indicate that democratic leadership most satisfactorily produces constructive group participation, at the same time as instilling capabilities of self government in students. Similar results have been produced in research by other behavioral scientists.

If school administrators decide that emphasis should be placed on democratic group leadership, assistance must be given to teachers in understanding and carrying out the concept. This can be accomplished through in-service training sessions, which are discussed in the section of this chapter on Teaching Techniques and Training. Studies show that changing from autocratic to democratic leadership is difficult for all persons involved,[5] so the introduction of new techniques should be carefully planned and phased.

Strong emphasis on democratic group leadership in a school that has previously relied on autocratic methods should be accompanied by positive publicity directed toward parents and the community in general. When not fully understood, use of democratic techniques is often labeled "undisciplined," and the allegation is made that students are "running the school." Administrators should stress the fact that democratic leadership *is* leadership. Work is accomplished and order is maintained, but the forces behind student behavior are internal ones—meaningful goals, pride in work, and responsibility to the group. Strong internal forces of these types are extremely important to students once they leave school and no longer have teachers available to lead them.

POLICY.   Students should be allowed to participate in making decisions
(C-2)   on school policies that affect them, particularly those involving
              sensitive issues in desegregation.

Students both need and desire to participate in decision-making that directly affects them. They are capable of understanding limits determined by laws, lack of funds, safety, and so forth. School administrators should identify the decisions and responsibilities that appropriately fall to the student body and then should encourage participation in policy determination and execution.

Suggested Techniques

1.   Student Desegregation Planning

As discussed in Chapter 3, students should be included in early planning for school desegregation and in subsequent reviews of progress. The general areas suitable for initial student consideration include: planning student government in desegregated schools, planning opening day procedures, making curriculum recommendations, proposing extracurricular activities, and preparing a ballot for choosing new school colors, team names, etc. A more specific list has been compiled from the literature on school desegregation and from the authors' interviews in ten school districts. Particular schools have encouraged student involvement in the following subjects and activities:

Dress codes.

Types of clubs, goals of clubs, and requirements for membership.

Social activities, such as school dances and picnics.

Student advisory committees on discipline.

Welcoming committees for new students.

Committees for improving human relations.

Committees to improve communications between teachers and students.

Commencement exercises.

Tutoring.

Newspapers.

Monitors.

Recess activities.

Choice of school colors, team names, new uniforms, yearbook and news-paper names.

Writing a new alma mater.

Making new school cheers to represent the whole student body.

Creating fair procedures for selecting queens, cheerleaders, student council, and class officers.

Analyzing and recommending curriculum needs and changes.

2. Guidelines on Sensitive Issues

Student involvement can be extremely important in resolving some of the very sensitive issues in desegregation. This includes such subjects as cheerleading, queen selection, class plays and student government. If bi-racial student committees representing merging schools can make or influence decisions on these subjects, the total student body will be more willing to accept and follow the established policies.

A group of students in North Carolina produced a detailed set of guidelines for student involvement in desegregation. With modification, these policies could be adopted by other desegregating districts. Excerpts from the portion of the guidelines dealing with especially sensitive issues are presented on the following pages.

D. Improvement of Self-Images, Achievement and Interaction Through Student Activities

PROBLEM: In the desegregated school, many students do not participate in activities because of limited access or interest. Yet student activities can have a great impact on self-images, achievement,

Example of Student Guidelines on
Sensitive Issues in School Desegregation

Cheerleaders—Cheerleader selection has been and will continue to be a potential trouble spot in high school. Selection procedures must be fair to all students, and justly allow cheerleaders to serve as leaders of all students. Hence, the following policy is recommended in cheerleader selection:

A.   Cheerleaders should be selected not elected. The position of cheerleader, like that of the football player, should be one which is gained by ability, not popularity. Judgment should be made upon the characteristics necessary to being a cheerleader: poise, leadership, personality, physical ability to do cheers well, coordination, creativity, and ability to work well with other girls and with large crowds.

B.   No grade requirements, activities records, or conduct requirements should be made of any prospective cheerleader. (After a student is selected to the squad, perhaps she should be required to maintain the same academic standing that students on athletic squads must hold—the passing of three academic subjects.) By eliminating these requirements before selection is made, any and all students may try out for the squad. Thus, more interest will be created, more students will be involved in tryouts, and less dissatisfaction will occur because certain students were "discriminated" against.

C.   The judging panel should be made up of impartial people, preferably from outside the school staff. The panel should represent fairly all races and cultural groups. Selection of panel members should be based on ability to judge cheerleading styles, judge personality and leadership, and to be fair in appraising all strong and weak points of each student trying out for the squad.

D.   Judgment should be made on merit; hence, the use of a scoring sheet is highly recommended. This sheet should allow each judge to score independently each student on several different categories (see I.-A. of this group of recommendations) with points being used in the manner of: five—excellent, four—good, three—satisfactory, two and one—unsatisfactory. In this manner the selection will be based on all students trying out, with only the tabulation picking the final winners. Tabulation should be done by an impartial person, witnessed by students. (Tabulator should not be a student nor one of the judges.)

E.   Cheers used for selection proceedings should be truly reflective of all cheers liked in the school. Differences between white and black cheers do exist, as do differences for other cultural groups. Utilization of all types of cheers will eliminate any subtle discrimination.

F.   Tryouts should be well announced to all students, with area for tryouts and selection procedure outlined well in advance of opening tryouts.

*Homecoming Courts—May Queens—Christmas Queens—*Beauty contests should be constructed so as to give all students a fair and representative chance at selection. The following procedure may be utilized as one method of selection:

A.   Allow any club, athletic team, homeroom, or individual to sponsor a girl for the crown. No standards as to academic standing or conduct record should be made of any girl, and "black-balling" by any teacher or student, individual or group, is highly discouraged.

B.   Selection should be done by popular vote, with plurality serving as the deciding vote, rather than by majority.

NOTE: No selection of queens or other beauty emblems can ever be done fairly until all students recognize the worth and dignity of all their fellow students. Continuation of beauty being defined as the "fair young maid with waxen hair and sky-blue eyes" will only lead to further difficulties. Encourage girls of all races and ethnic groups to be sponsored for the crown.

*Superlatives—*Superlatives are generally traditions carried over from the day of small schools from one community only. However, in a day of consolidation and enlargement, superlatives are not the same commodity as before. Today few students really emerge as "Best All Around" or "Best Looking." In addition, such titles as "Best Dressed" emphasize wealth rather than personality. Superlatives should be expanded with more students involved. Or, superlatives should be dropped all together, with selection of more students to such groups as the National Honor Society or a "Who's Who" in the school.

The main thought behind any honor is to acknowledge those students who are performing up to or beyond their own capabilities. Serious consideration should be given to the concept that "Every student in my school will succeed and be acknowledged for his success this year." With greater involvement and recognition for achievement, even of a minor nature, students take greater interest and pride in their school. "Involvement breeds involvement" is quite true, and with greater student involvement the educational process will surely improve. Though not a business, school functions much like any enterprise: it is only as productive as each of its members turns out to be.

Source: Task Force on Student Involvement, *Student Involvement: A Bridge to Total Education* (Raleigh, North Carolina: State Department of Public Instruction, August 1969), pp. 9–10.

---

and skills gained through interaction. Without explicit policies, this impact may be negative rather than positive.

POLICY.   School officials and teachers should understand the relationship
(D-1)   between participation in school activities and students' self-
                  images, achievement and social interaction.

Everyone has an image or concept of himself as a unique person, psychologically and physically. The people and experiences in a child's life tell him wha⁺

he is: his successes and failures and other people's response and labels are incorporated into his self-image. The child then lives out this image. A student with a good self-image is more likely to be successful and to be better behaved than a student with a poor one.[6]

Black students have unique problems with their self-images, as a result of segregation and alienation from society. These problems include feelings of inferiority, conflict and resentment; hostility towards self and whites; poor self-respect; poor personality development; and others.[7] Through desegregation, the schools are given the opportunity of changing these undesirable self-images.

Participation in extra curricular activities can have a profound effect on the self-image of a student and can be influential in establishing peer group social relations. Student participation in activities beyond the classroom can affect the self-image in the following ways:

Positive	Negative
1. Provide status.	1. Deny or lower status by exclusion.
2. Raise status of one's race.	2. Deny status of one's race by exclusion.
3. Provide opportunity for achievement and recognition.	3. Deny opportunity for achievement and recognition.
4. Provide peer group acceptance.	4. Provide peer group rejection.
5. Label one "popular", "star", "athlete", "beautiful", etc.	5. Label one "unpopular", not good enough", "a nobody", etc.
6. Develop skills and talents.	6. Deny opportunity for development of skills and talents.
7. Provide opportunity for success.	7. Give proof of failure.
8. Provide realistic self-image through fair competition.	8. Provide unrealistic self-image through preferential or prejudicial treatment.

There are some indications that involvement in student activities increases interest in the total school program and results in raising achievement and lowering drop-out rates.[8] Some students feel so alienated from school when excluded from activities that they lose all interest and achievement suffers.[9] There are also indications that social interaction of minority-group students with the rest of the student body is the critical factor leading to improved achievement among minority students in the desegregated school.

Student activities have a potential for either increasing positive interracial contact among students or creating racial tension and cleavage. Gains in interracial contact will only be made in proportion to the quality of the contact experience.[10] Some activities provide positive interracial contact among students, while others almost always lead to hostility. After illiciting student opinion on this subject, H.L. Winecoff prepared the following list indicating the activities considered most acceptable and least acceptable for interracial contact:[11]

Acceptable	Unacceptable
Sports	Home and slumber parties
Interest clubs	Dances and school socials
Student paper	Cheerleaders and majorettes
Service clubs, student government	Dramatic presentations (lead roles)

The literature and interviews with school staffs and students indicate that sports provide the most acceptable and positive interracial activity. They often lead to other interracial activities, such as parties, as well. With the exception of the home and slumber parties, the unacceptable activities of Winecoff's chart relate to high status positions in the schools, to which many students aspire. Selection procedures for these activities and racial composition of the participating groups must be given special consideration in desegregated schools, or racial cleavage will result. Many students have expressed bitterness over unfair selection or lack of representation of one race in such key activities in indivudual schools.

Although there are many indications that a positive correlation exists between participation and achievement, there is nothing to indicate that increased participation would lead to striking improvements in the achievement of a total student body. On the other hand, participation in and access to activities can have great impact on the self-images of students and the extent of true social interaction that occurs. If handled poorly and restricted to one race, activities can be damaging. If handled well, they can play a positive role in the process of education and in racial interaction.

POLICY.   Schools should encourage maximum participation in student
  (D-2)   activities under a variety of circumstances.

Suggested Techniques.   A list of techniques that could be used to encourage student participation in activities follows. The techniques are grouped by particular circumstances that can affect the degree and quality of participation likely to occur in a school. Information for this list was gathered from both literature and interviews.

Circumstances	Techniques
1. The smaller the proportion of minority students in the school, the smaller the degree of their participation.	1. If possible, create a racial composition that will provide large enough numbers of minority students to allow them to have some influence,

status, peer support and
confidence.

2. There is often little or no participation
by minority students when selection for
an activity is based upon a popular vote.

2. Eliminate the popular vote
whenever possible.

Select rather than elect
cheerleaders, pep squad,
and majorettes.

Have clubs nominate
queen candidates with
final selection made by an
inter racial, impartial
group.

Choose student council
representatives by wards
or districts where they
live. If housing is segregated by socio-economic
level and race, this will
guarantee better representation.

For the first year, choose
student officers the pre-
ceding June at the two
merging schools. Have
them work together or al-
ternate for specific time
periods.

3. Regardless of racial mix, there is more
participation when the student body is
smaller. A desegregation plan involving
the merger of two schools to create one large
school will tend to decrease participation
of all students.

3. Divide the large school
into one or two smaller
units, each with its own
activities.

Use the class divisions and
have more activities con-
ducted within the class
groups. A large school
might go so far as to have

a cheerleading squad for each grade level, while a smaller one might add junior varsity activities.

In a large school, communication regarding tryouts, sign-ups, and meetings must be more formal, using school newspapers, posters, and public address systems for announcements.

Active recruiting for membership should be done each semester. An assembly program is good for this.

Organizations should have opportunities throughout the year to show the student body what they do or achieve. Assemblies, bulletin boards, demonstrations and displays can be used for this purpose.

4. Academically poor students who might be able to achieve success or status through student activities are often prevented from participating because of grade average requirements.

4. Eliminate or lower the grade average requirement.

When grade requirements are regulated by the state, there should be some consideration for the students of a desegregating school.

If many students get lower grades in a new school because of greater competition, higher standards, or problems in adapting, allow them to participate based upon marks earned the previous year at their former school.

5. When desegregation makes one large school from two or more schools, there are more students competing for the available high status positions so many will not be allowed to participate.

5. Expand sports program to increase available positions.

Popularize existing sports to raise their status value.

Expand and diversify the activities program so it will have a better chance of offering something for everyone.

Work to make all activities more interesting and attractive.

Use student records and questionnaires to determine interests in activities.

6. Minority students may feel intimidated in the new school situation and hesitate to try out for activities.

6. Recruit actively for membership.

Ask official or unofficial student leaders to encourage participation.

Coaches should contact athletes from all contributing schools prior to opening day and invite them to join the teams.

Make a policy that anyone who tries out or signs up is automatically accepted whenever this is possible.

Make information of all activities available to everyone. A handbook is good for this.

7. Different schools may have stressed different activities and developed different skills among students. Students should have an opportunity to continue in the activities they value, and to demonstrate their skills.

7. If a group happens to have unique skills (an outstanding choir, for example), use this to show how the group can contribute to the school.

Teachers and students from contributing schools should work out the activities program for the new school.

8. Some students may be eliminated from participation because they are unable to pay fees or purchase equipment and uniforms.

8. Eliminate the costs of participation.

If the school cannot pay such costs, it can solicit aid from people in the community to defray costs for students who need this help.

9. Some students may be unable to participate in activities because of lack of transportation.

9. Hold activities during school time so students who take buses can participate.

Have late buses for students who participate in after-school activities.

10. Some school activities have community affiliations, and some community activities have traditionally used schools for promotion and facilities. For example, the Kiwanis sponsored Key Club for honor students. Boy Scouts and 4H clubs often conduct membership drives through the school.

10. School administrators can appeal to community organizations for cooperation in promoting school integration.

School policies can prohibit the use of the school

in promoting or carrying out any prejudicial or segregated children's activities. (For example, an all-white Boy Scout troop could not have its membership applications passed out in school.)

11. Students want and need to have members of their race represented in the status activities.

11. Racial composition requirements can be specified for status activities. such as cheerleading and majorettes.

Drop activities that are not integrated to some degree.

Use fair selection practices and all other techniques mentioned above.

12. Students and parents feel it is unacceptable to have lead roles in school plays given to students of different races when there is any sort of male-female relationship in the plot. Students are chosen for parts on the basis of race, not ability.

12. Choose plays to be produced in school very carefully so there are no racial overtones and so that there are a number of lead roles.

The use of a set of skits rather than one long play will increase the number of roles and reduce emphasis upon the traditional leading role.

13. Extracurricular activities can be used to develop exceptional talents and abilities among students. A school that produces a star of some sort develops pride and morale, and increases community support.

13. In the lower grades, art, physical education and music teachers should try to spot those with ability and encourage and prepare them to participate

when they get into upper grades.

Recruit good coaches in sports who will work for getting scholarships in these sports.

Take groups on field trips to see professionals in action. (For example, take the drama club to see a play.)

14. Extracurricular activities are going to have some impact on the self-images of students.

14. Use all techniques to increase participation in all activities and to improve access to high status activities.

Provide activity groups with adult leadership. This may require special training for the teachers involved or the use of a full-time activities coordinator.

Encourage and allow groups to make concrete and obvious contributions to the school and receive recognition for their achievements.

(The audio-visual club can do the lighting for a drama club play. The art club can put on an art show, make scenery, and provide posters. The sewing club can put on a fashion show. The auto mechanics club can change oil in teachers' cars.)

Conduct projects that can have some impact on the community. (Science club working on pollution, future teachers club conducting a tutoring program, etc.)

Work on projects that will be successful and avoid those that are likely to fail.

15. Cohesiveness and quality of the group experience is better when the group has a meaningful task and everyone is able to contribute to the achievement of that task.

15. Use suggestions cited above in choosing meaningful group tasks.

Use a democratic style of group leadership and have group members choose their projects.

The adult leader or advisor can help everyone have a chance to participate and contribute his ideas. Sometimes he can do this by helping the student leader of the group to learn better techniques of leadership.

E. Use of Curriculum to Improve Student Behavior, Adjustment and Achievement

PROBLEM: "Desegregation will bring to the school a student body with greatly varying educational and vocational aspirations and abilities." [12] Providing for individual differences has always been a responsibility of the school, but it becomes more important in the newly desegregated school because dissatisfaction with the learning process frequently leads to behavior problems.[13] Schools' traditional techniques for handling individual differences in children—tracking and ability grouping—tend to limit social interaction, which is critical to effective desegregation.

POLICY.   Modify the curriculum and teaching techniques.
(E-1)

Techniques for achieving this policy are discussed in the sections of this chapter on Curriculum Adaptation and Teaching Techniques and Training. In considering use of techniques, however, special attention should be given to the following points:

Children's need for genuine success.

Students need to be taught on their own grade levels.

Students need to be spared the frustration of redoing difficult tasks.

Students want to avoid boredom.

Students need learning tasks that are relevant to their present lives and future aspirations.

Students need evaluation procedures that are realistic, but not too discouraging.

Students need to save face in front of their peers.

Minority students need to maintain their identities.

F. Use of Guidance Services to Improve Behavior, Adjustment and Achievement

PROBLEM: Guidance services may be performed by teachers, principals or specialized guidance personnel. They "should be concerned with the whole individual in his total environment and with specific needs and problems."[14] When school desegregation occurs, many aspects of the student's total environment are substantially disrupted. Students develop needs and problems that schools have not encountered before.

POLICY.   When desegregation occurs, schools should provide some additional, unique guidance services, and should perform common
(F-1)   ones more meticulously.

Suggested Techniques

1. Orientation

The mere fact that change occurs can often lead to disruptive behavior among students, but some of the effects of change can be offset by a slow transition or preparation for change. Many schools have held orientations for new students during the spring preceding the opening of the desegregated school.

Typically, groups of students are taken by bus to the new school. They attend an assembly where they are briefed by school staff, and this is followed by a question and answer period. They are usually given a tour of the building and sometimes are allowed to sit in on classes and eat in the school cafeteria. A school handbook or other written account of the school activities and rules should be available at this time as well.

At the elementary school level, parents can be invited to accompany students on the visit to the new school. This helps to reduce apprehensiveness about having young children go to an unfamiliar school at some distance from home. Joint field trips to zoos and museums have also been used to expose children to interracial experiences prior to opening day.

2.   Guidance Counsellors

Ideally, guidance counsellors familiar with student behavior and psychology should be available for conferences with students who feel that they have problems. A guidance counsellor with a sense of the emotional climate of the school and rapport with the students can identify potential problems and work to alleviate their causes. For example, after receiving several complaints about the attitudes or methods of a teacher, a counsellor might offer to work with that teacher to correct the problem. Guidance counsellors should also be available to answer teachers' questions regarding student behavior, particularly that of students not of a teacher's race.

3.   Improved Educational and Vocational Guidance

If a district's curriculum is diversified to accommodate the abilities and interests of all students, there will be a need for additional guidance counselling to help students in choosing their electives and planning for their futures. Homeroom teachers or student advisors might have to be given special training to assist with this task.

Counsellors should try to appraise students' potentials objectively, and testing should be introduced where school budgets are adequate. Because desegregation places a new emphasis on equality of opportunity, information on college requirements, student loans, scholarships and other educational opportunities should be given to everyone. No student should miss an opportunity for higher education simply because he does not know about it. Students who do not have the ability or interest for higher education should not feel that they have been prevented from making their own decisions or that information has been withheld from them.

Older students perform better in school when they can see that it will lead to success after graduation. For this reason, a good guidance counsellor might aggressively seek part-time and summer employment for students, as well as jobs for graduates. Counsellors might even go so far as to form babysitting groups for girls or to organize odd job and lawnmowing services for boys.

Guidance counsellors should be well informed on vocational job opportunities and requirements for union membership, apprenticeship programs, armed services training programs and community college courses for specialized employment preparation.

4.   Home and Community Agency Contact

Students are required to make great adjustments when school desegregation occurs, and many children who already have exceptional problems may need special help. Guidance personnel should attempt to identify special problems among students and make appropriate referrals or contacts with parents. They should look for learning disabilities, visual or auditory handicaps, emotional problems, poor health or nutrition, and family problems. Once such problems are identified, help can often be obtained from clinics, health and welfare agencies, and college departments.

5.   In-Service Teacher Training

Many teachers have only a rudimentary understanding of psychology of individual and group behavior and of characteristics of exceptional children. Their understanding of home backgrounds, values, and problems of children of another race may also be limited. Through informal group meetings in an in-service training program, guidance counsellors can provide some of the knowledge and understanding that teachers will need to be effective in the desegregated classroom.

6.   Research on Behavior, Adjustment and Achievement

In many schools, guidance personnel conduct research appropriate to their needs. This may involve comparing achievement scores before and after establishing a new reading program, determining the positive and negative effects of a particular grouping policy, and so forth. When schools desegregate, records should be kept and data compiled to determine the effectiveness of the programs and possible needs for improvement. (Such records might be useful in public relations as well.) In working out a research program, the guidance personnel might consider the following:

Conducting sociometric tests at the beginning and end of the year to determine attitude changes.

Analyzing sociometric tests to see if any particular teacher or course had a more positive effect on racial attitudes than the average.

Testing and comparing achievement data from before and after desegregation.

Using questionnaires to determine student attitudes toward activities and curriculum.

Conducting simple tests to determine changes in teacher attitudes toward children and co-workers of another race, and, if necessary, using test results to attempt to improve those attitudes.

Keeping records of behavior problems that occur and the methods used to handle them, particularly those methods that were singularly effective or ineffective.

Compiling information on teaching techniques that were particularly effective or ineffective in the newly desegregated school.

Keeping information on any incidents that were controversial in nature, so that confrontations or accusations could be handled with detailed, accurate information.

G. Maintaining Discipline in the Desegregated School

PROBLEM: Discipline problems are intensified in newly desegregated schools because students have trouble adjusting to new rules, teachers and peers. In some cases, desegregation has been a controversial issue in the community so strong emotional feelings have built up and students have seen adults set an example of complaining, protesting, and perhaps even violating the laws. At the same time, discipline takes on added significance because students, parents and community members make judgments about the success or failure of desegregation based upon the ability of the schools to maintain order and avoid protests and violence.

POLICY.   Modify traditional approaches to behavior control and group
(G-1)   management.

Discipline, or behavior control, is foremost in the minds of everyone concerned with school desegregation—administrators, teachers, parents, students and the press. Our review of the literature and interviews with school staffs and students revealed no clear method for solving this problem. Therefore, the following techniques simply offer approaches that can be taken to avoid some of the difficult situations that have arisen in districts where physical desegregation has occurred.

Suggested Techniques

1.   Provision of a Satisfactory Academic and Social Experience

Considered as behavior control, discipline can be viewed positively. All of the suggestions made thus far in this section of Chapter 4 could be used by a school district to further effective desegregation and reduce the likelihood of serious behavior problems developing. To summarize, the most important points in providing a desegregated student body with a satisfactory academic and social experience are as follows:

Fair, democratic rules and procedures to remove many causes of frustration, complaint and rebellion.

Comprehensive written rules and disciplinary procedures carried out consistently to avoid or limit prejudicial treatment, and charges of such treatment.

Student participation in planning and decision-making to induce student acceptance and observance of regulations.

Fair selection and assured access for participation in extracurricular activities to maintain morale and interest in school.

Curriculum adaptation and remedial education to give every student an opportunity for success and a meaningful academic school experience.

Guidance services to help all students adjust to desegregation, to help children with special problems, and to work toward correction of some of the health and family problems that manifest themselves in deviant behavior.

Positive social interaction among students to ease tensions and help all students feel that they belong to the school and have a responsibility for behaving in a manner that is conducive to learning.

2.   Change Student Attitudes as Well as Surface Behavior

One important issue brought out in literature and in interviews with school personnel is the question of control of surface behavior versus change of attitudes. If disruption and disorder occurr in a desegregating school, administrators are forced to control surface behavior to insure survival of all students. However, when placed under pressure to maintain order, principals and teachers often exercise control of surface behavior almost exclusively, neglecting methods that could contribute to changing student attitudes.

Obviously, a compromise is needed. When student actions are dangerous, or destructive, surface behavior must be managed quickly. However, noisy, uncooperative children in a class, for example, can be helped to change their attitudes to effect permanent, rather than temporary, improvement. To do this, a teacher must determine the cause of disruption and then act upon it. The action might be to introduce more interesting work, to give students a break from academic concentration, or to clarify the assignments or make them more relevant.

Though changing the major concern from surface behavior to underlying attitudes is one way of approaching the behavior control problem in desegregated schools, such a change is difficult for several reasons:

It has been suggested that little technical skill is needed to successfully control surface behavior. The personality of the teacher is the key factor.[15] In contrast, discovering and handling sources of problems require knowledge and skill. Some teachers whose "classroom control" has earned them success and praise will not be capable of treating the causes, and they will resist change.

Many teachers do not have the professional training necessary to understand causes of behavior and will revert to control of surface behavior when they fail at attitudinal change.

Many principals are concerned primarily with the appearance of their schools and student bodies and they insist upon tight control of surface behavior.

Working with the causes of behavior problems often requires that teachers spend more time in interviews with students, conferences with parents and formation of cooperative plans with other members of the faculty.

3.   Consistent Student Punishment
     Explicit rules should be established on the use of physical correction for misbehavior. No matter what regulations are adopted, no discrimination should be made in punishment on the basis of color, religion or national origin. Both teachers and students should fully understand the grounds for physical correction, as well as the method and degree of correction to be applied.

4.   Reduction in Corporal Punishment
     School boards should consider eliminating corporal punishment and focusing on development of internal control in students. Many children come from home and school backgrounds in which corporal punishment is used commonly. While schools should be aware of these past practices, it is incumbent upon them to structure a fair policy on the use of this form of discipline in order to reduce the number of offenses for which corporal punishment is to be administered. This policy should strongly emphasize self-discipline among students in the hope that corporal punishment may be abolished.

     Behavioral scientists view corporal punishment as a form of coercion that does not involve demonstration of the proper way to behave and allows return to the undesirable behavior when coercion is not enforced.[16] Since much of the law and order in American society depends upon self-control of citizens, it is important that schools accept responsibility for teaching self-discipline. Although physical restraint of students is sometimes necessary, behavior control need not include corporal punishment. This is demonstrated by the fact that schools teaching disadvantaged and emotionally disturbed children have found ways of dealing with exceptionally bad behavior without using corporal punishment.[17]

     When administered by an understanding teacher, physical restraint can be extremely effective. The intention is to allow the student time to gain self-control and then to talk over the cause and effect of the disruption. This form of behavior control generally requires a firm and patient instructor who is familiar with the needs of individual students. When applied conscientiously, physical restraint has a greater long-term effect on students than most corporal punishment.

In desegregated schools, use of corporal punishment can raise specific problems:

> When white teachers hit white students or black teachers hit black students for recognizable behavior deviations the punishment is usually accepted in a traditionally authoritarian district. However, allegations of prejudice can arise when white teachers hit black students or black teachers hit white students.
>
> If white teachers hesitate to hit black students for normally punishable offenses, the black students either feel the teachers are afraid of them or that they are indifferent to how the students act. The same is true of black teachers failing to discipline white students.
>
> White teachers who do hit blacks often do it in a manner that blacks do not understand. (For example, black students usually expect punishment at first offense; when that does not occur, the assumption is that the teacher is allowing the behavior. When hit the first time after the fourth offense, students do not view the punishment as fair.)
>
> There have been incidents in desegregated schools where teachers have hit students and then been hit back.

Because of the above problems, corporal punishment should only be administered in accordance with well-defined and widely distributed policies. Districts should also consider assigning corporal punishment to particular staff members and thereby removing the responsibility from classroom teachers. All such punishment could be inflicted by the principal, an assistant principal or a physical education instructor.

5.   Effective Style of Group Leadership

Redl suggests that perhaps 30 percent of students' behavior problems are related to the style of group leadership being used.[18] A problem child may function well in a "good" motivated group, and a "good" child's behavior may deteriorate in a dysfunctioning group.

As mentioned earlier, the study by Lewin, Lippitt and White indicated that autocratic group members displayed fighting, scapegoating and non-productive behavior in the absence of the leader. Other studies indicate that autocratic leadership leads to fighting among group members who compete for approval of the leader and do not feel responsibility toward one another or toward the group or its goals. This has important implications for the newly desegregated school that wants to foster social interaction.

Behavioral scientists who specialize in group dynamics use the democratic style of leadership as a technique for producing a cohesive group in which all members gain a sense of belonging and contributing to the group. Group members assist in planning their own activities and rules. They exercise self-discipline out of a desire to fulfill their responsibilities to the group and to help achieve group goals. A great deal of knowledge and skill is required to develop a cohesive "group" out of students gathered together in a newly desegregated classroom, but administrative emphasis should be placed on a form of leadership conducive to positive social interaction and not to one that tends to lead to hostility and fighting. Ideally, a desegregating school district would hire a consultant who is a specialist in group dynamics to give intensive training to principals and supervisors and provide in-service training for teachers.

Notes

1. George V. Sheviakov and Fritz Redl, *Discipline for Today's Children and Youth* (Washington, D.C.: National Education Association, 1956), p. 12.
2. *Ibid.*, p. 13.
3. David Ausubel and Pearl Ausubel, "Ego Development Among Segregated Negro Children," in *Education in Depressed Areas,* A. Harry Passow, ed. (New York: Columbia University, 1963), p. 113. See also H. Greenberg and D. Fane, "An Investigation of Several Variables as Determinants of Authoritarianism," *The Journal of Social Psychology,* Vol. 49 (1959), pp. 105–111.
4. L. Joseph Stone and Joseph Church, *Childhood and Adolescence* (New York: Random House, 1957), pp. 260–262.
5. Ruth Cunningham and Associates, *Understanding Group Behavior of Boys and Girls* (New York: Columbia University Teachers College, 1951), p. 32. See also Sheviakov and Redl.
6. Camilla M. Anderson, "The Self-Image: A Theory of the Dynamics of Behavior," *Mental Hygiene* (April 1952), pp. 227–244.
7. U.S. Supreme Court, Record of the District Court Trial in *Briggs vs. Elliot,* pp. 15, 86.
8. Grace Graham, *Improving Student Participation* (Washington, D.C.: National Association of Secondary School Principals, 1966), pp. 1–2.
9. W.H. Riggle, *The White, the Black, and the Gray: A Study of Student Sub-Cultures in a Suburban California High School* (Unpublished doctoral dissertation, University of California, 1965), pp. 80–175.
10. J.R. Thornsley, *The Superintendent's Leadership Techniques for Inter-Group Racial and Ethnic Relations in Desegregated Schools* (Unpublished doctoral dissertation, University of Southern California, 1969), p. 175.
11. H. L. Winecoff, *Problems in School Desegregation: Real or Imaginary?* (School Desegregation Consulting Center, University of South Carolina), p. 8.
12. H.L. Winecoff and Paul Masem, *School Desegregation: A Challenge to Quality Education* (School Desegregation Consulting Center, University of South Carolina), p. 7.

13. Sheviakov and Redl, p. 46.
14. Don Edward Halverson, *A Study of the Organization and Administration of Guidance Services in the Elementary Schools* (Unpublished doctoral dissertation, University of Southern California, 1959), p. 14.
15. Sheviakov and Redl, p. 60.
16. William J. Gnagney, *Controlling Classroom Misbehavior* (Washington, D.C.: National Education Association, 1965), pp. 21–23. See also Sheviakov and Redl, p. 2.
17. Fritz Redl and David Wineman, *Controls From Within—Techniques for the Treatment of the Aggressive Child* (New York: The Free Press, 1952), pp. 153–245.
18. Sheviakov and Redl, p. 45.

Bibliography

Anderson, Camilla M. "The Self-Image: A Theory of the Dynamics of Behavior," *Mental Hygiene* (April 1952).

Ausubel, David and Pearl Ausubel. "Ego Development Among Segregated Negro Children," in A. Henry Passow, ed. *Education in Depressed Areas.* New York: Columbia University, 1963.

Baruch, D.W. *New Ways in Discipline.* New York: Whittlesey House, 1949.

Bowman, H.J. "Review of Discipline," *National Association of Secondary-School Principals Bulletin* 43: 147–56, September 1959.

Bradford, L.P. "Group Forces Affecting Learning," *Journal of the National Association of Women Deans and Counselors,* 23:3 (April 1960).

Cameron, Norman. *Personality Development and Psychopathology.* Boston: Houghton-Mifflin Co., 1963.

Coleman, J.S. "Academic Achievement and the Structure of Competition," *Harvard Educational Review,* 29 (Fall 1959).

Cunningham, Ruth and Associates. *Understanding Group Behavior of Boys and Girls.* New York: Columbia University Teachers College, 1951.

Cutts, N. and N. Moseley. *Teaching the Disorderly Pupil.* New York: Longmans, Green & Co., 1957.

D'Evelyn, Katherin E. *Developing Mentally Healthy Children.* Washington, D.C.: American Association of Elementary, Kindergarten and Nursery Educators.

"Discovering One Another in a Georgia Town," *Life Magazine* (February 1971).

Falk, Herbert Arnold. *Corporal Punishment—A Social Interpretation of its Theory and Practice in the Schools of the United States.* New York: Columbia University, 1941.

Fancher, Betsy. *Voices From the South: Black Students Talk about Their Experiences in Desegregated Schools.* Southern Regional Council, 1970.

Flanders, Ned A. "Personal-Social Anxiety as a Factor in Experimental Learning Situations," *Journal of Educational Research,* 45: 100–110; 1951.

Gnagney, William J. *Controling Classroom Misbehavior.* Washington, D.C.: National Education Association, 1965.

Graham, Grace. *Improving Student Participation.* Washington, D.C.: National
　　Association of Secondary School Principals, 1966.

Greenberg, H. and D. Fane. "An Investigation of Several Variables as Deter-
　　minants of Authoritarianism," *Journal of Social Psychology,* Vol. 49
　　(1959), 105–111.

Halverson, Don Edward. *A Study of the Organization and Administration of
　　Guidance Services in the Elementary Schools.* Unpublished Doctoral Dis-
　　sertation, University·of Southern California, 1959.

Hymes, J.L., Jr. *Behavior and Misbehavior.* Englewood Cliffs, N.J.: Prentice-Hall,
　　1955.

The Journal of Negro Education, Vol. 28, No. 3 (Summer 1969).

Prichard, Paul Newton. *The Effects of Desegregation on Selected Variables in
　　the Chapel Hill City School System.* Unpublished Doctoral Dissertation,
　　University of North Carolina, 1969.

Redl, F. *Understanding Children's Behavior.* New York: Teachers College,
　　Columbia University, 1949.

Redl, F. and W. Wattenberg. *Mental Hygiene in Teaching.* Second edition. New
　　York: Harcourt, Brace and Co., 1959. Chapter 13, "Influence Techniques."

Redl, Fritz and David Wineman. *Controls From Within–Techniques for the
　　Treatment of the Aggressive Child.* New York: The Free Press, 1952.

Riggle, W.H. *The White, the Black, and the Gray: A Study of Student Sub-
　　cultures in a Suburban California High School.* Unpublished Doctoral Dis-
　　sertation, University of California, 1965.

Sheviakov, G.V. et al. *Discipline for Today's Children and Youth.* Revised
　　edition. Washington, D.C.: National Education Association, 1956.

Smith, L.M. and B.B. Hudgins. *Educational Psychology: An Application of
　　Social and Behavioral Theory.* New York: Alfred A. Knopf, 1964. Chapter
　　9, "Classroom Discipline."

Stone, L. Joseph and Joseph Church. *Childhood and Adolescence.* New York:
　　Random House, 1957.

Symonds, P.M. "What Education Has To Learn from Psychology. III. Punish-
　　ment," *Teachers College Record* 57: 449–462; 1956.

Ten Houten, Warren David. *Socialization, Race, and the American High School,*
　　Unpublished Doctoral Dissertation, Michigan State University, 1965.

Thornsley, J.R. *The Superintendent's Leadership Techniques for Inter-group
　　Racial and Ethnic Relations in Desegregated Schools.* Unpublished Doctoral
　　Dissertation, University of Southern California, 1969.

U.S. Supreme Court, Record of the District Court Trial in *Briggs vs. Elliot.*

Vredevoe, L. E. "School Discipline," *National Association of Secondary-School
　　Principals Bulletin* 49: 215–226; March 1965.

Williamson, E.G. and J.D. Foley. *Counseling and Discipline.* New York: McGraw-
　　Hill Book Co., 1949.

Winecoff, H.L. *Problems in School Desegregation: Real or Imaginary?* School
　　Desegregation Consulting Center, University of South Carolina.

Winecoff, H.L. and Paul Masem. *School Desegregation: A Challenge to Quality
　　Education.* School Desegregation Consulting Center, University of South
　　Carolina.

Curriculum Adaptation to Achieve Effective Desegregation

The Function of Curriculum in Student Adjustment

A school district's curriculum is comprised of subjects and activities intended to serve two basic functions. The first is meeting the students' learning needs, which include preparation for dealing with situations both now and in later life. The second is motivating students in directions that are socially desirable. Consequently, curriculum content in a district is an expression of both community policies and educational theory.

In developing a curriculum, three factors must be taken into account: the development of the student, the organization of the material, and the content of the material to be taught. Broad objectives regarding these factors are necessary to perform the functions described above. Although periodic revisions of the objectives are required to keep pace with social change in the nation, there is general agreement that the curriculum should attempt to:

Assist students in realizing personal and social objectives.

Provide opportunities for social contacts and participation in democratically organized groups.

Provide the skills and knowledge that the student will require for participation in society.

Teach children to be self-reliant, to govern themselves and to participate in planning, carrying out and evaluating activities.

Guide and motivate students in understanding the relationships between subject content and their personal and social growth.

Provide experiences and insights that will contribute to healthy personality development.

Basic Curriculum Problems Caused or Aggravated by Desegregation

1. In most schools, the instructional program is oriented toward subjects needed in professional careers. Subjects are often taught in isolation from each other, and teachers consequently tend to direct students toward specific tasks involving the use of a limited range of classroom procedures and materials. The details of a subject-oriented curriculum—especially specific materials and procedures--may be unfamiliar to many minority-group and disadvantaged children entering desegregated schools. Since these students often enter the new environment with feelings of self-doubt, the unfamiliarity with the method of presenting the core subject matter makes it more difficult for them to adjust. If they experience humiliation or rejection by their teachers and peers, they may lose

interest in their classroom performance and withdraw. Thus, the classroom experience can reinforce initial negative feelings of self-doubt.

2. Because of their home backgrounds, many minority-group and disadvantaged students respond more readily to tangible and clearly useful activities than to more abstract forms of learning. They have often had little incentive to develop skills in problem-solving and critical thinking, which are both intellectual approaches unrelated to their expected future opportunities for employment or their home backgrounds. These factors may significantly reduce the interest and ability of the students to achieve in the classroom.

3. Although all students need to learn salable skills and develop employable habits, attitudes, and personalities, many minority-group and disadvantaged students have parents who are unable to teach them the basic skills and knowledge needed for conducting personal affairs effectively. Not many schools have courses with subject matter appropriate for performing this vital function.

Basic Objectives in Desegregation to Remedy These Problems

1. Evidence indicates that use of some group-centered activities in the classroom tends to increase the interaction of all students and increase the self-confidence of the minority-group and disadvantaged students. Desegregated schools should provide more opportunities for group-centered activities, especially those stressing democratic decision-making processes.

2. It is essential that the curriculum offer students who have been made to feel inferior by their status in society many opportunities to experience success and social interaction so they can develop pride and self-esteem. Since many students will enter the desegregated school with inferior academic backgrounds and limited worldly experiences, they will need some special help in achieving academic, personal, and social growth.

3. The school system should consider curriculum revisions to provide subjects that are more relevant to the needs of all students. These revisions could include diversification of the curriculum to offer a wider range of courses, especially courses relevant to the future occupational needs of non-college bound students.

4. The school system should evaluate the possibilities for community-based learning and work experiences to assist students in selecting future occupations.

5. Schools should attempt innovations in classroom organization as a means of providing time for teachers to work with individuals and small groups.

6. Teachers, principals, and other school officials should realize that, in the first stages of desegregation, establishing positive self-images and reinforcing feelings of adequacy among many minority-group and disadvantaged children is far more important to their long-term academic success than exposing them to specific academic subjects. This fact should significantly influence the way the curriculum for such students is designed.

Specific Problems, Policies, and Techniques

A. Developing a More Student-Centered Curriculum

PROBLEM: Available evidence indicates that peer group acceptance is an
              important factor in both the interest and achievement of minority-
              group and disadvantaged students. However, the interaction of
              peers is difficult to achieve in the traditional classroom, which is
              dependent upon the teacher for direction and relies heavily upon
              a subject-centered curriculum.

POLICY.   Teachers should examine their curricula to discover as many op-
  (A-1)   portunities for group-centered activities as possible.

To provide opportunities for peer interaction in the classroom, the teacher
should structure special group situations. Group work is not, of course, appropriate for all, or perhaps even most, instruction. But in the areas of the social
sciences and language arts, for instance, a teacher can create group-centered
learning situations. Peer interaction within a carefully structured situation guided
by a sensitive teacher should result in greater peer acceptance.

Suggested Techniques.

The teacher can provide more group-centered experiences in the classroom
within the formal structure of the curriculum. Particular techniques that can be
used to encourage group activity in a variety of subject fields are presented
below.

One way in which children can be encouraged to interact as a group is
through dramatic play. When they become so involved in their experience that
they identify with the characters and roles played, students are provided with a
rich opportunity for clarification of ideas, enlargement of concepts, and
deepening of understanding and appreciation. An example of this type of group
experience is described on the following page.

2.   Group Purposes

Another technique for effecting peer interaction is the creation of situations
in which groups must cooperate to achieve an objective. An example of a way
in which a whole class can work together toward a common goal would be for
the students to write to a foreign embassy for information on a country they
are studying. Such an experience teaches children that they can obtain information through research and requests to specialized persons and also encourages
all the members of the class to participate in a group effort. Another example of
this type of peer interaction would be caring for an animal or raising potted
plants.

In a similar group effort, students from several Los Angeles high schools
worked together to create an anthology of self-descriptive poems, letters and

Example of Dramatic Play

"In the development of any unit of work there are always a variety of situations that can be 'played' by the children. For example, during a unit of work on ships and their cargoes, children will become harbor masters as they enforce the regulations on the use of the harbor; pilots of tugboats as they bring the freighters into the harbor; stevedores as they unload cargo; truck drivers as they haul the materials away. And as they gain information about the correct procedures in relation to how ships enter and leave a harbor, how tugboats are obtained to ensure safe passage in and out of a harbor, how clearance for entering or departing ships is obtained from the harbor master, their dramatic play will take on authenticity and will become organized into a pattern that affords vital and worthwhile educational learning. The teacher's part in making such play truly educative is to provide many firsthand experiences, ample reading material, many pictures, and opportunities for discussion after each play period to help the children evaluate their play."

Source: Lavone Hanna, et al, *Unit Teaching in the Elementary School* (New York: Holt, Rinehart & Winston, 1963), pp. 133–134.

---

articles entitled "Pages of My Mind." This paperback has been screened, financed and distributed to other students on a pilot basis by the school system's curriculum development program. The freedom and initiative that students experience through innovations of this type contribute significantly to effective learning.

3.   Intergroup Competition

In most public schools, great emphasis is placed on interpersonal competition. This tends to generate frustration, anxiety and hostility among many students. In intergroup competition, the competing unit is changed from the individual to the group.

An important consideration in using this technique is to be sure that the groups be constructed heterogeneously in terms of motivation and ability. This way better students will serve as models for poorer students. A motive for helping each other will be provided because the grade or reward each student receives is partially dependent upon group performance. Groups can compete within the same classroom, against groups in another classroom, or against a standard set by the teacher.

An excellent demonstration of the value of intergroup competition occurred in Chapel Hill, North Carolina. In an effort to test the hypothesis that group purposes are a stronger motivation for achievement than personal competition, an experiment was conducted among four groups of students.

The experimental procedure was based on the administration of two tests per week. For their performance on the test, individual students earned tokens that could be spent in a school store. However, the tokens could only be spent if a Master token had been earned. For the control group, the Master token was obtained on the basis of the combined average of weekly individual test scores. For three other groups, the Master tokens were earned for achievement of high scores by the whole group. The competition varied: in one case, subgroups competed with one another; in a second case, classes were in competition; and in a third case, an artificial standard was set for the group to attain.

At the end of the marking period, the performance of the control group of individual competitors had decreased by 70 percent, while that of the three sets of intergroup competitors had increased by 62 to 83 percent. Although differences among the experimental groups were not significant, they did suggest that competition with another group is more motivating than competition with an abstract standard. Between-class competition seemed to lead to less intergroup interference than did within-class competition.[1]

4.   Coordinated Intergroup Projects

Intergroup projects offer an opportunity for students to work in both large and small groups to plan and carry out specific activities. No direct competition is involved; instead, groups of students handle different aspects of a large project. The project may be one assigned by the teacher or it may arise out of a student need or problem. An example of a seventh-grade coordinated project is given on the following page. At all levels of intergroup activity, each student should play an important role in the activities of his group.

5.   Process Approach to Curriculum Development

The process approach to teaching science was developed by a major corporation. It matches learning capabilities of students at various age levels with graded portions of a comprehensive science curriculum designed for presentation over a span of years from K through 12. This approach stresses small-group work in laboratories from an early age. At each age level, it concentrates on presenting concepts and experiments that typical students of that age can easily grasp. Yet the entire set of activities over the thirteen-year period comprises a comprehensive program of scientific knowledge, methods and procedures. If the program is followed in its entirety, each student will have been exposed to a very complete and integrated scientific curriculum without having been either "overloaded" or "underused" in relation to his capabilities at each age level. This approach is too complex to be designed in a local school. However, teachers can incorporate it into their own curriculum after it has been developed elsewhere—as with this science curriculum.

POLICY: Teachers should structure their curricula so that opportunities
(A-2)   for learning democratic values will be provided.

Example of Coordinated
Intergroup Project

Seventh-grade students, who were concerned because so many children had had accidents with their bicycles, attempted to solve a problem on "How Can We Prevent Bicycle Accidents?" In analyzing the problem, they decided they needed to know many things: the causes of accidents, the safety devices on bicycles and how they work, the rules regulating the riding of bicycles, how to take care of their bicycles, the attitudes of adults toward bicycle riders, and the like.

Various committees within the room were organized. Each one was to handle a particular phase of this prevention problem and report to the class. One committee of six made a list of all the causes of accidents they could think of. A local traffic policeman was asked by another committee to come to talk with the group. He talked about the local rules regulating the riding of bicycles and left copies of these rules.

It was evident from the discussion of the rules regulating bicycle riding that a new ordinance was needed. The class accepted the challenge to write a new ordinance which they later presented to the city council. In the course of their project, the class also worked together to sponsor a school safety assembly in which they presented the rules of bicycle safety to all the other students.

The unit on "How Can We Prevent Bicycle Accidents?" evolved because of a need, a problem about which the children were frustrated and concerned. It ended when they, working together, had solved the problem to their satisfaction and had put their solution into operation so that accidents were reduced.

Source: Lavone Hanna, et al, *Unit Teaching in the Elementary School* (New York: Holt, Rinehart & Winston, 1963), p. 133.

The application of democratic principles in the classroom means that through the curriculum, every child—regardless of his or her capabilities—should have the opportunity to grow to his full mental, emotional, physical and social potentials.[2] Each disadvantaged child should be put in situations where he can achieve and experience success. Each individual should be encouraged to take responsibility, to solve problems and to reach decisions. And each student should be given opportunities to become involved in group decision-making.

Suggested Techniques

1. Planning the Curriculum to Cover Sensitive Subject Matter
Skillfully teaching sensitive subjects and dealing with sensitive situations that arise in the classroom are especially important for the teacher of minority-group students who may be uncertain of their positions in a democratic society.

Coverage of such subjects and matters of opinion is appropriate when the teacher can use the opportunity to clarify the student's role, to distinguish fact from opinion, to differentiate between rational and emotional responses, and to develop critical thinking skills.

It is the teacher's responsibility to plan a curriculum that will include subject matter that is sensitive, and therefore may be ambiguous or emotionally charged. For example, the Harvard University Committee on Programmed Instruction designed a presentation of two Supreme Court cases: *Plessy vs. Ferguson* and *Brown vs. Board of Education.* [3] In this material, the student is presented with the attitudes of American society toward human rights, the intent of the Fourteenth Amendment, and instances where the intent was violated. In conjunction with the subject matter presentation, the teacher guides the students in a discussion of the meaning of "equal treatment for all."

Often, in a newly desegregated classroom, the students and/or teacher do not know how to openly and appropriately recognize the differences between classmates and/or teacher. The teacher needs to consciously guide interaction to promote better understanding. Mrs. Opal Harper, a black teacher in Little Rock, Arkansas, found herself in such a situation when she was transferred to a previously all-white school.[4] As part of a study of dialects, one of her students commented, "When you are talking to someone over the phone, you can usually tell whether the person is Negro or white." As soon as the word "Negro" was spoken, the class reacted with hushed silence and tension. Mrs. Harper met the situation with humor and good will by telling the students that "Negro" and "white" are perfectly good words and that she had been a Negro all her life and was not likely to change. After this incident, she noted that her students showed increased tolerance and restraint.

2.   Decision-Making

One way of enabling students to act out democratic processes is for the teacher to provide experiences in which they can participate in decision-making. The teacher should structure the curriculum so that each student has continual opportunities for making choices, resolving differences and planning in a group.

Teacher-pupil planning can enter into every phase of the teaching-learning situation at some time or other. Selecting the unit to be studied, defining the problem or goal, formulating the objectives and deciding upon the activities can all be the result of joint decision-making at least some of the time. An example of how this process was introduced in an American history class is described on the following page.

3.   Debate or Moot Court

Role playing in debates or moot court situations offers an excellent opportunity for students to act out democratic principles. In such activities, the

Example of Decision-Making

Mr. Sanders, a history teacher in a large northern high school, was disappointed with his results of the previous year. He had found that the students were bored in class, seldom did the assigned work, and were not creative. Determined not to repeat his failure, Mr. Sanders asked his new class to help plan the curriculum, reminding them that he was required by law to cover the period of American history from the Civil War to the present. Before the class could plan, however, he suggested they had to decide what they wanted to do. To diagnose students' curriculum interests, Mr. Sanders asked each one to write a short essay telling what he or she would like to learn during the term. He also distributed the following questionnaire:

Instructions: Please mark those subjects that you would most like to learn more about this term.

	I would like to learn about this	I don't care	I would not like to study this
1. Civil War battles			
2. Slavery			
3. Political reconstruction			
4. Populism			
5. Black legislators after the Civil War			
6. Growth of "Jim Crow" segregation			
7. Presidents of the United States			
8. American Indians on the frontier			
9. Immigrant groups coming to U.S.			
10. Growth of urban life			
11. Economic development at turn of the century			
12. 19th century fashions			
13. Others:			

He tried to concentrate on those issues and methods that appealed to most students. He also decided to have a "free unit" of time for those people whose interests were not covered through the rest of the units in the depth they desired. Thus, if the students were accurate and honest in stating their preferences, they should have been working most of the time on something that a large portion of the class wanted to do. By asking detailed questions on the methods students wanted to use, he was able to design activities and arrange time schedules to accommodate special interests.

Mr. Sanders also asked the students to identify the kinds of instructional methods and materials they preferred. For example:

I like to—yes	I don't like to—no
_read textbooks	—
_work with some of my friends on a separate project	—
_work with lots of different classmates	—
_work alone	—
_use the library	—
_write reports	—
_present projects to the class	—
_draw and paint	—
_act in plays	—
Others:	

Toward midsemester Mr. Sanders wanted to know how the students felt about the class and subject matter. He asked them the following questions:

1. Have you enjoyed the work you have been doing this term?
   a. a little more than usual
   b. about the same as usual
   c. not as much as usual
   d. a lot more than usual
   e. much less than usual
2. Would you like to continue the course in the same way as we have been working? Yes_ No_ If No, what would you like to change? Be specific_
3. When you're in this class, do you
   a. usually feel wide awake and very interested?
   b. feel pretty interested, bored part of the time?
   c. feel not very interested, bored quite a lot of the time?
   d. dislike it, feel bored and not interested at all?
4. How hard are you working these days on learning American history?
   a. very hard
   b. quite hard
   c. not very hard
   d. not hard at all

Source: Mark Chesler, Carl Jorgensen and Phyllis Erenberg, *Planning Educational Change,* Vol. III: *Integrating the Desegregated School* (Washington: U.S. Dept. of Health, Education and Welfare, Office of Education), pp. 54–55.

---

student sees a direct conflict of ideas and has to decide which viewpoint is correct and why. At the same time, of course, he gains an understanding of differing points of view.

An example of a role-playing debate situation is provided in the inset that follows. In this case, two student groups examine an historical situation from both sides, rather than just from the viewpoint that is usually presented. This

---

Example of Role-Playing Assignments
in American Colonial History

From the Point of View of the British:

The American Revolution Against British Authority
London, 1773 to 1776: How Does it Look from Here?

You are in London. During the 1770's, crucial events occur in the colonies of North America, where ever-enlarging groups of colonists are challenging first the authority of the British Parliament and then the authority of the King. Such challenges are met by acts of Parliament and statements of policy by the King.

"How is this story told in London?"

"How do the colonists upset the British?"

To answer these questions, you will find in this envelope a set of news stories (on cards) describing the events of the 1770's, as they might have appeared in London.

From the Point of View of the Colonists:

The American Revolution Against British Authority
American Colonies, 1773 to 1776: How Does it Look from Here?

You are now in the American colonies. The events of the 1770's force groups of British colonists to turn against the British Parliament, then the British King, and finally to separate and withdraw from the British Empire.

"How is this story told in the American colonies?"

"How do the British upset the colonists?"

"How does the American story compare with the British story?"

To answer these questions, you will find in this envelope a set of news stories (on cards) describing the events of the 1770's, as they might have appeared in the American colonies.

Source: Social Studies Curriculum Program, *How Does It Look from Here?*, from "The American Revolution Against British Authority," (Cambridge, Mass.: Educational Services, Inc., 1964). Material was taken from an experimental edition.

---

study of the way in which the colonists protested against British authority could provide a parallel for discussion of protest and revolution today.

Such an exercise can be used to demonstrate every person's right to have and express his or her own opinion. It is therefore important to be certain that minority-group and disadvantaged students are actually given equal opportunities to form and express their own opinions during this type of activity. It also helps teach all students to base their opinions upon logical thought and factual information, rather than customary beliefs.

B. Diversification of the Contents of the Curriculum

PROBLEM: In some schools, the curriculum strongly emphasizes subjects needed in professional careers, even though many students will not pursue such careers. Consequently, some students lose interest in classes not relevant to their present or future lives. Moreover, traditional texts and materials often fail to recount contributions of minority groups to American history. Narrow curriculum content also fails to provide opportunities for many students to learn occupational and other skills directly useful to them as adults. Emphasis throughout the curriculum upon use of "perfect" English may discourage students who come from bi-lingual backgrounds or homes where dialects are dominant.

POLICY.   Teachers should strive to improve communications with their
(B-1)   students, especially those students who use unfamiliar speech styles.

Suggested Techniques

1.   Teachers Meetings
     In a newly desegregated school, white teachers may be at a loss to interpret the language and behavior of the minority-group students, while minority-group teachers may have trouble understanding the attitudes and behavior of whites. From year to year in most schools teachers exchange information about students on an informal basis to help a student's next teacher better understand his behavior. A newly desegregated school cannot take advantage of this natural mechanism. Therefore, it would be beneficial to hold a teachers meeting before opening day for the purpose of sharing notes on the behavior characteristics of individual students. Depending upon the mechanism employed for desegregation, such a meeting might involve teachers from one school only, several schools in the same area, or in the case of small districts, the whole district.
     A generalized picture of the behavior of different student groups can also be gleaned from these meetings. This information will be helpful in planning curriculum as well as in handling disciplinary problems. The section of this chapter on Teaching Techniques and Training includes further discussion of this technique.

2.   Student Human Relations Sessions
     Students can often benefit from discussion sessions in which their relationships with each other are clarified. Interaction alone is not enough to overcome interpersonal barriers. Teachers can create an atmosphere of acceptance, however, and guide discussions toward achievement of greater interpersonal understand-

ing. For students to begin to accept each other, they must first understand each other's normal communication and behavior patterns.

A teacher may structure the curriculum so that student discussion groups are meeting for another purpose, yet better bi-racial understanding is a by-product. Or the actual focus may be on interracial collaboration, as in the example described below. In that case, the teacher asks for written answers to questions that relate to interracial attitudes. The teacher should share some of the information from such questionnaires with the students and encourage free and open discussion of the feelings expressed. This exercise helps the students learn acceptable ways of expressing their feelings toward each other and provides better understanding of how others think and feel.

3.   Language to Suit the Occasion

Modern linguists have shown that language is used in very different ways for different purposes.[5] For example, the level of usage one employs in a speech is different from that which one employs with friends or family. Some texts are now available based upon this approach.

Example of Student Human Relations Analysis

A fifth grade teacher, Miss Wilentz, recognized the existence of some serious interpersonal and intergroup problems among the students in her class. She wanted to understand some of these problems in order to create an environment where blacks and whites would feel comfortable working together and being friends with each other. She decided to begin by trying to discover what students felt about some of their classmates.

Instructions: Write in the space next to each question the way you would answer that question. Tell me just how you feel.

1. My parents told me that people with different colored skins are   _____
2. Who are three people in this class you like the most?   _____
3. Who are three people in the class you don't like?   _____
4. What are the things that people do to make you angry?   _____
5. How do you show someone that you like them?   _____
6. How do you show someone that you want to study with them?   _____
7. What are the things that you do when you are very angry?   _____

With these data, Miss Wilentz was able to diagnose some patterns of friendship and rejection in class and to identify some of the barriers to interracial collaboration.

Source: Mark Chesler, Carl Jorgensen and Phyllis Erenberg, *Planning Educational Change,* Vol. III: *Integrating the Desegregated School* (Washington: U. S. Department of Health, Education and Welfare, Office of Education), p. 55.

Applying this technique in the classroom means teaching students the appropriateness of various levels of language usage. Rather than forcing disadvantaged or minority-group students to abandon familiar speech in favor of "acceptable English usage," the teacher should convince them that some language is acceptable at home, but a different usage is appropriate for the classroom. Such instruction should avoid any stigma of "badness" or inferiority with respect to informal speech.

4.   Study of Speech Patterns

A helpful device for improving teacher-pupil and peer communication is to study the dialectic speech patterns and colloquial expressions used by class members. The teacher could simply, for his own benefit, draw up a list of unfamiliar words and their definitions as used by students in his class. Or class members could discuss individually or together unfamiliar words used by classmates. The teacher should establish the concept that, with words or expressions, there is no absolute right or wrong but rather *different* ways of communicating an idea, which may be appropriate to different audiences or occasions. This type of discussion can be extended to looking at variations in regional dialects and slang across the country, or variations in slang between generations. The results are amusing, and also show how diversity helps make life more interesting.

5.   Language Arts Courses

A formal technique aiding communications would be inclusion in the curriculum of a study of different racial speech patterns. This could be covered in an overall study of the development of the English language, or in a specific unit on American regional or dialectical speech.

6.   Bilingual Education Programs

Bilingual education projects are designed to use the child's first language as the medium of instruction until his competence in English permits the use of both languages in a balanced instructional program. It is necessary in all bilingual projects to strive to maintain the child's self-esteem and legitimate pride in both cultures.

Under Title VII of the Elementary and Secondary Education Act of 1965, the Office of Education awards grants for bilingual educational programs. The goal behind this funding, as outlined by the Office of Education, is to produce bicultural students.[6] Anglos and non-English speaking students are given combined instruction based on the assumption that one learns best from peer interaction. A second benefit to desegregated schools is that resegregation is often avoided. A description of a program funded by the Office of Education follows.

POLICY.   Considering the predominance of basic communication skills and
  (B-2)   the lack of prereading skills among the disadvantaged, a first

Example of Bilingual Program

A bilingual education program has been established in Las Vegas, New Mexico, to provide for 540 children in the first grade the development of language processes in both Spanish and English, improvement of cognitive functioning, development of positive self-concepts, and desire for academic achievement. This project will also establish effective parent-teacher-school-community relationships. Teachers and parents will receive training, with mothers serving as second educators of their children. Educational concepts will be presented in the mother tongue of the children, with reinforcement of concepts in the second language; independent learning will be stressed. The curriculum will include English and Spanish literacy skills, concept development, culturally-oriented program and self-image development. Project components are the instructional program, staff development, and parent involvement. The long range objectives are to: 1) develop cultural awareness of the two predominant cultures; 2) extend the program through the fifth grade by adding an additional level each year; 3) raise the achievement level of students to that of the national norm by completion of the fifth grade; 4) provide worthwhile programs that will enable participants to become more productive members of society; 5) prepare teachers for bilingual education programs; and 6) develop evaluation methods and techniques that will provide a true picture of achievement.

Source: Office of Education, *Notification to Members of Congress,* June 30, 1970.

priority should be given to developing these communication skills in a desegregated school.

The disadvantaged child enters school with few prereading skills. He does, however, have other communications skills.[7] He has a highly selective aural facility and can, at will, hear what he wishes to and tune out what he does not want to hear. Another communication skill prevalent among the disadvantaged is the use of gestures to convey meaning: hand and body movements are more heavily relied upon than verbal expression. The skills that the disadvantaged student does have need to be developed further so that he will be prepared for reading and other language arts. To implement this policy, programs emphasizing concrete experiences, coupled with the communication skills of listening, speaking and gesture, should be offered to provide children with the cognitive and perceptual abilities they will need for reading.

Suggested Techniques

1.   Development of Listening Skills

The *Programmed Experiences in Creative Thinking* study of the University of Minnesota is a good example of a program that extends and refines listening skills. A set of audio tapes and lessons designed for fourth grade use has been developed. An example of how these tapes are used to "stretch the imagination" and to stimulate children to listen to sounds appears in the following inset.

Example of Listening Skill Exercise

The following excerpt is from an audio tape:

Now, this recording contains four separate sounds. Each sound will be repeated three times. As you listen to these sounds, try to picture them in your mind. Then write them down. Some of them, however, you won't recognize at all. You'll probably have a little trouble in picturing and describing them. These are the sounds I want you to use your imagination on, and write down the word pictures they make you think of. The first sound will be easy to describe, but the others are a bit mysterious and are guaranteed to make you stop and wonder. As you listen to them, use your imagination while writing down the word pictures these sounds suggest to you. The chances are, the sounds will also call up many different feelings, and hold onto them long enough to write them down.

I am now going to play those sounds again, exactly as before. Only this time I want different answers from you. I want you to let your imagination FLY this time, so that even everyday sounds will take on new meanings for you.

Now, take your paper—and write down the word pictures you think of as I play the sounds a third time. This time, the sky's the limit, for I want you to push the walls of your imagination out as far as they'll possibly go.

I'll bet your answers this time really had a different twist! Now then: Take a look at all twelve of your answers. I want you to choose from them the one answer which you think is the most interesting of all—and put a dark circle around it. Then, draw or paint a picture about that answer. And, if you have time, write a story to go with it. Be very careful to choose the one answer you think is the most unusual, though, because the more unusual the answer, the more unusual will be your picture of your story. And the more fun you'll have in the long run.

Source: E. Paul Torrance and Ram Gupta, *Programmed Experiences in Creative Thinking* (Minneapolis: Bureau of Educational Research, College of Education, University of Minnesota, 1964).

---

2.   Role-Playing

Role-playing experiences not only allow for discussion and oral exchange, but make it possible for children to express themselves physically while acting out a problem; hence, disadvantaged children can build on what might be, for them, a successful means of expression (physical), at the same time that language is subtly introduced through the dialogue.

In the Wilmington, Delaware, Three-Year Experimental Project on Schools

in Changing Neighborhoods, the focus is on developing language skills through
planned experience units that will help children grow in human relations skills,
knowledge, and information. One of the media through which these units
are taught is that of role-playing—aloud or in pantomime. Children will often
find the roles of other people easier and more fun to deal with than their own
roles in life.

POLICY.   Desegregated schools should diversify the content, course
  (B-3)   offerings, materials, and procedures used in presenting the cur-
                 riculum to appeal to a broader range of personalities and
                 cognitive learning styles.

Suggested Techniques

1. Black Studies Programs
    All children need to feel pride in themselves and identification with some-
thing or someone important. Some of this feeling can be given to students
through the use of literature about their heritage. Many schools have included
black studies programs or Indian history courses in their curricula in an attempt
to provide adequate treatment of the historical significance and the important
role of these groups in the growth and progress of the United States. The
Cleveland Public School System has published a textbook titled, *The Negro
American: His Role, His Quest.*

The inclusion of ethnic-studies material in the curriculum accomplishes both
a substantive and a personal-social goal. Various approaches have been tried, two
of which are described on the following page. The policy in Flint, Michigan, of
integrating the black studies program into the rest of the curriculum is representative of many other school districts. In Portland, Oregon, for example, most
students have lost interest in separate programs; and the district will now integrate ethnic studies materials into the required American or U.S. History
courses.

2. Intercultural Materials
    The incorporation of intercultural materials into the curriculum serves to
bolster a minority-group child's self-pride, to clarify history, and to broaden
students' understanding of the multi-racial and interdependent characteristics of the
world.

Interviews with various officials in the Colorado Springs, Colorado, public
schools produced several excellent examples of this technique. The curriculum
personnel have established an intercultural relations committee made up of
one teacher from each elementary school, plus supervisors. The committee
examines multicultural material for appropriate inclusion within the curriculum. Guides have been published for K-6 demonstrating the types of

---

Examples of Black Studies Programs

Many Philadelphia, Pennsylvania schools have developed their own curriculum materials. For instance, 103 schools created their own materials in 1968–
69. These materials most often consisted of guides, outlines, and reference
materials (31 schools); slides, tapes, and transparencies (17 schools); fictional
stories, poems, and plays (13 schools); costumes and dances (11 schools); arts
and crafts exhibits (10 schools); bibliographies (10 schools); and photographic displays (9 schools). One school prepared African-style food. Another constructed
student genealogies. Still, 80 percent of the schools with some kind of black
studies program say that they need "more good texts and reference books" and
60 percent would like at least one more teacher with a black studies background.

The Flint, Michigan Board of Education policy requires that the emphasis
be on an integrated curriculum, not on separate black studies courses. As a result,
the district has a 238-page curriculum guide for an integrated English program
for grades 10, 11, and 12. But the district actually offers 35 separate high school
English courses, including The Literature of Minority People and Harlem Renaissance. Flint's standard American literature course is called Rebellion and
Conformity.

Source: National School Public Relations Association, *Black Studies in Schools*
(Washington, 1970), pp. 8 and 12.

---

interracial material that should be incorporated. An example of a unit for grade
three is described in the following inset.

Example of Grade Three Intercultural Material

Understandings: Contributions have been made and are being made by all races
in all aspects of community life in the Pikes Peak Region.

Topic: History and Geography of the Pikes Peak Region

Part One—Indians

1. Have the class read *Indians of the Pikes Peak Regions* and *Red Shirt* by
   Virginia McConnell.
2. Discuss and list contributions of the Indians (music, literature, food, art, etc.).
3. Listen to stories and music of the Indian. Discuss the art of the Indians.
4. Listen to the tapes *Legends of the Pikes Peak Region* and *Chief Ouray* by
   Rowena Roberts.
5. Discuss the role of the Indian today. (Write for free and inexpensive material:
   Literature on Indians, United States Department of the Interior, Bureau of
   Indian Affairs, Washington, D.C. 20240.)

(continued)

Example of Grade Three Intercultural Material
(Continued)

Part Two—Pioneers

1. Have the children read the multi-racial biographies of people of the Pikes Peak Region by Inez Hunt. (These biographies are scheduled for production in 1970–71.)
2. Make a Hall of Fame of pioneers of the Pikes Peak Region showing their multi-racial composition.

Our Community Today

1. Show participants in all areas of community life are multi-racial (civic, professional, business).
2. Make a booklet of pictures (original, newspaper, camera, etc.) of the people of the community showing their multi-racial composition.

Note: For additional suggestions, refer to the following units in the third grade Social Studies guide:

A. *History and Geography of the Pikes Peak Region* (Part One—Indians; Part Two—Pioneers)
B. *Our Community Today*

Source: *Inter-Cultural Relations: A Supplement to the Social Studies Curriculum.* (Colorado Springs, Colorado, October 1970).

Residents of Colorado Springs, including some teachers, have written books on the histories of local minority-group members who have been successful. These attractively published texts are distributed with detailed study guides to all elementary schools.

Colorado Springs also has a closed circuit TV network on which multi-racial programs are presented. "Cultural Understanding" is the name of the fourteen-program TV series that examines the culture of four ethnic groups in America—Asian Americans, American Indians, Hispanic Americans and American Negroes. A guide is furnished to all 5th and 6th grade teachers. The guide to the program on Hispanic Cultural Arts is reproduced on the following page.

3. Student Participation in Course Preparation

Another form of curriculum innovation is direct student participation in design of elective courses. A group of several students and teachers in Seattle have introduced contemporary issues and politically relevant subjects to the curriculum, along with a course on jazz appreciation. In West Hartford, Connecticut, students alone created and implemented a series of summer school courses dealing with problems of the inner city.

Example of Intercultural Program
on Closed Circuit TV

Description of Telecast on Hispanic Cultural Arts

The host, Mr. Manuel Andrade, greets his viewers in a classroom setting to help bring understanding of five of the important Hispanic cultural arts. Language, music, dance, architecture and art are discussed and explained with visual techniques to help make children aware of the influence that these parts of culture have had in the region. Musical artists will play, sing and dance. We will visit historical and modern homes to learn of the influence of Spanish architecture. Folk art of wood carving and the making of Santos will introduce the students to artists such as Elido Gonzales and the famous santero, George Lopez.

Preparation Before Viewing

1. The following words may need explaining:
   arid—dry
   sala—living room
   vigas—log rafters in a Spanish pueblo style home
   portales—porch
   central plaza—a central square around which the main buildings of
     an Hispanic town were built
   Santos—images of saints
   santero—maker of Santos
2. The states of the West and Southwest have hundreds of Spanish-named places. The class or a committee could help prepare a list of some of these for display on a bulletin board.
3. How is adobe made? Several students could prepare a report on adobe and its importance in the history of the Southwest.
4. Discuss with students the meaning of the word "culture." Help them discover what things go to make up a culture.

Concepts Developed within the Program

1. A language is important to any group of people. It is usually the central thread by which customs and heritage of a culture are kept alive.
2. Much of the Hispanic music is characterized by its rhythm and use of percussion instruments.
3. The Spanish pueblo type of architecture found throughout our Western region is a mixture of Spanish and Indian influences.
4. Folk art such as wood carving and the making of Santos developed as a result of early Hispanic settlements in the Southwest being almost cut off from the supply routes of trade in Mexico.

Follow-up Activities

1. Pictures, dioramas or simple adobe-like models could be part of group work to emphasize the influence of Hispanic architecture in a region.

(continued)

Example of Intercultural Program
on Closed Circuit TV (Continued)

2. Spelling lessons could include a few of the Spanish-named places found either in your city, state or region.
3. Dances such as la Raspa or la Varsoviana are easy to teach and are ones that students would enjoy learning.
4. Music teachers could supplement the experiences of boys and girls in this cultural area with Spanish and Mexican songs.
5. Games such as "Who Am I?" or "Where Am I?" centering about Hispanic words and places are fun for students to play. Choose a student leader who gives the class the clues. The one who guesses correctly becomes the leader.

Source: "Cultural Understanding," *Teacher's Guide* (A Title III Operational Project of the Denver, Colorado, Public Schools, 1968), pp. 20–21.

---

4. "Concrete" Experiences

The disadvantaged child is familiar with the concrete. His normal activities are "motoric" and are likely to be related to concrete objects.[8] Because of this, he has difficulty moving into conceptualization and abstract thinking.

To meet the needs of a student in this stage of cognitive development, the curriculum should provide experiences that encourage the child to form concepts and generalizations by working with real things and with actual materials and processes, and by feeling, counting, and grouping things. From such experiences the child should be able to draw simple generalizations. Then, when presented with a new experience he should be able to apply these abstract generalizations.

The Nuffield Mathematics Teaching Project exemplifies this technique, as described below:

The object of the Nuffield Mathematics Teaching Project is to produce a contemporary course for children from five to thirteen. This is being designed to help them connect together many aspects of the world around them, to introduce them gradually to the processes of abstract thinking, and to foster in them a critical, logical, but also creative, turn of mind.

A synthesis is being made of what is worth preserving in the traditional work with various new ideas, some of which are already being tried out. These cover presentation as well as content, and emphasis will be placed on the learning process. A concrete approach will be made to abstract concepts, and the children should be allowed to make their own discoveries whenever possible. The work of the project is set against the present background of new thinking concerning mathematics itself.

The Nuffield Project bases its program upon experience working with physical materials. The project seeks to identify clearly defined developmental stages in the child's growth, and to plan its curriculum accordingly.

The verbally handicapped disadvantaged student may find pictures more interesting and informative than the conventional textbook. Too often in the classroom, pictures are equated with recreation instead of being considered as a basis for learning. Consequently, the potential of the field of visual arts is still being realized. Visual aids—silent or sound films, television, photographs, slides, charts, paintings, or film loops—can become the intermediate steps between concrete objects and the written word.[10] An example of a district that has recognized the importance of visual arts is Muskogee, Oklahoma which has a media center that distributes to the whole school system. The head of the center indicated that a fairly good supply of materials is maintained and noted that *Ebony* magazine is popular with white teachers who are attempting to understand and show their children about black fashions, etc.

There has been increased emphasis in the last ten years on use of laboratories, particularly in the early grades. J.A. Campbell, Director of the Chemical Educational Material Study Project, says, a "surprising number of supposedly less able students seem to do well in a course that is based almost completely upon laboratory experimentation."[22] One cannot, then, underestimate the role of physical equipment and experience in both science and mathematics programs.

5.   Vocational, Commercial, and Occupational Education

Desegregation has prompted greater use of vocational education, particularly as schools have increased in size and diversity. It provides subjects more meaningful to many students than academic courses, and therefore increases their interest and motivation. Also, students from poor families who are not likely to attend college benefit from learning skills that can improve their economic welfare as adults. The type of vocational program adopted is not uniform, however.

Many small school districts that cannot bear the cost of implementing extensive vocational programs have had to provide practical training on a very small scale. Some schools are adding arts and crafts or a similar elective at the junior high level, whereas some high school programs seem to stem from club functions such as photography.

Chapel Hill, North Carolina, largely in response to school desegregation, has expanded the vocational and commercial course offerings in the district. A list of their subjects appears in the following inset.

In one community the financial problem has been partially overcome through the use of a mobile shop that visits several junior high schools for a specified time period each week. This idea could be extended to include mobile typing or sewing facilities and art workshops. High schools that cannot afford

Example of Vocational Course Offerings

Commercial Courses

Notehand	Basic Business
Personal Typing	Business Law
Data Processing	Cooperative Office Practices

Vocational and Occupational Courses

Home Economics Courses	Auto Mechanics I and II
Distributive Education	Bricklaying
Industrial Cooperative Training	Carpentry
Electronics I and II	Commercial Art
Architectural Design	Photography and
Radio & TV Broadcasting	Multimedia

Source: Chapel Hill, North Carolina, Senior High School registration form, 1971–72.

the machinery and staff needed for a fully diversified vocational program can join with other schools in the same geographic area to form a complex where each provides a portion of the course offerings in the full program.

When a school district can include a broader, more intensive, vocational education program in its curriculum, it should develop one based on the results of a survey of four main aspects of the school and community. The survey needs to: 1) inventory the community's resources—its people, industry, agriculture, and other economic activities; 2) analyze factors affecting economic growth in the area; 3) determine local employment opportunities; and 4) predict long-range needs for occupational education.[12] Utilization of information from a survey such as this is vital in the creation of a successful, relevant program.

6.   Inclusion of Courses on Personal Business and Home Management

Many students from low-income homes do not learn from their parents how to conduct personal business affairs very effectively. Schools serving such students can benefit them greatly throughout their lives with one or a series of courses on such practical subjects as home management, budgeting, borrowing and interest, use of installment credit, income tax matters, efficient consumer buying, basic child care, how to find and obtain public services, and how to find information in a community.

7.   Community-Based Schools

A unique concept first proposed by John Martin in Jackson, Mississippi, is that of the community-based school in which students spend part of their classroom time in local industrial plants. This allows students to be trained in skills for which the school cannot afford to provide instruction. Another aspect of the community-based school is that it provides an opportunity for blacks and whites to meet and work together in a "neutral" area outside the schools.

A more sophisticated version of this concept was undertaken in South Bend, Indiana, where the Home Builders Association, in conjunction with a local high school, directed the building of a complete house as part of a vocational project. Members of the high school Building Trades Corporation board of directors, who were directly responsible for the building program, were: the director of vocational education at the high school, the business manager for the school system, and five builder members. The building program will continue, with the profits from each year's house used to finance land and materials for the next year's project. This kind of experience obviously draws·the school into closer contact with the community.

The new house was a well-planned, three-bedroom ranch style home with a full basement, two full baths, double garage and family room with fireplace. It has a brick facade and attractive landscaping. In addition to the building group itself, girls in home economics classes planned kitchen cabinets, appliances and color schemes, and the architectural drafting class drew plans for a house to be built by the next year's class.[13]

C. Changing Classroom and Scheduling Organization to Promote Small-Group Work

PROBLEM: Difficulty in maintaining discipline and teacher control in the classroom often makes it hard to develop a small-group orientation.

POLICY.

(C-1)   Desegregated schools should provide opportunities through classroom and scheduling organization for small group and individual work.

Approaches to organizing the classroom and scheduling the curriculum are diverse. They range from simply making changes in seating arrangements in order to maintain control in the classroom to larger-scale alterations that provide opportunities for group interaction.

Suggested Techniques

1.   Seating Arrangements

For years, teachers have based student seating assignments on maintaining behavior control, but some seating arrangements can also provide good physical organization for discussion or group work. In fact, some schools buy easily movable desks and chairs deliberately so they can be quickly rearranged to provide for different types of activities: in small circles to encourage small-group discussions or projects, moved to one side to create space for some activities, in rows for more traditional learning, etc. Use of carpets even allows children to sit on the floor for some activities.

2.   Multi-Age Grouping

When rigid standards are set for regulated sequences of educational growth, the programs often demand a conformity that many children find impossible to attain. For others, the standards are not challenging enough. Some schools avoid adherence to inappropriate standards by organizing multi-aged classes. In such classes, self-selected activities and exploratory learning occur. They are not based on standardized grade expectations, but on individualized goals. Multi-age grouping offers many opportunities for social interaction and a climate for continuous learning.[14]

As the example in the following inset indicates, all students in a multi-age group are not at the same ability level, nor do they play the same role in instruction. Often the older children help the younger.

Example of Lesson for a Multi-Aged Group

Instructional Situations: At one elementary school some ten- and eleven-year old children wrote down stories as dictated by six- and seven-year old youngsters. Some of the older children's reactions we recorded follow:

TOM: "Sometimes they get stuck and I have to help them over the hump. I find the best way is to read the story back to them and say, 'What do you think should come next?' "

STEPHANIE: "It takes time for them to get the hang of telling stories, but after they do it once it's always easier the second time. I tell them, 'You should have a story of your own. Why don't you tell about a place you have been?' It's always easier to get a story before or after a holdiay; they have something real to talk about. They may exaggerate, but I think that's all right."

BILL: "It's a real good feeling when they learn your name and call you when they pass you in the hall."

CHANG: "It did bother me that one girl always told a story about a rabbit or some other animal. So I brought in my sister's doll, and, you know, she told a wonderful story about it."

SCOTT: "They have the most trouble ending the story, but so do we."

These same children, as part of their class work, decided to write books expecially designed for the younger children. They worked out plots they thought would interest their younger schoolmates, included plenty of lively conversations to hold their interest, drew illustrations for every page, and, finally, bound them sturdily in decorated bindings.

Source: American Association of Elementary-Kindergarten-Nursery Educators, *Multi-Age Grouping: Enriching the Learning Environment* (Washington: National Education Association, 1970); p. 22.

---

3.   Team Teaching

The objective of team teaching is to "maximally utilize the strengths of each teacher." In essence, each teacher should be assigned to the subject area and group size for which he is best suited. A teaching team can consist of as many as six or seven teachers and teacher aides or as few as two or three persons. It is the administrator's responsibility to select the best combination of personnel for each team and to provide the space for their activities within the existing facilities.

A major advantage in team teaching is that teachers are freed to work with individuals and small groups. A discussion of further applications of team teaching is included in the section of this chapter titled Teaching Techniques and Training to Achieve Effective Desegregation.

4.   Mod-Scheduling

An organizational technique now being applied in several schools is flexible or "modular scheduling." In recognition of the diversity of a student body, administrators attempt to place each student in an educational program geared to his individual needs—within the boundaries imposed by time, professional personnel and physical space. A description of the mod-scheduling at Chapel Hill Senior High School in Chapel Hill, North Carolina, follows.

Example of Mod Scheduling

The regular six period day is divided in twelve modules of 25 minute intervals. The schedule is based on a three-day cycle during which the student spends six mods in each subject area. On one day there is one mod (25 minutes), another day two mods (50 minutes), and on the third day in the cycle three mods (75 minutes). Through the use of modular scheduling, the individual student spends his school day in learning situations of four types: large group lectures by teachers possessing special talents or abilities, small student-centered group discussions with a member of the faculty present nearby, and individual study. The amount of time spent in any one of the learning experiences during a school day is dependent upon the student's progress, ability and interest.

Source: Chapel Hill, North Carolina, Senior High School organizational description.

The underlying philosophical and psychological bases for the mod-scheduling program are as follows:

Students can be taught best in classes of varied sized and of varied lengths.

Students should be given the opportunity to plan and manage their time during the school day.

Students should learn *how* to learn.

The four phases of instruction will give the student the variety of learning experiences he needs for a more interesting and profitable school day.

Mod-scheduling generally works most effectively with students who possess considerable self-discipline and so is usually not recommended for students who have not had practice in self-discipline. Also, parents are often skeptical of flexible scheduling, so public relations efforts should accompany introduction of mod-scheduling in a school.

5. Individualized Instruction

When this approach is used, the institutional level of each student is determined, and he is assigned tasks he is capable of accomplishing. Common materials are individualized reading kits and S.R.A. reading lab. Although the primary emphasis of this technique is not upon the creation of small-group learning opportunities, it does generate them upon occasion. When most students are working independently, the teacher can hold small-group conferences as well as help other individuals.

Notes

1. Desmond P. Ellis and James A. Wiggins, *Preliminary Report of the Classroom Organization and Academic Performance Project* (Chapel Hill, North Carolina, September 1969).
2. Lavone A. Hanna, *et al, Unit Teaching in the Elementary School* (New York: Holt, Rinehart and Winston, 1963), Chapter 3.
3. Joseph O. Lorentan and Shelley Umans, *Teaching the Disadvantaged: New Curriculum Approaches* (New York: Columbia University, Teachers College Press, 1966), pp. 116–121.
4. National Education Association, *Issues and Alternatives* (Washington, D.C.: National Education Association, 1968), p. 15.
5. Editorial Department of American Book Company, *What's Happening to Our Language Today?* (New York: American Book Company, 1970), p. 13.
6. Office of Education, *Notification to Members of Congress* (Washington, D.C., June 23, 1971).
7. Loretan, p. 17.
8. *Ibid.*, p. 12.
9. Robert B. Davis, *The Changing Curriculum: Mathematics* (Washington: National Education Association, 1967), p. 27. More information on this program is available from: The Nuffield Foundation, Mathematics Teaching Project, 12 Upper Belgrave Street, London, S.W. 1, England.
10. Loretan, p. 91.
11. "An Approach to Chemistry Based on Experiments," in Robert W. Heath, ed., *New Curricula* (New York: Harper and Row, 1964), p. 91.
12. National Association of Secondary School Principals, *The Bulletin*, Vol. 49, No. 301 (Washington: 1965), p. 54.

13. Home Builders Association of Indiana, *The Indiana Builder,* Vol. 1, No. 6 (June 1970), p. 7.
14. American Association of Elementary-Kindergarten-Nursery Educators, *Multi-Age Grouping: Enriching the Learning Environment* (Washington, D.C.: National Education Association, 1970), p. 22.
15. H. Larry Winecoff, *School Desegregation: A Challenge to Quality Education,* Part II (University of South Carolina: S.C. School Desegregation Consulting Center), p. 7.

Bibliography

American Association of Elementary-Kindergarten-Nursery Educators. *Elementary School Media Program: An Approach to Individualizing Instruction.* Washington, D.C.: National Education Association, 1970.
——. *Multi-Age Grouping.* Washington, D.C.: National Education Association.
Bloom, Benjamin. *Compensatory Education for Cultural Deprivation.* New York: Holt, Rinehart & Winston, 1967.
Campbell, J.A. "An Approach to Chemistry Based on Experiments," in Robert W. Heath, ed., *New Curricula.* New York: Harper & Row, 1964.
Carithers, Martha W. "School Desegregation and Racial Cleavage, 1954–70: A Review of the Literature," in *The Journal of Social Issues,* Vol. 26, No. 4 (1970).
Chesler, Mark, Carl Jorgensen and Phyllis Erenberg. *Planning Educational Change,* Vol. III *Integrating the Desegregated School.* Washington, D.C.: U. S. Department of Health, Education and Welfare, Office of Education.
Colorado Springs School District No. 11. *Intercultural Relations: A Supplement to the Social Studies Curriculum.* Colorado Springs, Colorado, October 1970.
Conant, James B. *Slums and Suburbs.* New York: McGraw-Hill, 1961.
The Consultative Center for Equal Educational Opportunity. Dr. Joe Garrison, director. *Teaching Units.* University of Oklahoma: Arrowhead Materials & Techniques Workshop, January 1970.
Davis, Robert B. *The Changing Curriculum: Mathematics.* Washington, D.C.: Association for Supervision and Curriculum Development, 1967.
Denver Public Schools. *Cultural Understandings: Teacher's Guide.* A Title III Operational Project of the Denver, Colorado Public Schools, 1968.
Editorial Department of American Book Company. *What's Happening to Our Language Today?* New York: American Book Company, 1970.
Ellis, Desmond P. and James A. Wiggins. "Preliminary Report of the Classroom Organization and Academic Performance Project," Chapel Hill, North Carolina, September 1969. (Mimeographed).
Hanna, Lavone A., Gladys L. Potter and Neva Hagaman. *Unit Teaching in the Elementary School: Social Studies and Related Sciences.* New York: Holt, Rinehart and Winston, 1963.
Hillway, Tyrus. *Education in American Society: An Introduction to the Study of Education.* Boston: Houghton-Mifflin, 1961.

Home Builders Association of Indiana. "Home Builders Sponsor Building Class in High School; Success Leads to Second Project," *The Indiana Builder*, Vol. 1, No. 6 (June 1970).

Horn, Thomas D., ed. *Reading for the Disadvantaged: Problems of Linguistically Different Learners*. New York: Harcourt, Brace and World, Inc., 1970.

Katz, Irwin. *Problems and Directions for Research on Public School Desegregation*. University of Michigan, 1967.

Loretan, Joseph O. and Shelley Umans. *Teaching the Disadvantaged: New Curriculum Approaches*. New York: Teachers College Press, Columbia University, 1966.

MacBeth, Edwin W. "A Study of Group Interaction and the Process of Change in a Team Teaching Program," Unpublished doctoral dissertation. Department of Education, Columbia University, 1966.

National Association of Secondary School Principals. *The Bulletin*. Vol. 49, No. 301. Washington, D.C.: National Association of Secondary School, Principals, 1965.

National Education Association. *Issues and Alternatives*. Washington, D.C., 1968.

National School Public Relations Association. *Black Studies in Schools*. Washington, 1970.

Otto, Henry J. and David C. Sanders. *Elementary School Organization and Administration*. New York: Appleton-Century-Crofts, 1964.

Roberts, John L. "A Study of Business Education in the Negro Public Secondary Schools of Tennessee," Unpublished doctoral dissertation, State University of Iowa, 1962.

Stephens, J.M. *Educational Psychology: The Study of Educational Growth*. New York: Holt, Rinehart and Winston, 1956.

Stephens, J.M. *The Process of Schooling: A Psychological Examination*. New York: Holt, Rinehart and Winston, 1967.

Thayer, V.T. and Martin Levit. *The Role of the School in American Society*. New York: Dodd, Mead and Co., 1969.

Torrance, E. Paul and Ram Gupta. *Programmed Experiences in Creative Thinking*. Minneapolis: Bureau of Educational Research, College of Education, University of Minnesota, February 1964.

U.S. Commission on Civil Rights. *Racial Isolation in the Public Schools*, Vol. 1. Washington, D.C.: Government Printing Office, 1967.

Williams, Johnetta King. "The Development of the Process of Curriculum Improvement in the Negro Schools of Chattanooga, Tennessee," Unpublished doctoral dissertation, Department of Education, New York University, 1952.

Winecoff, H. Larry. *Problems in School Desegregation: Real or Imaginary?* S.C. School Desegregation Consulting Center, University of South Carolina.

———. *School Desegregation: A Challenge to Quality Education*, Part II. South Carolina School Desegregation Consulting Center, University of South Carolina.

About the Authors

Al Smith, an assistant vice president with Real Estate Research Corporation, has a wide range of experience in dealing with political and administrative problems at all levels of government. In supervising the preparation of this handbook, he has brought new techniques of public administration to bear on the sensitive social issues surrounding the process of school desegregation. Mr. Smith holds an M.R.P. degree from the Maxwell School at Syracuse University.

Anthony Downs, senior vice president of Real Estate Research Corporation, is a consultant on urban affairs, government organization and land use economics. He wrote several chapters of the *Report of the National Advisory Commission on Civil Disorders*, and he was a member of the President's National Commission on Urban Problems. The U.S. Civil Rights Commission has published his essay, *Racism in America, and How to Combat It*. Dr. Downs is the author of *An Economic Theory of Democracy, Inside Bureaucracy* and *Urban Problems and Prospects*, as well as numerous articles and reviews. His study, *Federal Housing Subsidies: How Are They Working?*, is also published by Lexington Books.

M. Leanne Lachman is a senior analyst with Real Estate Research Corporation, focusing on public affairs analyses. In addition to school desegregation, her areas of concentration include low- and moderate-income housing problems, urban growth patterns, and property assessment methodology. Ms. Lachman received her academic degrees from the University of Southern California and Claremont Graduate School.